AFRICAN STUDIES
HISTORY, POLITICS, ECONOMICS, AND CULTURE

T0300050

Edited by
Molefi Asante
Temple University

A ROUTLEDGE SERIES

African Studies

History, Politics, Economics, and Culture

Molefi Asante, *General Editor*

CONTENDING POLITICAL PARADIGMS IN AFRICA

Rationality and the Politics of
Democratization in Kenya and Zambia

Shadrack Wanjala Nasong'o

Routledge
Taylor & Francis Group

NEW YORK AND LONDON

Published in 2005 by
Routledge
Taylor & Francis Group
711 Third Avenue,
New York, NY 10017

Published in Great Britain by
Routledge
Taylor & Francis Group
2 Park Square
Milton Park, Abingdon
Oxon OX14 4RN

First issued in paperback 2012

International Standard Book Number-13: 978-0-415-97588-9 (Hardcover)
International Standard Book Number-13: 978-0-415-64696-3 (Paperback)
Library of Congress Card Number 2005011570

Library of Congress Cataloging-In-Publication Data

Nasong'o, Shadrack Wanjala.
   Contending political paradigms in Africa : rationality and the politics of democratization in Kenya and Zambia / Shadrack Wanjala Nasong'o.
        p. cm. -- (African studies)
   Includes bibliographical references and index.
   ISBN 0-415-97588-3 (hardback)
   1. Africa--Politics and government--1960- 2. Democratization--Africa.
   3. Democratization--Kenya. 4. Democratization--Zambia. 5. Comparative government. I. Title. II. African studies (Routledge (Firm))

JQ1879.A15N27 2005
320.96--dc22

2005011570

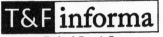

Taylor & Francis Group
is the Academic Division of T&F Informa plc.

Visit the Taylor & Francis Web site at
http://www.taylorandfrancis.com

and the Routledge Web site at
http://www.routledge-ny.com

To all activist scholars, committed social reformers, and genuine democrats in Africa, past, present, and future. For, the logic of their epic struggles constitutes the essence of this narrative.

Contents

viii Contents

List of Tables

Acronyms

AFORD	Alliance for Democracy
ANC	African National Congress
AZ	Agenda for Zambia
BAG	Bloc Africain de Guinée
CCCC (4Cs)	Citizens Coalition for Constitutional Change
CCM	Chama Cha Mapinduzi (Revolutionary Party)
CCU	Chama Cha Umma (People's Party)
CHAKA	Christian Alliance for the Kingdom of Africa
CJPC	Catholic Justice and Peace Commission
CKRC	Constitution of Kenya Review Commission
CNU	Cameroon National Union
COTU	Central Organization of Trade Unions
CPP	Convention People's Party
CRIC	Civic Resource and Information Centre
CSO	Civil Society Organization
CTSP	Comité de Transition pour le Salut de Peuple
ECK	Electoral Commission of Kenya
ECWD	Education Centre for Women in Democracy
EPLF	Eritrean People's Liberation Front
EPRDF	Ethiopian People's Revolutionary Democratic Front
FDD	Forum for Democracy and Development
FORD	Forum for Restoration of Democracy
FORD-A	Forum for Restoration of Democracy Asili
FORD-K	Forum for Restoration of Democracy in Kenya
FORD-P	Forum for Restoration of Democracy for the People
FRELIMO	Mozambique Liberation Front
GEMA	Gikuyu Embu Meru Association
HP	Heritage Party
ICEDA	Institute for Civic Education in Africa

ILO	International Labor Organization
IMF	International Monetary Fund
IPPG	Inter-Parties Parliamentary Group
KADU	Kenya African Democratic Union
KANU	Kenya African National Union
KENDA	Kenya National Democratic Alliance
KNC	Kenya National Congress
KPU	Kenya People's Union
KSC	Kenya Social Congress
LAZ	Law Association of Zambia
LDP	Liberal Democratic Party
LPF	Liberal Progressive Front
LSK	Law Society of Kenya
MCC	Mwanakatwe Constitutional Commission
MCP	Malawi Congress Party
MDP	Movement for Democratic Process
MFJ	Movement for Freedom and Justice
MGG	Middle Ground Group
MMD	Movement for Multiparty Democracy
MUZ	Mineworkers Union of Zambia
NADA	National Alliance for Democracy
NCC	National Citizen's Coalition
NCCK	National Council of the Churches of Kenya
NCEC	National Convention Executive Council
NDP	National Development Party
NEC	National Executive Committee
NGO	Non-Governmental Organization
NLD	National Leadership for Development
NLP	National Lima Party
NP	National Party
PAC	Public Affairs Committee
PAN	National Action Party
PCD	Presidential Committee on Dialogue
PRI	Institutional Revolutionary Party
PDG	Parti Democratique de Guinée
PF	Patriotic Front
RENAMO	Mozambique National Resistance
SAPS	Structural Adjustment Programs
SDP	Social Democratic Party
SIDA	Swedish International Development Agency

SPK	Shirikisho Party of Kenya
SONU	Student Organization of the University of Nairobi
SUPKEM	Supreme Council of Kenyan Muslims
TANU	Tanganyika African National Union
TPLF	Tigrean People's Liberation Front
UDF	United Democratic Front
UN-ECA	United Nations Economic Commission for Africa
UNIP	United National Independence Party
UNZA	University of Zambia
UON	Universitiy of Nairobi
UP	United Party
UPND	United Party for National Development
UPP	United Progressive Party
USAID	United States Agency for International Development
ZANU	Zimbabwe African National Union
ZCTU	Zambia Congress of Trade Unions
ZDC	Zambia Democractic Congress
ZFE	Zambia Federation of Employers
ZINCOM	Zambia Industrial and Commercial Association
ZRP	Zambian Republican Party

Foreword

Like the legendary Phoenix that ascended from ashes, so a new order emerged from the rubble of the Second World War. A world dominated by a handful of imperial dominions gave way to a Cold War overshadowed by the ambitions of the United States and its Western allies in opposition to the Soviet Union and its Eastern partners. Capitalism was juxtaposed to state-managed economies. Likewise, the West presented itself as a bastion of civil liberties and free elections vis-à-vis the totalitarian one-party political systems of the Communist bloc. This dichotomous view of the post-war period shrouds the political heterogeneity of the supposedly democratic states west of the Iron Curtain. Standing alongside the United States, the United Kingdom, and France in opposition to Soviet aspirations were Franco's Spain and Salazar's Portugal—two right-wing authoritarian states. In addition, the Western powers could count on a host of allies in Latin America and certain parts of Asia; many of these were also non-elected regimes. The missionary zeal to spread democratic rule to Eastern Europe was toned down considerably when it came to virtually all other parts of the globe. Indeed, throughout the third quarter of the twentieth century many Western allies were forced to come to grips with their own hypocrisy. If democracy and self-determination were good for East Europeans, why were they inappropriate for their colonial subjects?

Scholars, pundits, and many casual observers asked why certain countries embraced democratic rule while others did not. A common issue running through many post-war political analyses was the question of culture. One of the most celebrated works centered on this framework was published in the early 1960s—Gabriel Almond and Sydney Verba's *Civic Culture*. What made the U.K. and U.S. strong and stable democracies as opposed to Germany, Italy, and Mexico? In brief, they answered that the two Anglo-American societies shared a common "civic culture," a set of mores lacking in the three other countries in their study. A logical deduction of their research was that societies desirous of establishing and maintaining democratic regimes would have to embrace not just general European norms but their American and British subvariants. Thus developing states aspiring to become democratic polities would have to change more than just their regime structures and economic policies. Culture shift was presented as a prerequisite of democratic governance. It should not be surprising that this approach, while popular with many Western academics and policy makers, was frequently accused of ethnocentrism.

Beyond its ethnic and racial biases this perspective was battered by the emergence of democratic regimes in unlikely settings—societies quite distinct from civic culture prototypes. Spain, Portugal, and Greece joined the democratic club in the 1970s. In the following decade genuinely competitive party systems arose in several Latin American and Asian states. The generals moved back to their barracks in Argentina and Turkey. People power in the Philippines brought down the rule of Ferdinand Marcos. By the last decade of the twentieth century democratic governments emerged in parts of the former Soviet bloc and Africa. Free and fair elections were becoming the norm in Poland and the Czech Republic as was the case in South Africa and Botswana. This democratic wave may have started in Europe but it did not end there. Democratization sprouted, and in some cases took root, without gravitating towards Anglo-American cultural norms or even industrialization. Although institutionally weak compared to their West European counterparts, democratization was clearly appearing in terrain the political culturalists of the 1950s and 60s would deem unfavorable to popular rule.

Still democratization is far from an inevitable process. Pinochet's rule illustrated that even a long-running democracy like Chile was not immune to military dictatorship. The demolition of the Berlin Wall did not inaugurate democracy uniformly throughout Eastern Europe. Authoritarianism remains alive and well in post-Soviet Belarus. The 2004 presidential elections in the Ukraine highlighted the fragility of free and fair elections in a society emerging from decades of authoritarian rule. The fall of the Pahlavi family in Iran marked a new period of multiparty competition. Still, Iranian theocrats engineered election results by limiting the participation of political parties and candidates. Accusations of neo-authoritarianism surfaced in Chávez's Venezuela as they did in Fujimori's Peru. Far from certain is the political system that will emerge in the wake of George Bush's invasion of Iraq. As some have suggested, the United States, as an instructor in the art of Democracy, certainly could have benefited from a few lessons as the 2000 presidential election illustrated. Just as democratic governance is not inevitable, geographically or culturally determined, neither is authoritarianism. The mixed record of the past half-century leaves us back where we started. What leads to democracy's inauguration and subsequent consolidation?

Shadrack Nasong'o tackles these pressing questions head on. After reading this book we understand that democratization is not a product of any particular cultural upbringing or geographic happenstance. Its materialization and consequent coalescence are the result of a dynamic process involving civil society and ruling elites. Leaders may design democratic systems but ultimately the superstructure of democratic governance will stand on the foundations of civil society. This is the realm lying outside the parapets of the state. Here economic conditions and socio-cultural divisions interact in a sphere represented by an array of actors and institutions.

Defying a long held supposition in Western political folklore Shadrack Nasong'o points out that ethnic heterogeneity, in and of itself, is neither a hindrance nor a facilitator of Democracy. Dr. Nasong'o departs from some of the more popular notions relating to government relations with its ethnic communities. Analyses of Nationalism concomitant with the Civic Culture presumed that ethnic strife was symptomatic of a society's growing pains—an inevitable consequence of modernization. They deduced that since North American and West European societies were already modern the anguish of nationalism was an agonizing phase the rest of the world would have to endure. The appearance of vibrant nationalist movements throughout Western Europe and North America in the late 1960s severely impugned that hypothesis. Fears of ethnic strife are often exploited to justify one-party rule or a caudillo's tenure in office. Ethnic solidarity and pan-ethnic alliances, Dr. Nasong'o points out, can become tools for promoting or sustaining virtually any regime type. Calls for democracy from civil society merge or clash with the short- and long-term aspirations of rulers.

Ultimately those in command must choose whether to suppress calls for greater freedoms or negotiate an end to authoritarian rule. Theirs is not a decision preordained by cultural norms but rather a rational assessment based on what appears to be in their best interests. An unquestioned part of that computation is the price the regime is willing to expend in order to maintain the status quo alive. Here again, Dr. Nasong'o highlights the importance of testing the universality of theoretical models often formulated by Western scholars. If, as these academics often assume, politicians in industrialized democratic states engage in cost-benefit analyses the same should also hold true for their political counterparts in developing countries. And what bigger prize is there to mull over than the fate of the regime itself.

This book represents a new generation of scholarship and a significant contribution to our understanding of democratization and political development. While familiar with the research of previous generations Dr. Nasong'o is not bound by dubious theoretical conjectures and outdated cultural and ideological assumptions. This work focuses principally on two African states: Kenya and Zambia. While centered primarily on the experiences of these two former British colonies the findings in this book extend to other parts of the continent and, indeed, to other societies. Here Dr. Nasong'o combines new approaches to the study of politics in general, and democratization in particular, with an ever-growing literature on culture, politics, and society in Africa. Students in developing countries are often taught to learn from American and European examples. This book switches that ordering. It is time for those in Europe and the Americas to learn from Africa.

AMÍLCAR ANTONIO BARRETO
Northeastern University, Boston

Acknowledgments

The fruitful completion of a book is a complex and tedious process with input from many quarters. Accordingly, I would like to express my gratitude first, to the Department of Political Science, Northeastern University for awarding me a two-year adjunct lectureship, which facilitated the research and writing of this book. Second, my gratitude goes to Professor William Crotty of the Center for the Study of Democracy, Northeastern University, for providing me with office space and access to the Center's resources during the preparation of the book. Third, I feel greatly indebted to Professor Amílcar Antonio Barreto of the Department of Political Science, Northeastern University for his critical comments on my draft chapters and for constantly bringing to my attention new sets of literature relevant to my study in the course of my research and writing. Professor Barreto was a dependable source of inspiration and invaluable advice and readily accepted to write the foreword to this book, for which I am very grateful.

Fourth, I would like to most sincerely thank my respondents, both in Boston, and in Nairobi, for taking time off their busy schedules to respond to my inquiries and share their experiences with me in the spring of 2002 and summer of 2003, respectively. In particular, I would like to single out Dr. Neo Richard Simutanyi for special mention. I attended a political science summer institute for foreign scholars in 1998 at the Southern Illinois University, Carbondale, with Neo during which time, his witty insights into Zambian politics and views on President Fredrick Chiluba inspired my interest in Zambian politics and thus laid the foundation for this comparative study of the politics of change in Kenya and Zambia.

Fifth, I am indebted to Karolina Hulterström of the Department of Government, University of Uppsala, Sweden, for her express permission to cite Table 4.1 on the effect of ethnicity on party support in Zambia and Kenya, originally part of her conference presentation in 2002. Sixth and most importantly, the publication of this book would not have happened, at least when it did, without the crucial role played by Mr. Benjamin Holtz-man of Routledge (Taylor & Francis Group), New York. I wish to therefore register my gratitude to Ben for his advice, support, and patience during the final revision of the book manuscript.

Finally, my sincere thanks and appreciation go to my family, wife Irene and sons Amos and Alfred for their love and companionship.

SHADRACK WANJALA NASONG'O, PH.D.
Assistant Professor of International Studies
Rhodes College
Memphis, Tennessee

Introduction

This study examines, and seeks to explain the conjuncture of contending political paradigms between democratization and enduring authoritarianism in Africa by focusing on the cases of Kenya and Zambia. It is noteworthy that virtually all states in Africa emerged from the depredations of colonial domination into political independence under the guidance of vibrant nationalist movements that transmuted into political parties. On attainment of independence, however, the process of political consolidation saw the emergence of single-party regimes that were rationalized as the most viable means for maintaining national integrity and engendering nation and state-building. This eventuality led to the rise of the phenomenon of the single-party state system and personal rule in Africa.

The reality of single-party monolithism witnessed increasing consolidation of power in the hands of the executive in a conjuncture that led to the overwhelming dominance of the state in the African political economy. This development undermined the basis and dashed hopes for the possibilities of democratic practice on a continent that was just emerging from oppressive, repressive, and exploitative colonial control. Indeed, available evidence indicates that in the first three decades of African independence (1960–1989), even partially democratic states accounted for fewer than five out of the forty-eight sub-Saharan African countries. These were Botswana, Gambia, Senegal, and Mauritius. More specifically, Mauritius was the only unambiguous democracy, which witnessed the alternation of power between political parties through the electoral process.

Single-party authoritarianism as the established paradigm of governance in Africa was seriously challenged both by political dynamics internal to the African states as well as by external political exigencies, especially following the end of the Cold War and the disintegration of the Soviet Union at the end of the 1980s. At the continental level, a concerted push for democratization saw three quarters of sub-Saharan African countries (37 out of 48) hold multiparty elections between 1990 and 1996. These elections, according to Bratton and Posner (1999), offered voters real choices about who would govern them, often for the first time since independence. By 2000, 43 of the 48 sub-Saharan African countries (89.56%)—all except the Democratic Republic of the Congo, Eritrea, Rwanda, Somalia, and Swaziland—had conducted multiparty elections. Consequently, between 1991 and 2000, there were 78 top leadership elections in Africa. The electoral results, however, were mixed. Of the 78 top leadership contestations, only twenty-one (26.92%) led to the ouster of incumbent heads of government in nineteen countries (39.58% of the total), representing fewer than half of the countries that conducted multiparty elections.

This outcome raises a pertinent question as to what factors accounted for the defeat of some authoritarian regimes and the victory of others over the forces of democratization. This question assumes great significance when it is considered that some countries with similar colonial experience, comparable socio-political circumstances, ethnoregional composition, and civil society vibrancy such as Kenya and Zambia had different results. The incumbent regime in Zambia was vanquished in 1991 while the one in Kenya prevailed over the forces of democratization in 1992 and 1997. Furthermore, even where regime change occurred, as was the case in Zambia, authoritarian tendencies persisted. Whereas there are a number of factors that may account for this eventuality, this study contends that the three principal explanatory variables include the role of civil society, ethnicity, and electoral system design in the politics of transition.

This study is guided by three key assumptions. First, it is significant to note that the role of civil society as political norm setter and agent of democratization is taken for granted (see Diamond, 1999; Harbeson, 1994; and Chazan, 1994). However, an examination of the work of some civil society organizations reveals some unmistakable ambivalence towards their presumed role of pushing the democratic agenda (see for instance Ndegwa, 1996; Callaghy, 1994). This study thus hypothesizes that the nature and structure of the politically active civil society organizations is an important factor in determining the success of the new democratic paradigm over the old authoritarian forces. Secondly, the study hypothesizes that the instrumentalist mobilization of politicized ethnicity and its deployment in the service of ethnic bossmen is an important explanatory variable in the electoral victory or defeat of incumbent authoritarian regimes. Finally, it is hypothesized that the third key determinant of the electoral victory or defeat of the incumbent authoritarian regimes in their first contest with opposition political parties was electoral system design.

Overall, the phenomenon of enduring authoritarian leaders in Africa and democratization issues has concerned a number of African and Africanist scholars in recent times. However, studies on these issues have largely tended to be country-specific (see for example Brown, 2001; Nasong'o, 2001a; Adar, 2000a, 2000b; Murunga, 2000; Ajulu, 2000; Ihonvbere, 1996a; Bratton, 1994; Hamelengwa, 1992; and Mbikusa-Lewanika, 1990). The significance of this study lies in the fact that it seeks to rise above the level of country-specific analysis to a comparative approach in examining the social struggles for democracy in Africa, explaining why some authoritarian leaders triumphed over the forces of democratization while others fell victim to such forces, and evaluating the prospects for democratic consolidation on the continent.

Towards this end, the study employs the rational choice approach to the study of social phenomena as its theoretical frame of reference, which is developed and elaborated in Chapter One. Nonetheless, it suffices to mention here that the utility of rational choice theory lies in its ability to reveal how intentional and rational actors generate collective outcomes and aggregate behavior. The strength of rational choice in comparative analysis, according to Margaret Levi (1999: 20), is evident in three ways. First is its capacity to spawn testable theory with clear scope conditions. Second is its ability to make sense of a correlation of a set of events by providing a plausible and compelling story that identifies the causal mechanisms linking the independent and dependent variables. And third is its universalism that reveals generalizable implications applicable to cases beyond those under immediate investigation. The emphasis of this model is on rational and strategic individuals who make choices within constraints to obtain their desired ends, whose decisions rest on their assessment of the probable actions of others, and whose personal outcomes depend on what others do (Levi, 1999: 23). Although the approach is methodologically individualist, therefore, its focus is not on individual choice but on the aggregation of individual choices.

With regard to the principal research questions herein, the assumption is that both authoritarian regimes in Kenya and Zambia, as elsewhere in Africa, aimed at maintaining their power positions in the face of electoral competition. They sought to do so by taking rational decisions based on their assessment of the probable actions of opposition political parties and other forces of democratization. Similarly, opposition political parties are also assumed to be rational actors who rationally responded to the actual and probable actions of the incumbent regimes. The difference in the outcomes with regard to incumbent authoritarian regime victory in Kenya and loss in Zambia, for instance, may be explained in terms of the relative strength of the constraints within which the two regimes operated as well as the relative strength and capacity of their respective opposition parties. It is in this sense that Levi (1999) observes that the rational choice approach is essentially an equilibrium analysis in which actors are assumed to respond to each others' decisions until each is at a position from which no improvement is possible. "Sometimes, of course, there is no such position, and the result is either cycling or chaos" (Levi, 1999: 23).

Based on the assumption of rationality, therefore, the task of this study is to delineate the nature of the strategic interaction among the key political actors in Kenya and Zambia; the forms of constraint appertaining thereto; the search for equilibrium between the political forces at play, and how these processes impacted upon electoral outcomes in the two countries in the period 1991 to 2002. Towards this end, Chapters One and Two set the pace for the analysis. Chapter One is an exposition of the emergence of authoritarianism on the continent as manifested in the rise, consolidation, and maintenance of the single-party system. It examines the ways in which the incumbent elite rationalized the single-party system and elevated it to the status of a hegemonic ideology. Chapter Two analyzes the dynamics of democratization and opposition to the single-party dogma with specific reference to the cases of Kenya and Zambia.

For its part, Chapter Three compares the politically active civil society organizations in Kenya and Zambia in terms of their nature, organization, and resources with a view to accounting for their seemingly differential contribution to democratization in the two countries. In doing so, the study seeks to contribute to the debate about civil society and democratization in general and to inform civil society organizations engaged in democratization projects and the deconstruction of authoritarianism in Africa in particular. Chapter Four focuses on the variable of politicized ethnicity and posits that some key political players generally perceived emergent political pluralism as a zero-sum game with definite winners and losers among a country's ethnoregional groups. As such, they sought to mobilize ethnically by playing on ethnic fears and sentiments. This eventuality had important implications for electoral outcomes in the first multiparty elections in Africa in the early 1990s, which Chapter Four delineates and analyzes with special reference to Kenya and Zambia.

Chapter Five grapples with the role of electoral system design as it relates to incumbent regime electoral loss in Zambia in 1991 and incumbent regime electoral victory in Kenya in 1992 and 1997. In addition, the chapter flips over the issues and examines the dynamics of an entrenched new incumbent regime in Zambia vis-à-vis the opposition in the 2001 electoral contest; and the new-found unity in the opposition ranks in Kenya that vanquished the perennial incumbent in 2002. The key argument here is that the low rate of incumbent regime turnover in Africa in spite of the reintroduction of multipartyism in the 1990s is a function of political liberalization without transformation of the political institutions and rules of the political game. Whereas regime change occurred mainly in countries that effected some significant changes to their constitutions towards fair political competition, most multiparty elections in the 1990s were held within the political and legal structures of the single-party era, thus effectively constraining possibilities for democratic transformation.

Chapter Six summarizes the study's findings, juxtaposing them with the key assumptions of rational choice theory. It evaluates the findings vis-à-vis the hypotheses outlined above with a view to assessing the veracity of the hypotheses. In the final analysis, Chapter Seven attempts an exposition of the prospects for democratic consolidation in Africa. The chapter juxtaposes the pessimistic prognosis on the prospects for democratic consolidation in Africa with an optimistic perspective and, using various indicators and measures, the study concludes that in spite of the numerous false starts, reversals, and lingering authoritarianism on the continent, Africa is definitely moving toward a democratic political dispensation. Although this is no reason for celebration given the many structural obstacles still standing in the way of genuine democracy, it is a basis for cautious optimism that the shift of paradigms in Africa from authoritarianism to more democratic modes of governance is well nigh.

Chapter One
Emergence of Authoritarianism

The anti-colonial struggles for political independence in Africa were struggles for democracy. They sought to replace the exclusive, exploitative, and oppressive colonial establishment with political systems based on the notion of government by the consent of the governed, formal political equality, inalienable human rights, including the right to political participation, accountability of power to the governed and the rule of law (see Ake, 2000). It was expected that the new democratic African states would place emphasis on concrete political, social, and economic rights to redress the injustices of colonial tyranny and kleptocracy, and invest heavily in the improvement of people's health, education, and capacity so that they could participate effectively in their political economies (see Ake, 1996). Towards this end, virtually all states in Africa emerged from the depredations of colonial domination into political independence under the guidance of vibrant nationalist movements, and nascent political parties that constituted the institutional basis for vibrant competitive politics in the envisaged new democratic era.

After attainment of independence, however, the process of political consolidation saw the emergence of single-party regimes, which were rationalized as the most viable means for maintaining national integrity and engendering nation and state-building. This turn of political events resulted in the rise of the phenomenon of the single-party state system and personal rule in Africa. This eventuality witnessed increasing consolidation of power in the hands of the executive in a conjuncture that led to the overwhelming dominance of the state in the African political economy. Michael Neocosmos (1993) argues that this phenomenon of statism simultaneously provided a vehicle of accumulation from above by large sections of the ruling class as well as the systematic economic plunder and political oppression of the masses of Africa. Within this framework, the relations between the state and the mass of citizens in Africa remained directly coercive and oppressive.

In reference to the exploitative and coercive relationship between the elite and the masses, Robert Jackson and Carl Rosberg (1982) observed that the state in Africa in the late twentieth century was an arena in which individuals could obtain great power. Jackson and Rosberg posited that what the Church represented for ambitious men in medieval Europe or the business corporation in nineteenth and twentieth century America, the state was in the late twentieth century for ambitious Africans with skill and fortune because it remained the major arena of privilege. In this context, the African political class simply adapted colonial-based political structures and processes to presidential authoritarianism (Nyong'o, 1989), or what Richard Sandbrook (1987) calls "neopatrimonialism." This neopatrimonialism[1] had a high propensity of degenerating into an economically irrational form of personal rule in which "a chief or strongman emerges and rules on the basis of material incentives and personal control of his administration and the armed forces" (Sandbrook, 1987: 89). This political process spawned conditions under which corruption and other forms of white-collar crime flourished with far-reaching implications for economic development (see Mutoro et al., 1999; Chikulo, 2000; Mbaku, 2000a, 2000b). A number of explanations have been advanced to explain the rise of authoritarianism as the dominant governance paradigm, exemplified by the emergence of the single-party political system on the continent.

THE RISE OF "PARTY-STATES"

The emergence of the authoritarian paradigm of governance in Africa was particularly epitomized by the rise of the single-party state system. Aristide Zolberg (1966), in a seminal study on the party system in Africa, analyzed the rise of the "party-states" of West Africa and posited that the philosophy behind their establishment was quickly replicated in the rest of the African countries with variations based on local context. According to Zolberg, the rise of the West African "party-states" is explicable in terms of the absence of agreement on rules of the political game. Zolberg traced the search for electoral monopoly by incumbent parties and the emergence of the party-state to six kinds of pressures. These included (1) the perception that the opposition was led by people who challenged the fundamental values of the incumbent party. (2) The perception that resource scarcity made politics a zero-sum game, with the winners taking all and the losers receiving nothing. (3) The belief that fellow politicians had not internalized the rules of the game, and that adherence to standards of political civility that normally attend the adoption of a Westminster parliamentary system could not be assumed. (4) The absence of factors that normally limit the kinds of issues up for negotiation. (5) The record of assassinations of heads of state in Africa, which induced fear of opposition. (6) A pattern of international involvement that made it possible for opposition groups to acquire more financial support than they could succeed in amassing from domestic constituents and that consequently undermined the legitimacy of the electoral system (see Zolberg, 1966: 37–65). This view, as Jennifer Widner (1992: 10) observes, suggests that the rise of "party-states" had roots in characteristics common to many African countries after independence, some social and cultural, others economic and even psychological. The gist of Zolberg's thesis is that the party-states were established as a means for creating political order.

The second explanation of the rise of the party-state in Africa is rooted in the underdevelopment perspective. Scholars such as Walter Rodney (1981), Immanuel Wallerstein (1979), James Caporaso (1978), Colin Leys (1975), Richard Sandbrook (1975), Johan Galtung (1971), and Andre Gunder Frank (1967; 1970), among others, have elaborated the neocolonial and dependent nature of Third World economies in general and the African political economy in particular. According to this school, Western colonialism suppressed the economic, social, and political development of the Third World and the West is still to blame for the poverty therein. The essential argument here is that underdevelopment was, and is still, generated by the same historical processes that also generated economic development namely the development of capitalism. The logic of the world capitalist system, it is argued, is to keep the periphery perpetually in a dependent relationship with the center for purposes of further exploitation. Hence, in spite of these countries having gained political independence, they remain poor and economically subjugated to the West in a conjuncture that has been summed up as neocolonialism.

Accordingly, scholars such as Anyang' Nyong'o (1989) and Mukum Mbaku (2000a; 2000b) identify the economic dependence of African elites on foreign enterprises and foreign governments as the source of African authoritarianism. According to this perspective, local political elites who manage subsidiaries of multinational corporations or who sit on the boards of these businesses depend on the survival and success of their foreign patrons and try to influence domestic policy-making to protect these interests. Hence government policies, inasmuch as they are responsive to foreign imperatives, prove inappropriate for generating economic growth. The policies benefit only local elites allied with multinational enterprises. As a result, Anyang' Nyong'o argues, "[i]ndependent governments thus preside over the impoverishment of local majorities and have to be strong enough to master the tensions and conflicts generated among the mass of the people by the process of underdevelopment" (cit. in Widner, 1992: 15). This conjuncture inevitably leads to rule by fiat, of which single-party authoritarianism is emblematic.

Concentration of power and political departicipation is provided as the third explanation of the rise of the party-state. This focuses attention on the behavior of entrepreneurs vis-à-vis state officials. In Africa, economic power is overwhelmingly concentrated in the office of the head of state. As such, dependence on government officials for licenses, capital, infrastructure, foreign exchange, police protection, and protection against competition leads local entrepreneurs to invest in the careers of the bureaucrats on whose services or favor they depend to reduce the regulation-induced costs of business and make their enterprises profitable (Mbaku, 2000a: 13). In return, entrepreneurs pay back government officials through appointment to boards of trustees, hiring of relatives, or outright payment, which is an important source of extra-legal income for most African civil servants according to Mukum Mbaku. Once these transactions have taken place, the private-sector entrepreneurs seek to defend their investments and do so in direct proportion to the difficulty of maintaining their standards of living through occupations independent of government control. It is against this background that efforts at maintaining monopoly over power by incumbents through political corruption including vote buying, election rigging, solicitation of illegal campaign contributions, and outright repression may be understood.

Jennifer Widner (1992) provides a fourth explanation of the rise of the party-states in terms of bureaucratic authoritarianism in which high-level technocrats restrict electoral competition and the influence of electoral outcomes on policy choice. They do so, according to Widner, by seeking, not to mobilize followers, but to promote apathy on the part of citizens. Towards this end, bureaucratic authoritarianism eschews cultivation of corporatist links between groups in society. Instead, "the links between civil society and the bureaucratic-authoritarian regime are achieved through the co-optation of individuals and private interests into the system" (Widner, 1992: 19). This form of authoritarianism, however, is more applicable to Latin America than to Africa, and, in any event, it varies only slightly from the third explanation.

The fifth explanation differs from the foregoing four in the sense that it shifts from the state-centric approach to explaining the rise of the party-state in terms of the notion of weak states confronting strong societies.

This explanation is attributed to Joel Migdal (1988) according to whom the difficulty of securing agreement on the "rules of the game" in African politics traces back to characteristics of economic and social structures. Dispersion of power among multiple, contending centers of authority including ethnic and religious communities and local economic strong men, creates special difficulties for policy implementation. This is especially so when most production and consumption takes place through the kinds of lineage structures that are the common ways of organizing labor in Africa and given the limited economic dependence of residents on observable, official market transactions. For Migdal, the state in the Third World remains weak and is indeed subverted by the actions of the provincial-based strongmen and power brokers who maintain alternative organizational structures and are even more able to garner the loyalty, support, and obedience of the masses. In short, center-periphery relations in most Third World countries remain an endless struggle for social control between the state elites on the one hand and local moneybags and petty despots on the other. This view, as Widner (1992: 11) notes, holds that political "departicipation" of which the shift to a party-state is symbolic, derives from the difficulty in policy implementation in African settings where weak states confront strong societies. Herein, the rise of the party-state, or the authoritarian paradigm for our purposes, is seen as an effort by the national elite to effect some semblance of control and mobilization of the masses.

Most of the above explanations of the emergence of authoritarianism have a number of faults and limitations. With regard to the first explanation based on Zolberg's study of West African states, Widner (1992: 10) rightly argues that Zolberg's exposition is less of a theory than an inventory of circumstances that correlated with the shift to a party-state in the West African cases. The perspective does not seek to identify necessary and sufficient conditions, leaving the reader to wonder whether party-states emerge when all of the six circumstances, or only some of them, obtain. With respect to the power concentration thesis, Widner argues that to be useful, the approach must pursue the relationship between particular kinds of economic policies and the character and strength of the interest groups they spawn. It is important to ask, she asserts, what conditions give rise to groups with countervailing power, groups that are simultaneously independent of the government for their incomes, but sufficiently affected by government actions to have a stake in the quality of public management and thus in the preservation of the political space necessary to contest policy choices (Widner, 1992: 19).

Three key limitations can be attributed to the bureaucratic authoritarianism explanation. First, as Widner has noted, neither the military nor the bureaucratic establishments in Africa exhibited the same self-confident claim to technical mastery, much less the ideological commitment to a national capitalist development strategy as, for example, their Latin American, especially Brazilian, counterparts. Second, she points out that in Africa, popular classes display little programmatic political organization and are insufficiently strong to repeatedly press for platforms antagonistic to the interests of business. And finally, she argues that the tactics used to generate apathy among popular classes by some Latin American governments differ substantially by those favored by African heads of state. "Except in a few extreme cases, military or police 'death squads' are not part of the tactical repertoire in most African authoritarian systems. Detention without trial and petty harassment are more common" (Widner, 1992: 21).

Similarly, Widner argues that the underdevelopment perspective, even in its modified form, fails to explain preferences for specific strategies, institutions, or forms of authoritarian rule and " . . . therefore supplies little intellectual leverage in understanding the rise of party-states. It operates at too high a level of generality" (Widner, 1992: 17), she laments. She also finds that the "weak states, strong societies" approach fails to explain adequately the variations between and within countries. Indeed, Although Migdal's weak state, strong society thesis is compelling and analytically insightful, his conclusion lends credence to the pessimistic prognosis that most modern Third World countries are not engaged in state building but plagued by state disintegration. In addition, Migdal does not clarify whether strong states in Africa are based on democratic foundations or are products of effective employment of instruments of coercion as manifested in most military dictatorships in Third World countries. Migdal's analysis can also be faulted for failing to deeply explore the cultural normative basis of mass allegiance and loyalty to the state, which is crucial for the perpetuation of strong states. Furthermore, Migdal's thesis amounts to a "soft" form of cultural determinism, in which case, the "strong" societies should promote sub-state units rather than the central state.

In spite of the flaws that Widner finds with the above explanations, she goes on to build her hypotheses on elements of the same views in her examination of the rise of the party-state in Kenya. She in particular proceeds from Anyang' Nyong'o's thesis and blends this with Zolberg's exposition in regard to West Africa. Indeed, as noted above, Widner is cognizant of the fact that Zolberg's postulation is less of a theory than an inventory of circumstances that correlated with the shift to the party-state in West

Africa. Yet this notwithstanding, she is more than content to elevate Zolberg's "inventory of circumstances" into a theoretical framework capable of theorizing the transition from a single party to a party-state in Kenya (Ajulu, 2000: 139). Widner's study thus falls victim to the same flaws and limitations. The gist of this study's argument is that the emergence of authoritarianism in Africa as exemplified by the rise of the party-state—as well as the advent of democratization—can best be explained by the rational choice perspective.

THE RATIONAL CHOICE APPROACH

The emergence of the rational choice approach in social analysis is traced to the writings of Jeremy Bentham (1781), especially his enunciation of the principles of utilitarianism. The approach was subsequently elaborated by, among others, Von Neumann and Morgenstern (1944), Anthony Downs (1957), and Olson (1965). It has since been applied and critiqued by many scholars within the realm of political science.[2] According to Margaret Levi (1999: 20), rational choice reveals how intentional and rational actors generate collective outcomes and aggregate behavior. The strength of rational choice in comparative social analysis, she writes, is evident in three ways. First is its capacity to spawn testable theory with clear scope conditions. Second is its ability to make sense of the correlation of a set of events by providing a plausible and compelling story that identifies the causal mechanisms linking the independent and dependent variables. And third is its universalism that reveals generalizable implications applicable to cases beyond those under immediate investigation. The emphasis of this model is on rational and strategic individuals who make choices within constraints to obtain their desired ends, whose decisions rest on their assessment of the probable actions of others, and whose personal outcomes depend on what others do (Levi, 1999: 23).

For his part, George Tsebelis (1990) points out that the rational choice approach assumes that individual action is an optimal adaptation to an institutional environment while interaction between individuals is assumed to be an optimal response to each other. Hence the prevailing institutions, or the rules of the game, determine the behavior of actors, which in turn produces political or social outcomes (Tsebelis, 1990: 40). Although the approach is methodologically individualist, therefore, its focus is not on individual choice but on the aggregation of individual choices. The rationality implied in this approach is one in which individuals are assumed to act consistently in relation to their preferences. Amílcar

Barreto (2001) points out that before embarking on a course of action, rational individuals assess not only the factors favoring a particular action but also those against it. Accordingly, there are five characteristics of a rational actor:

> (1) He can always make a decision when confronted with a range of alternatives; (2) he ranks all the alternatives facing him in order of his preference in such a way that each is preferred to, or indifferent to or inferior to each other; (3) his preference ranking is transitive; (4) he always chooses from among the possible alternatives that which ranks the highest in his preference ordering; and (5) he always makes the same decision each time he is confronted with the same alternatives. (Downs, 1957:6)

In applying this approach, the trick is to define the preferences in general, ex ante to a particular application. Generally, this involves observation of what is of principal concern to the class of actors under consideration (Levi, 1999: 24). For the typical *homo economicus,* it is maximization of wealth; for *homo politicus,* maximization of power; for *homo sociologicus,* it is maximization of prestige, honor, or social status (Barreto, 2001: 83). Overall, the assumption is that whatever rational actors do, be they individuals, political parties, interest groups, or governments, they consider net payoffs, which may be material or psychological, egoistic or altruistic. Nonetheless, as Levi (1999: 20) points out, although the choice of each actor may be intentional and individually rational, the results may seem unintentional and socially irrational to many. It is in regard to this that Tsebelis (1990) argues that seeming suboptimal choices by actors indicate the presence of "nested games" wherein events or strategies in one arena influence the way the game is played in another arena.

Against the foregoing, it is the contention of this study that the actualization of the authoritarian paradigm in Africa was a deliberate rational choice on the part of the dominant political elite to maximize and monopolize power and thus reign supreme. This eventuality was a result of the strategic interaction between the incumbent political elite and the nascent opposition politicians within the rubric of weak political institutions and fragile constitutional frameworks, what Okoth-Ogendo (1991) calls "constitutions without constitutionalism." As Anyang' Nyong'o (1989) has argued, sections of the nationalist coalitions in Africa favored this establishment of authoritarianism, seeing in it an opportunity to have access to state apparatuses and thereby acquire avenues for capital accumulation and personal enrichment.

Fredrick Wanyama (2000: 31) rightly observes that African leaders wished to also enjoy the privileges, which the authoritarian colonial administration had exclusively afforded colonialists. Having witnessed the efficiency with which control of state institutions had enabled the colonial elite to convert the "national" economy into some kind of private estate, emergent African leaders simply sought to inherit the same institutions intact for their own benefit. They thus rejected the pluralistic political structures that were part of the negotiated independence package soon after assuming political power. The dominant political elite, however, camouflaged their realist self-interest in idealistic nationalist rhetoric. To justify their ill motives, they hid behind the call for national unity as the precursor of rapid economic development:

> They convincingly argued that a defused political structure would simply divide people along ethnic lines (given the ethnic plurality in African countries) rather than unite them. Reference was also made to the much-cherished traditional African society and argued that a plural political structure was incompatible with the traditional African lifestyle that was essentially communal and, hence, united. (Wanyama, 2000: 32)

Wanyama notes that the above arguments provided African leaders with a "sound" backing to return to the authoritarianism and autocracy of the colonial period after a brief stint with plural politics. Once in power, therefore, the first generation of African political leaders closed the door of politics and co-opted the colonial discourse of "development" (Young, 1994: 231). To discourage opposition and perpetuate their power positions, " . . . they argued that the problems of development demanded complete unity of purpose, justifying on these grounds the criminalization of political dissent and the inexorable march to political monolithism" (Ake, 1991: 32). The kind of political centralization that followed seemed to suggest that the essence of decolonization was simply the replacement of alien rulers with indigenous ones (Wanyama, 2000: 32). To this extent, as Rok Ajulu (2000: 150) observes, the colonial state was simply deracialized but it was never democratized; the colonial governor was replaced by the African president but the provincial administration and its entire legal paraphernalia, through which the governor had ruled was left more or less intact. "The new elites' economic fortunes rested heavily on access to state power. Any attempts to democratize the post-colonial state would obviously threaten the new political class' access to the state and the privileges that accrued from such control" (Ajulu, 2000: 151).

The emergence of single-partyism in Kenya and Zambia amply illustrate this rational choice approach to engineering authoritarianism in Africa, which was achieved through a combination of carrot-and-stick strategies.

THE CASE OF KENYA AND ZAMBIA

Both Kenya and Zambia are former British colonies. The two countries attained their political independence in 1963 and 1964 respectively. Both emerged into their independence with multiparty political systems defined by their respective constitutions. The two main political parties in Kenya were the ruling Kenya African National Union (KANU) and the opposition Kenya African Democratic Union (KADU). In Zambia the parties were the ruling United National Independence Party (UNIP) and the opposition African National Congress (ANC). It would seem, however, that the founding presidents of Kenya and Zambia, Jomo Kenyatta and Kenneth Kaunda respectively, were keen on establishing a single-party system and this they attained through different ways.

One-Partyism in Kenya

The process of political consolidation in Kenya began with nipping in the bud the constitutional provisions for a *Majimbo* (quasi-federal) system of government. The opposition KADU had pursued this philosophy of *Majimboism* that would allow semiautonomous ethnically-based regions to have substantial decision-making power over agricultural land, primary and intermediate education, local government, and public health among others.[3] The central government was responsible for external affairs, defense, customs, international trade, major economic development, and sourcing of foreign economic assistance. At the center was a bicameral legislature. The Lower House consisted of elected representatives from single-member constituencies while Senate was made up of elected members, one from each of the country's then 41 administrative districts. "Senate was constituted to guard the constitution from arbitrary amendment, as such amendment would require a 75 percent majority in the Lower House and a 90 percent majority in Senate" (Nasong'o, 2001a: 121). In effect, Senate was given powers to delay bills except those dealing with finances, powers that paralleled the delay powers of the United Kingdom's House of Lords.

Whereas KANU was dominated by the Kikuyu and Luo, KADU was essentially a coalition of politicians from the Luhyia, Kalenjin, and Mijikenda, and was led by Ronald Ngala, Masinde Muliro, and Daniel arap

Moi. These leaders argued that *Majimboism* was the only way of ensuring that no single large ethnic group could dominate the country. It was thus a strategy to counter the domination of KANU by the then two largest ethnic groups in the country, the Kikuyu and Luo. KANU acquiesced to the *Majimbo* constitution during the independence constitutional negotiations at Lancaster House, London. This acquiescence was, however, merely a strategic move on the part of KANU leaders to hasten the granting of independence. As V. G. Simiyu argues, it looks like all African leaders took the advice of Kwame Nkrumah very seriously when they were negotiating constitutions for their independence and could not agree on democratic checks and balances:

> Nkrumah said, at least in the case of Kenya, he told Koinange, 'go and tell Kenyatta in London [the second Lancaster House conference] to just accept what the British are telling him. If they want regionalism, and what-have- you, accept, let it be in that constitution, get independence then do what you like.' So for Kenya the 1962 constitution was only good for getting the independence.[4]

After independence, the new KANU government set about systematically dismantling the system that had been agreed upon. President Kenyatta was quite uneasy about opposition to his rule and the decentralized nature of the *Majimbo* system. He was devoted to a single-party dictatorship within the framework of a unitary state right from the beginning of Kenya's independence. Speaking at Bungoma's Kanduyi stadium, in the then Western Region in March 1964, he asserted that the opposition KADU—the champion of *Majimboism*—was a dying horse and predicted: "very soon, the country would see to it that Kenya had only one party—KANU" (Nasong'o, 1997: 10). The then Minister for Information, Broadcasting and Tourism, Achieng' Oneko added that this would facilitate accomplishment of the country's requirements as Kenya would "speak with one voice." KADU President Ronald Ngala reacted sharply to this one-party state idea and argued:

> . . . for a democratic government to rule properly it must have a constructive opposition. The opposition is in fact the watchdog of the ordinary persons in the country [and] government ought to use its majority in parliament to fulfill the country's demands or else resign and pave way for the opposition to rule. (Nasong'o, 1997: 10–11)

Nonetheless, by year's end, through the politics of intrigue, arm-twisting, and outright denial of resources to the Regional Authorities, the

opposition KADU was forced to dissolve itself. Walter Oyugi recounts the
deliberate strategy used by KANU to frustrate the opposition:

> . . . the strategy involved ignoring the stipulations of the constitution.
> When it came particularly to matters relating to financial allocations,
> regions were deliberately starved as a result of the center's refusal to
> release funds that were due to them. Development projects stalled and
> ministers went around reminding the opposition that no development
> funds could be released to their constituencies. In the meantime they
> were also denied permits to hold political meetings by the provincial
> administration which, contrary to the stipulations of the Majimbo con-
> stitution, continued to be answerable to the center. The message sank
> and KADU disbanded in October 1964, thereby enabling Kenya to
> become a de facto one party state under KANU, with KANU emerging
> thereafter as a multi-ethnic party soon to become an arena for factional
> ethnic infighting. (Oyugi, 1992:13)

In announcing the dissolution of KADU to parliament, Ronald Ngala, the
party president said: " . . . in the interests of Kenya, I have full mandate to
declare today that the official opposition is dissolved and KADU joins the
government under the leadership of Mzee Jomo Kenyatta . . . we intend to
face the national issue with one purpose" (Mutoro et al., 1999: 73). Two
years later, the two Houses of parliament were merged. The dissolution of
KADU saw President Jomo Kenyatta declare enthusiastically that " . . .
opposition for opposition's sake has died for ever and ever, Amen"
(Gertzel, 1972: 110). The absorption of KADU members of parliament into
KANU, however, swelled the ranks of the KANU left wing thereby height-
ening the ideological polarization between the left wing, led by Vice President Oginga Odinga, and the right wing led by President Kenyatta. The
subject of contestation between the two groups revolved around the question of land and the kind of post-colonial state to be crafted.

On the issue of land, the progressives argued that social justice
demanded the return of the three million hectares of prime land expropri-
ated by the colonial settlers to the landless Africans without cost to them or
to the government. However, in the independence negotiations, the British
government had, on behalf of the settlers, secured an agreement to the effect
that a smooth transfer of land would be on the basis of willing-seller-willing-
buyer. The conservatives thus held that social justice demanded protection
of private property and just compensation if an individual's property had to
be taken over. They ruled out nationalization of the "White Highlands."
The progressives viewed this as a dereliction of nationalist duty and a
betrayal of the nationalist struggle for independence. Indeed, because of his

fervent criticism of government agrarian policies, especially the slow pace of Africanization, Bildad Kaggia, a veteran of the radical trade union movement of the 1950s and an ex-Kapenguria trialist,[5] was dismissed as an assistant minister for education in early 1964 (Ajulu, 2000: 141). The issue of land remained a thorny one with great socio-economic implications.

With regard to the kind of post-colonial state to be established, the conservatives were content to retain the capitalist colonial state apparatus to which they had succeeded. The progressives, on the other hand, pushed for the deconstruction of the colonial state and the crafting of a new one based on socialism and reflecting the people's aspirations. They urged for nationalization of the commanding heights of the economy and pushed for radical agrarian reforms. Observing that the socialist way of life was not entirely new to Africa, Oginga Odinga denounced capitalism arguing that Kenyans had not fought for independence so as to supplant colonial masters and adopt the same system of exploitation and plunder against the Kenyan masses. He took advantage of representing Jomo Kenyatta at a United Nations conference in 1964 to disclose that, " . . . the government of Kenya is dedicated toward the establishment of a 'Democratic African State' . . . [and] to take steps away from the Western orbit to redress the imbalance caused by former colonial ties" (Okoth, 1992: 86).

Inevitably, the ideological divide between the progressives and conservatives became linked to the Eastern and Western ideological blocs then engaged in a raging Cold War. In particular, the progressives identified with the Soviet Union and China while the conservatives were supported and bolstered by the United States and Great Britain. Washington was especially wary of Oginga Odinga whom it regarded as " . . . the opening wedge in the Communist attempt to penetrate Kenya" (Okoth, 1992: 88). Emboldened by Western support, Kenyatta moved to stem the rising tide of the radical socialists and to marginalize them from the center of power. First, Pio Gama Pinto, a veteran of the Mau Mau underground struggle and acknowledged tactical advisor to Oginga Odinga, who had just won special election[6] to parliament as the progressives' candidate, was assassinated in Nairobi in mid 1965. "At the trial, the man who pulled the trigger, Mutua Kisili, told the prosecution that he had only been an agent of the 'Big Man.' But nobody seemed keen to pursue the Big Man" (Ajulu, 2000: 141). Then at the March 11–13, 1966 American and British-sponsored KANU delegates conference in Limuru, which "took on the pattern of a closely stage-managed American-type political convention" (Okoth, 1992: 95), Odinga's position of deputy party president was scrapped and eight regional vice presidents elected in his place.

Odinga and Bildad Kaggia reacted by quitting KANU and establishing the Kenya Peoples Union (KPU). Ten Senators and nineteen Representatives defected to join Odinga and Kaggia on the opposition side and, as Rok Ajulu (2000: 142) argues, as a result of the build up of pressures in the constituencies, "there were indications that more members would follow Odinga and Kaggia into the opposition." To forestall this eventuality, a constitutional amendment was enacted (the fifth in the three-year old republic) requiring members of the National Assembly who changed parties to seek a new electoral mandate from their constituencies. In the "little general election" that followed in 1966, insurmountable obstacles were placed in the way of KPU candidates. The government used its monopoly of sanctions and economic rewards to close the party out of the rest of the country, leaving it to operate only in Nyanza, the KPU leader, Oginga Odinga's home province. In this event, KPU won only two of the ten contested Senate seats and only nine of the nineteen House seats (Ajulu, 2000: 142). The KPU Vice President, Bildad Kaggia, who hailed from President Kenyatta's Central Province, lost his Kandara seat where "Kenyatta and Koinange took personal charge of Kaggia's personal harassment. Kandara was too high a stake to be left to chance. Kaggia lost the election, but a few days later newspapers reported Kaggia's abandoned ballot papers floating on Chania River" (Ajulu, 2000: 142). Three years later, KPU was banned altogether, and its leaders detained following a heated verbal exchange during an official function in Kisumu between Odinga and Kenyatta and a riot by Odinga's supporters (see Mutoro et al, 1999: 74). This turn of events ushered Kenya into a de facto single party system.

Political developments in Kenya following the banning of the KPU saw an active people's participation in politics decrease and the steady emergence of institutional authoritarianism (Chepkwony, 1987). Once he had used KANU to marginalize the Odinga faction from power in 1966, Kenyatta felt so comfortably powerful that "he had no more use for the party and left it into abeyance with neither meeting of its top organs nor national party elections between 1966 and 1978 when he eternally left the political scene" (Nasong'o, 2001a: 122). It is this reality of a largely dysfunctional party under Kenyatta that Jennifer Widner (1992) describes as a loosely organized debating society with little policy influence. She contends that "Kenyatta perceived that the best way to maintain political order in a society where ethnic or community boundaries usually coincided with economic differences, and where no one community constituted a majority of the nation's voters, was to eschew central control of political views" (Widner, 1992: 73). Instead, she asserts, Kenyatta employed a unique extra-parliamentary bargaining system in the name of *Harambee* (self-help movement), and a loosely defined political party to focus the attention of politicians on local issues and on the formation of alliances across communities, while limiting their power to force agendas on one another. Arguably, however, Kenyatta and his faction simply used the party to entrench their power positions by shutting out their competitors after which the party became superfluous, at least for their purposes. As Anyang' Nyong'o (1989) argues, the disintegration of the nationalist coalition had enabled a strong authoritarian president to emerge. Consequently, the dominant faction maintained the party when it suited its interests to do so, and then allowed it to atrophy to deny any other organized faction the chance of using it politically to attain its objectives within the bounds of law.

The Kenyatta regime went further to create a power base disguised as a welfare association known as Gikuyu Embu Meru Association (GEMA),[7] which by the mid 1970s acted informally as parliament, cabinet, and quite often, as judiciary in the country. This reality prompted the late popular member of parliament for Nyandurua North, Josiah Mwangi Kariuki to remark thus: "I tell you the cabinet is not running the country. It is no use having ministers who do not take decisions, who have no control over their ministries" (Chepkwony, 1987: 169). In the same vein, Martin Shikuku, member of parliament for Butere, complained in parliament that the Kenyatta regime was intent on killing parliament the same way it had killed KANU; a remark that elicited calls for substantiation or withdrawal. The presiding Deputy Speaker, Jean Marie Seroney, member for Tinderet, wondered loudly how Shikuku could substantiate the obvious! In spite of provisions for parliamentary immunity, both Shikuku and Seroney were arrested within the precincts of parliament and detained without trial with Jomo Kenyatta metaphorically warning that "the hawk in the sky is ready to swoop on the chickens" (Nasong'o, 2001: 123; Chepkwony, 1987: 167). Later in 1977, the two were followed in detention by radical parliamentarians George Anyona and Koigi wa Wamwere (see Ajulu, 2000: 144).

For his part, when he assumed power following Kenyatta's death in August 1978, Daniel arap Moi released all political detainees, did away with detention without trial, declared war on *magendo* (smuggling), and, quite significantly, affirmed that he would follow in Kenyatta's *Nyayo* (footsteps). Moi thus remained popular for about four years up to the attempted coup of August 1982. After this, the clamp down on political dissenters was so intense that most dissenters either fled to exile or were forced to operate underground leading to the emergence of an underground organization known as *Mwakenya—Muungano wa Wazalendo wa*

Kukomboa Kenya (Patriotic Union for the Liberation of Kenya) with its publications *Pambana* (Struggle) and *Mpatanishi* (The Arbiter). In June 1983, detention without trial was reinstated as populism was replaced by repression on a scale unprecedented even by the Kenyatta standards. This saw the detention and conviction of members of the country's traditional left wing—university lecturers and student activists—as well as those associated with the former vice president and doyen of opposition politics, Oginga Odinga under the guise of a crack down on *Mwakenya*.

President Moi systematically dismantled Kenyatta's ruling coalition and established his own. He began by hounding the former attorney general and then minister for constitutional affairs, Charles Njonjo out of office by accusing him of plotting to overthrow the government in cahoots with a foreign power, and then instituting a commission of inquiry to investigate this. Then, demonstrating a remarkable reluctance to co-opt powerful regional figures into government, Moi dispensed with Stanley Oloititip (then minister for Local Government), G. G. Kariuki (minister of state in the President's Office), Charles Rubia, Zachary Onyonka (minister for Education), as well as Robert Matano, a cabinet minister and long-serving secretary general of KANU. "Even within his (Moi's) old KADU peers, men of independent minds like [Masinde] Muliro were sidelined" (Ajulu, 2000: 146). Whereas Kenyatta had dealt with the "problem" of regional party bosses with power bases independent of the center by simply letting the party to atrophy, Moi sought to solve the same by imposing his men at all levels of the party hierarchy. Towards this end, he set about reorganizing and strengthening the party, KANU, and accorded it pride of place in the country's political process. In 1982, he rushed through parliament a bill introducing the now infamous section 2(A) to the Kenyan constitution, making the country a *de jure* one-party state. He did this ostensibly to forestall the eventuality of an opposition political party, which Oginga Odinga and George Anyona were preparing to register at the time.

In 1986, the Moi regime pushed the frontiers of authoritarianism even further by removing the security of tenure for the constitutional offices of judges, the attorney general, and the comptroller and auditor-general. The regime affirmed that KANU "has supremacy over parliament and . . . the party is also supreme over the High Court" (*Weekly Review* [Nairobi], November 21, 1986). The regime went further to adopt the queue voting (*Mlolongo*) system which it put to use in the 1988 general elections, thereby ensuring complete top-down control of the electoral process to the extent that the 1988 general elections have gone down as the most rigged elections in Kenya's history. It is against these developments that Widner holds that Kenya made a transition from what she calls "a single-party-dominant system" to "a party-state." Widner rightly observes that the 1980s would best be remembered as the decade that saw the consolidation of the power of the State House to control the political life of the country through the ruling party (Widner, 1992: 199). The extent of personal rule in the country is well captured by President Moi's exhortation of his cabinet ministers to demonstrate blind loyalty to him the way he himself had done to Kenyatta. On his return from an official visit to Addis Ababa on September 13, 1983, he said:

> I call on all Ministers, Assistant Ministers and every other person to sing like parrots. During Mzee Kenyatta's period I persistently sang the Kenyatta tune until people said 'This fellow has nothing except to sing for Kenyatta.' I say: I didn't have any ideas of my own. Why was I to have my own ideas? I was in Kenyatta's shoes [sic] and therefore, I had to sing whatever Kenyatta wanted. If I had sung another song, do you think Kenyatta would have left me alone? Therefore, you ought to sing the song I sing. If I put a full stop, you should also put a full stop. (Human Rights Watch, 1993: 7)

Clearly, the 1980s were a period of time when authoritarianism had its high noon in Kenya. Whereas the pillar of order under Kenyatta was repression, Moi for his part built a monster of a leviathan (Mueller, 1984). By the end of the 1980s, as Ajulu (2000) rightly observes, Moi had for all practical purposes created an imperial presidency.

One-Partyism in Zambia

Whereas the ruling party in Kenya took immediate steps after independence to nip the nascent opposition in the bud, the situation was not the same in the case of Zambia. For several years after independence in 1964, the leadership of UNIP expressed the view that a one-party system in Zambia would only come through the ballot box and not through imposition. For instance, addressing a UNIP annual general conference at Mulungushi Hall on August 15, 1967, President Kaunda declared:

> If what has been happening at both the Parliamentary and Local Government levels is anything to go by, we are obviously very close to the attainment of the one-party state . . . being honest to the cause of the common man we would, through effective Party and Government organizations, paralyze and wipe out any opposition thereby bringing about the birth of a one-party state . . . We go further and declare that even when this comes about we would not legislate against the formation of opposition

parties because we might be bottling the feelings of certain people no
matter how few . . . I repeat, one-party state is coming to Zambia
because the masses of our people recognize that we are sincere and true
to each one of them . . . The masses of our people trust us because we
have said that the one-party state was going to come as a result of the
people voting for the party freely for a people's democracy and this has
continued to be our guideline. (Hamalengwa, 1992:136–137)

According to Munyonze Hamalengwa (1992), these optimistic views were
expressed as a result of massive electoral successes UNIP had been register-
ing in local elections between 1964 and 1967.

However, in 1966, political developments began to emerge that had
serious implications for the fledgling Zambian democracy. In January
1966, two Lozi cabinet ministers, N. Mundia and M. Nalilungwe were dismissed for alleged financial impropriety. Later in July 1966, the two former
ministers, together with Mufaya Mumbuna who had resigned from ANC in
1965 following the party's support of the Local Government Act that
sought to abolish the traditional Induna (chieftaincy) system so central to
his Lozi people, founded the United Party (UP). UNIP reacted by persuading ANC to join it in amending the constitution to provide for the compul-
sory resignation of any MP who changed his political party allegiance after
his or her election. This was the same weapon used by the Kenyatta regime
in Kenya to stem the tide of defections from KANU to KPU, also in 1966.
In the subsequent by-elections in February 1967, UNIP won both Mundia's
and Nalilungwe's former seats, one of which—Mazambuka—was in ANC's
stronghold of the Southern Province. Tordoff and Molteno (1974) note,
however, that only one third of the registered voters cast their votes and
there was a clear distortion of the democratic process due to widespread
intimidation and violence by UNIP activists, especially in the ANC stronghold Mazambuka constituency. "Mazambuka tactic" became part of the
political folklore of both parties. On the one hand, intimidation and violence signified the fragility of UNIP's commitment to multiparty competition and, on the other, gravely shook ANC's confidence in the legitimacy of
the system. As a result, four of the remaining nine ANC MPs anticipated
the early demise of their party and crossed the floor to join UNIP (Tordoff
& Molteno, 1974: 23). Nonetheless, ANC recaptured these four seats in
the subsequent by-elections.

Political rivalry within UNIP came to a head in August 1967 when
the first post-independence election for members of the Central Committee of the ruling party was held. Posts in this committee were crucial and
those who held them wielded tremendous power and influence over the

decision-making process that allocated scarce resources to regions, communities, and individuals in Zambia. Thus stiff competition arose in UNIP over posts in the Central Committee. Bemba leaders of Northern Province, whose followers had taken a prominent role in the independence struggle and who felt relatively under-represented and unrewarded, formed a coalition with the party's weak Tonga minority of Southern Province to unseat leading Lozi (Western Province) and Nyanja (Eastern Province) office holders. The openly ethno-regional appeals by both sides generated a vast amount of ill feeling in the party that undermined its national prestige. President Kaunda captured the gloomy picture of the intra-party factional fight when he stated, during the election, that:

> We have canvassed so strongly and indeed, viciously, along tribal, racial and provincial lines, that one wonders whether we really have national or tribal and provincial leadership. I must admit publicly that I have never experienced in the life of this young nation, such a spate of hate, based entirely on tribe, province, race, color and religion, which is the negation of all that we stand for in this Party and Government. I do not think that we can blame the common man for this. The fault is ours fellow leaders—we, the people here assembled. (Hamalengwa, 1992: 137)

According to Tordoff and Molteno, the consequences of the intra-UNIP factional struggle were manifold, damaging, and permanent. First, it introduced an era of cabinet reshuffles—sometimes three in a year—which proved very disruptive of continuity in the making and implementation of policy. Second, it resulted in the accession to the vice presidency of both UNIP and the republic of Simon Kapwepwe, the most senior Bemba politician, thereby increasing the impression that the party was Bemba-dominated. Third, the party's further image was tarnished by the necessity in December 1967 of setting up a commission of inquiry into the affairs of the Lusaka City Council, which subsequently revealed that certain UNIP councilors were feathering their own nests (Tordoff & Molteno, 1974: 24–25).

Any lingering hopes on the part of Kaunda that opposition parties in Zambia would die a natural death at the alter of the ballot box were dashed by the results of the 1968 general election. In the run-up campaign to the election, the UNIP-UP conflict culminated in a clash between the two parties in August 1968 on the Copperbelt resulting in six deaths. The government took the opportunity to ban the UP, even though it was not the sole culprit. The party had, however, won majority support in Western Province and its activists continued to campaign under ANC. As a result, ANC gained some seats due to the swelling of its ranks by former members of the UP and managed to wrest control of Western Province from UNIP, where UNIP lost 8 of the 10 seats to ANC (Momba, 1993: 188). The ANC now commanded 22.11 percent (23 of 104) seats compared to the 13.33 percent (10 out of 75) of the seats it commanded at independence in 1964. On the other hand, UNIP garnered 77.88 percent (81 of 104) of the seats compared to the 73.33 percent (55 of 75) it held at independence.[8] The December 1968 election results thus came as a shock to UNIP, though the party still won by a large margin. The election results, as Hamalengwa (1992) notes, were a clear indication that ANC was not going to suffer a natural death as had been envisaged.

Matters were further complicated by the endurance of the intra-UNIP factional competition that had been unleashed by the 1967 party election. By February 1968, the factionalism and sectionalism in UNIP was so intense that, disgusted by it all, Kaunda announced his resignation as president of both the party and the country to the party's National Council. He, however, rescinded the resignation after eight hours before it could take legal effect (Momba, 1993: 191). To stem the tide of sectional factionalism in the party, Kaunda suspended UNIP's Central Committee in August 1969 and assumed control of the party as the secretary general.[9] He initiated measures to reform the party, which culminated in a new party constitution that was finally ratified in November 1970. According to Gertzel, Baylies, and Szeftel (1984), the new constitution represented a further attempt to control intra-party conflict through structural change. The gist of the problem was provincial representation in the General Conference, UNIP's highest authority, which also elected the Central Committee. Since independence, representation in the General Conference was based on the party's administrative structure. In this event, the uneven growth of party regions across Zambia had resulted in an imbalance in provincial representation and the dominance of the Copperbelt as the province with the largest number of party branches. Quite inevitably given the sectional nature of Zambian politics, other provinces viewed Copperbelt dominance as the source of Bemba preponderance in the party, and thus of the Bemba success in the 1967 party election. The new party constitution sought to redress this imbalance by providing for equal provincial representation in the General Conference. On the positive side, this provision for equal representation effectively appeased provinces that had hitherto considered themselves underrepresented. Furthermore, it was a crucial factor that contributed to UNIP's ability to withstand the subsequent United Progressive Party (UPP) challenge. On the downside, however, it was, in fact, the source of disappointment and alienation by many on the Copperbelt and in

Northern Province that directly contributed to the emergence of the UPP in the first place (see Gertzel et al., 1984: 13–14).

In 1969, the politicians who had been edged out in 1967 began to form coalitions to fight the next round of party elections, which were to be held in 1970. Sensing the tension and possible electoral disaster in the 1970 party elections given the new constitution, and on allegations that his Bemba people were being persecuted, the vice president, Simon Kapwepwe, resigned his post in 1970. He eventually quit UNIP and government in August 1971 to found the United Progressive Party (UPP), the most formidable opposition party to Kaunda's UNIP at the time. Unlike ANC, whose stronghold was Southern Province, UPP threat to UNIP lay in the fact that it threatened UNIP's geographical base—Northern, Luapula, and Copperbelt Provinces (Momba, 1993: 190). Kapwepwe, whose constituency was based on the Copperbelt and in Northern Province, quickly gathered support from some key members from UNIP, the Copperbelt, Northern Province and elsewhere. Disgruntled petty bourgeois members of UNIP also defected to UPP. Gertzel et al. (1984) note that the many defections to UPP seriously impaired UNIP's capability for mobilization, especially in Copperbelt Province. The three scholars further observe that:

> The split at the national level was mirrored by divisions at the local level and, on the Copperbelt, led to a great deal of violence when party branches and constituencies either divided or defected wholesale to U.P.P. Indeed, U.N.I.P. lost many of its most efficient organisers and outspoken leaders. Furthermore, the great popularity of the U.P.P. leader, Simon Kapwepwe, among many Bemba-speaking people, presented U.N.I.P. with the very real possibility of losing much electoral support in Northern and Copperbelt Provinces, thus threatening to make U.N.I.P. itself a regionally defined party by default. (Gertzel et al. 1984: 14)

With the likelihood of a coalition between the UPP and ANC in the 1973 general election that was just around the corner, UNIP was clearly in a crisis and something had to be done or else it faced the possibility of going down in defeat (Hamalengwa, 1992: 138). UNIP's reaction was swift and hysterical. Through invocation of emergency powers, some UPP activists including its entire executive committee except Kapwepwe were detained under the pretext of threat to national security. Considerable violence and other intimidatory measures were used against suspected UPP supporters in the December 1971 by-elections that were occasioned by defections to UPP. Within this political conjuncture, UNIP won eleven of the twelve contested seats. Kapwepwe won the Mufulira seat on the Copperbelt against all odds.

In order to secure the popular loyalty and acquiescence under the circumstances, the Kaunda regime dished out large placatory salary increases throughout the public sector including the armed forces (Tordoff & Molteno, 1974: 33).

It was within this political context that the one-party political system in Zambia became inevitable. UNIP activists renewed their demands for a one party state. To forestall the eventuality of a UPP-ANC coalition in the 1973 general election, which was a foregone conclusion and about which UNIP was jittery, the UPP was banned altogether in February 1972 and its leader, Simon Kapwepwe and 123 of its leading members detained. Jotham Momba (1993) notes that with the seeming success of the one-party system in Tanzania, Kaunda seemed to have changed his mind about the need to shift to a one-party state.[10] Consequently, after the banning of UPP, a commission chaired by Vice President Mainza Chona was set up to recommend what form a "one-party participatory democracy" should take. In setting out to establish single-party authoritarianism, Kaunda argued on February 25, 1972:

> You know that since independence there has been a constant demand for the establishment of a one-party state in Zambia. The demands have increasingly become more and more widespread in all corners of Zambia . . . In the resolutions passed by almost every conference, whether political or non-political, unequivocal demands have been made for Government to introduce a One-Party system of Government . . . Indeed, the UNIP National Council sitting in Mulungushi Hall between the 1st and the 3rd October last year (1971) charged the Central Committee of the ruling party to work towards the achievement of a One-Party Democracy in which the liberties and welfare of the common man will be paramount. The Central Committee in its study of the subject noted that in this overwhelming public demand the objective for calling for a new system of Government is the fundamental need to preserve unity, strengthen peace and accelerate development in freedom and justice. (Hamalengwa, 1992: 138; Momba, 1993: 193)

Because of the "people's demands," Kaunda noted further, "the Government had decided that Zambia shall become a one-party participatory democracy and that practical steps should be taken to implement the decision" (Hamalengwa, 1992: 138–139). Towards this end, the Chona Commission began collecting and collating views for purposes of considering and recommending changes to the constitution of the Republic of Zambia and that of UNIP and matters related thereto necessary to bring about the establishment of a single-party state (see Donge, 1995: 195).

It is important to note President Kaunda's concern that one-party states take many different forms and his insistence on the best, arguing that Zambians deserved the most democratic of the one-party systems. As Momba writes, Kaunda required the commission to consider the key issues of the method of electing the president "including the important question" of whether an incumbent president shall be eligible for re-election;[11] relationships between the various structures of the party and the amount of freedom the people should have to form pressure groups along ethnic lines; and the kind of freedom citizens ought to have to stand for national and local elections. Of crucial importance to Kaunda in his consideration of the single-party system was an attempt to establish a system that would be able to stem the tide of political polarization along ethnic lines while at the same time ensure some considerable measure of popular participation (Momba, 1993: 194–195).

The single-party legislation was passed in December 1972 thereby abolishing ANC and other attempts at reviving the UPP. The final constitution that emerged in December 1972, did not only establish the single-party state, but also codified in its preamble President Kaunda's thoughts and prescriptions for Zambia. The new constitution institutionalized Kaunda's welfarist philosophy of "Humanism" as the official ideology of the new system and the guiding compass for Zambians as a whole (Hamalengwa, 1992: 139). Once the one-party state was inaugurated, the Kaunda regime now felt strong enough to release Kapwepwe and 35 other political detainees in January 1973.

The one-party constitution in Zambia provided for the supremacy of party organs over state organs. In this context, as Jotham Momba points out, the Central Committee took precedence over the cabinet. The Central Committee's role was to formulate policy for implementation by the cabinet. This state of affairs remained so from 1973 until 1988 when the UNIP Central Committee was expanded to include cabinet ministers as ex-officio members. The supremacy of the Central Committee over the cabinet also meant that it was the secretary general of UNIP rather than the Prime Minister that acted as president whenever President Kaunda was absent. Additionally, UNIP's National Council took precedence over the National Assembly. Nonetheless, its composition included members of parliament, two representatives of the labor movement, members of the Central Committee and party leaders at provincial and district levels. The new constitution further enhanced the powers of the president with regard to the composition of parliament and the party Central Committee. It gave him powers to personally nominate three additional members to the 20 elected members of the Central Committee, and ten members to the National Assembly. The constitution further provided for one presidential candidate to be elected by the party General Conference and then presented to the electorate for ratification. Although the original proposal was for an electoral competition between three presidential candidates, this was rejected on grounds that it would divide both party and country along ethnic lines since there would be no political party differences between the candidates.

With the new constitutional framework in place, ANC members, led by their leader, Harry Mwaanga Nkumbula, decided to formally join UNIP as a bloc under the famous Choma Declaration of June 27, 1973. Single-party authoritarianism was thus officially inaugurated in what was subsequently known as Zambia's Second Republic.

POLITICAL MONOLITHISM AS HEGEMONIC IDEOLOGY

Once the "party-states" were established in Africa, the single-party system was objectified in ways that elevated the single-party idea to the position of a hegemonic ideology. The first way in which these parties were objectified was by equating them with the spirit of nationalism that informed the fight for political independence. It is noteworthy that whether one is talking about KANU in Kenya, Tanganyika African National Union (TANU) in Tanzania,[12] UNIP in Zambia, Zimbabwe African National Union (ZANU) in Zimbabwe, Convention People's Party (CPP) in Ghana, or Parti Democratique de Guinée (PDG) in Guinea, all these parties started off as nationalist movements that led their respective countries to independence. In spite of existence of other political parties, as Zolberg (1966) notes, one political organization emerged which held the center of the stage and could more appropriately be called a nationalist movement than any of its opponents. These movements, he argues, were not necessarily devoid of ethnic and other traditional particularisms; "on the contrary, most of them grew by successfully incorporating a variety of ethnic and other groups. The difference was that these coalitions were large, and hence by definition had to be heterogeneous, while many of their opponents almost by default stressed specific affiliations" (Zolberg, 1966: 35). Elites thus presented the dominant party to the masses as the personification of nationalism, as the party that "brought independence." To express dissent from such a party was thus viewed as an act of betrayal; it was to be anti-nationalism, which, by default, meant being Eurocentric and thus pro-colonialism. Political dissenters were thus generally dismissed as agents of foreign masters bent on destabilizing the hard-won independence. For instance, President Kenyatta described the opposition KPU as "tribal malcontents concerned mainly with sectional interests, who would also drag Kenya into communism" (Barkan, 1987: 225).

Second, and as a corollary to the above, African leaders stressed historical differences between parties in Africa on the one hand and those in Europe and North America on the other hand. Julius Nyerere justifiably argued that the Anglo-American parties came into being as a result of existing social and economic divisions, with the second party being formed to challenge the monopoly of political power by some aristocratic or capitalistic group:

> Our own parties had a very different origin. They were not formed to challenge any ruling group of our own people; they were formed to challenge the foreigners who ruled over us. They were not, therefore, political 'parties'—i.e., factions—but nationalist movements. And from the outset they represented the interests and aspirations of the whole nation. (Nyerere, 1974:198)

Because of this, it was argued, alternative political parties were unnecessary; they were superfluous. Ghana's Kwame Nkrumah, the first African leader to institute a *de jure* single-party system, for instance, dismissed out of hand Anglo-American postulations that opposition political parties are a prerequisite to democratic practice. He argued: "I do not agree with those political theoreticians and theoretical politicians who would want us to believe that it is wrong for all the country to belong to one party, and that an opposition is necessary in a democracy . . ." (Zolberg, 1966: 48). For his part, Julius Nyerere (1974) argued that for as long as the single party's membership remained open to all citizens, and the party was identified with the nation as a whole, the foundations of democracy were firmer and the people could have more opportunity to exercise a real choice than where there are two or more parties, each representing only a section of the community.

Thirdly, the most erstwhile champions of the single-party system saw it as a moral community. They defined unity in a negative way by which was essentially meant the absence of opposition. Opponents could, and were invited to join the nationalist (dominant) party. Zolberg (1966: 46) writes, for instance, that in Guinea, Sékou Touré generously appealed to "our brothers BAG [Bloc Africain de Guinée] and socialists," but asked them to surmount their "self-love, complexes, rancor, selfishness and jealousy." In this way, as Zolberg notes, Touré implied that his opponents were not merely individuals who disagreed with his party on legitimate grounds, but rather, that they were morally defective, and if they wanted to become good men and women, they had to join the Parti Democratique de Guinée (PDG). The quality of the PDG as a moral community was stressed when, after a new election had strengthened and consolidated the PDG's majority, Sékou Touré hailed the party's most recent adherents by saying: "Here, allow me to solemnly salute all those men and women who, having definitely abandoned the path of sabotage and crime, have recently joined us in our exalted task of the construction of a new Guinea" (Zolberg, 1966: 46). Indeed, after Guinea's independence, the PDG viewed itself as the moral spearhead of all Africa: "We must know that our political task now goes beyond the borders of Guinea. Our party becomes that of all Africans who love justice and freedom" (Zolberg, 1966: 46). Having set itself this task, as all other dominant parties in Africa did, the PDG brooked neither opposition nor dissenting views, spontaneous or otherwise. Such opposition was regarded as an interference with the task of national mobilization.

In similar manner, Ghana's Kwame Nkrumah portrayed his CPP as a moral community and demonized the party's competitors for power. In a speech tracing the history of nationalism in Ghana, he hailed the legitimate ancestors who manned the pre-Second World War political groups, but damned the still-active predecessors of his CPP as a "petty bourgeoisie." He noted that these leaders despised the common people and the common people distrusted them. In contrast, "the masses recognized in the Convention People's Party the only hope for their salvation" (Zolberg, 1966: 57). Hence, like in Guinea, so it was in Ghana, the party was a moral community and the struggle between the CPP and its opponents was described in appropriate terms: "some of the people were led astray and all the forces of darkness, feudalism, and ignorance joined together to stab the revolution in the back and to rob our people of the fruits of their struggle on the very verge of independence. But the party successfully met the challenge and once more the people rallied to its side" (Zolberg, 1966: 57). The triumph of the CPP was thus seen as a revolution, the result of which was "political power vested in the people." Against this background, Nkrumah went further to legislate against other political parties via a constitutional amendment. The identity of the people then became synonymous with the party and that party with the nation.

The same situation obtained in Kenya where the Kenyatta regime saw its opponents in KPU as being crazy individuals who needed to "reexamine their heads" and return to KANU. At Nairobi's Kamukunji Grounds during a Kenyatta Day rally on October 20, 1967, President Kenyatta remarked with regard to the opposition KPU:

> Brothers, there are those who ask, 'What is the government doing?'
> And there are those who say, 'The Government has done nothing as
> yet.' But I am telling you, even if we have done nothing, I think every
> citizen should be proud of being free. Each man is free, and is no longer
> anybody's slave. For a man to say he is free, and that he is governing
> himself is a very important thing. . . . We all fought for *uhuru* [inde-
> pendence], and it is only the cowards who used to hide under the beds
> while others were struggling who go about asking what the KANU
> government has done. . . . You all know KPU. . . . Ask them where and
> how they fought for *uhuru*. . . . What have the KPU ever done for any-
> body? As from today, KPU are to be regarded as snakes in the grass.
> Let them try and reexamine their minds and return to KANU. If they
> do not do so, KPU should beware! The fight for our *uhuru* is on. Who-
> ever has ears to hear let him heed this. (Ochieng, 1995: 98)

For their part, ardent UNIP supporters in Zambia went further to regard
their party as a Church with a definite creed, which required regular atten-
dance. In a pamphlet on political solidarity, then secretary general of UNIP,
Manu Sipalo, wrote in 1960:

> U.N.I.P. is not a faction, not a group, a wing, it is an institution rooted
> like a tree in the centre around which men group themselves as best
> they could. It is a fundamental and self-evident thing like life, liberty
> and the pursuit of happiness or like a National Flag . . . It is in fact the
> synonym of patriotism (Nationalism) which is another name for
> U.N.I.P. . . . On this basis therefore it is inconceivable that any self-
> respecting man should not belong to. . . . U.N.I.P. . . . U.N.I.P. is in a
> sense a political church, which requires regular attendance and has a
> creed, which epitomizes the 'modernizing' approach. (Cit. in Gertzel, et
> al. 1984: 27)

In the same vein, while instituting single-party rule in 1972, Kaunda characterized the opposition as people who had become "professionals at man-
ufacturing lies, spreading rumours, creating confusion and despondency,
and pretending to oppose what they inwardly welcome and exploit for
their own personal benefits in the name of democracy which they have
abused and desecrated." He thus argued that "The One-Party Democracy
will help us to weed out [these] political opportunists" (Gertzel et al., 1984:
17). It was against this background that opposition politics was demonized
and ultimately legislated against.

Fourth, given the centrality of the state in the African political economy and the lack of distinction between the ruling party and the state, the
party was objectified as the agent of development. For instance, at the
height of the single-party system in Kenya in the mid-1980s, the ruling

party, KANU, simply became known as "Baba na Mama" (Father and Mother). It was the sole provider of the goodies and to partake of them, one had not only to be loyal to the party, but also had to be seen to be so— by singing praises to the party leader. Those with dissenting political opinions were labeled as *wasiotosheka* (disgruntled elements), *vinyangarika* (nondescripts/hirelings), and "enemies of development." It is in regard to this that Zolberg rightly observes that under the party-state, all possible dissenting political opinion and cleavages were illegitimized and defined out of existence. The people could speak only through the party, which had to be supreme and paramount because it, alone, represented the hyphen that bound all layers of the population, all those who, in the name of the population or of the party, were invested with even minimal responsibility. The people were one and, acting through the party, which directed the state, they built the nation (Zolberg, 1966: 47). The party was thus the basis of the legitimacy of all other socio-political institutions. Ultimately, it was the people, it embodied the nation and, therefore, it had to be one.

Fifth and finally, the single party system was viewed as the foundation and true reflection of "African democracy." This view had such wide appeal that it is worthy considering at length. The leading proponent of this perspective was Tanzania's Julius Nyerere. According to Nyerere, democracy is one thing that is as African as the tropical sun. The very essence of traditional African democracy inhered in the fact that "[t]he elders sit under the big tree, and talk until they agree" (Nyerere, 1974: 195). Nyerere argued that "where there is one party, and that party is identified with the nation as a whole, the foundations of democracy are firmer than they can ever be where you have two or more parties, each representing only a section of the community" (Nyerere 1974: 196). To him, a two-party system can be justified only when the parties are divided over some fundamental issue; otherwise it merely encourages the growth of factionalism. He emphasized:

> ... the only time when a political group can represent the interests of a section of the community, without being a faction, is when the group fights to remove a grievous wrong from society. But then the differences, between this group and those responsible for the wrong it fights, are fundamental; and there can therefore be no question of national unity until the differences have been removed by change. And 'change' in that context is a euphemism, because any change in fundamentals is termed 'revolution.' (Nyerere 1974: 196)

Nyerere argued that if you have a two-party system where the differences between the parties are not fundamental, then you immediately reduce politics to the level of a football match. "A football match may, of course, attract some very able players; it may also be entertaining; but it is only a game, and only the most ardent fans (who are not usually the most intelligent) take the game seriously" (Nyerere, 1974: 197). According to Nyerere, this is, in fact, what has happened in many of the so-called democratic countries where some of the most intelligent members of society have become disgusted by the hypocrisy of the party games called politics, and take no interest in them:

> They can see no party line they could support without reservation and are thus left with no way of serving their country in the political field, even should they wish to; except, perhaps, by writing a book! For the politics of a country governed by the two-party system are not, and cannot be, national politics; they are the politics of groups, whose differences, more often than not, are of small concern to the majority of the people. (Nyerere, 1974: 197)

Nyerere recognized that the theory behind the party-based method of conducting elections is that voters choose a policy rather than a personality. He argued, however, that where there is no difference over policy,[13] as was the case in Africa where all were agreed on the imperative need for nation building and economic development, the only choice which can make sense must be a choice between individuals—the choice of the best individual to do the job. Cognizant of the fact that as leader of a one-party government, he could be accused of special pleading in justifying one-party systems, President Nyerere pointed out that defenders of the two-party system could equally be well accused of the same thing:

> For, in spite of their professed conviction that democratic government demands an Opposition, I have never heard of a party fighting an election with the object of forming one! On the contrary each party fights with the hope of winning as many seats as possible. They fail however to win them all. And then, having failed, they quite blandly make a virtue of necessity and produce the most high-sounding arguments in praise of their failure. (Nyerere 1974: 198)

To Nyerere, in any human society, compromise between individuals is not only necessary but also desirable; it is the only means of arriving at that common denominator without which the very idea of society would be impossible. "But, if compromise is desirable, what makes it so is the common good—not sectoral interests. Individualism, therefore, should be tempered with, or subjected to, the good of society as a whole, not merely to the good of a part of society" (Nyerere, 1974: 200). Nyerere thus rejected the Anglo-American emphasis on organized and automatic opposition and embraced what he termed the African practice of spontaneous and there- fore free opposition within the rubric of a single party. He recognized, nonetheless, that "[t]o minds molded by Western parliamentary tradition and Western concepts of democratic institutions, the idea of an organized opposition group has become so familiar that its absence immediately raises a cry of 'dictatorship'" (Zolberg, 1966: 48). Given Nyerere's philo- sophical arguments in defense of the "party-state," it is no wonder that Tanzania's one-party model became the exemplar for other countries such as Zambia.

Against the foregoing, the authoritarian paradigm became locked in place in Africa, becoming the rule rather than the exception insofar as gov- ernance was concerned. Its establishment was not at all seen, at least on the part of the elite, as an antithesis to democracy. It was instead justified as the actualization of genuine African democracy rooted in traditional political ethos, and as a logical response to the imperatives of socio-economic devel- opment on the part of the emergent African states. As the Kaunda regime in Zambia argued, the objective of the establishment of the single-party state was " . . . the fundamental need to preserve unity, strengthen peace and accelerate development in freedom and justice" (Hamalengwa, 1992: 138; Momba, 1993: 193). Similarly, in orchestrating the formation of the Cameroon National Union (CNU) as the sole political party in Cameroon in 1966, President Ahmadou Ahidjo claimed that the "great unified party" would indeed promote the democratic process, safeguard freedom of expression and discussion, and tolerate various other democratic tendencies (Takougang, 1997: 52). At the end of the day, the single party became syn- onymous with the state and the nation-in-the-making. The slogan of the party in Kenya—*KANU Yajenga Nchi* (KANU builds the nation)—became part of the nationalist repertoire as was that of UNIP—One Zambia, One Party, One Leader!

CONCLUSION

This chapter has focused on the emergence of authoritarianism in Africa as embodied in the rise of the single-party state system soon after political independence. It has argued that virtually all African countries emerged into independence under nascent multiparty political systems but political consolidation by the dominant political elite saw the outlawing of opposi- tion political parties. The parties of independence in Kenya and Zambia, as elsewhere in Africa, were not all-encompassing nationalist movements. Their capacity for mobilization and control was increasingly circumscribed once independence was attained. The new political elite faced spirited opposition and challenge from both ethno-regional and ideological groups, which undermined their power positions. To maximize their power and insure themselves against competition, therefore, the dominant elite rationalistically opted for single-party authoritarianism, which they justified as a logical response to the politics of fragmentation and a basis for the onerous task of nation building. For all practical purposes, the emergence of single-party states in Africa was "part of the process whereby an acquisitive elite entrenched itself in power" (Gertzel, 1984: 3). It was, in Gertzel's view, an attempt to achieve an institutional balance between participation and control.

Indeed, the cases of Kenya and Zambia, especially the latter, amply illustrate how the single-party state rationally emerged out of a bitter and prolonged political conflict, which had demonstrated the difficulties the leadership faced in asserting control. The groups that faced each other in KANU in the mid-1960s were ideologically oriented, with leftists who espoused radical agrarian reforms, Africanization of the economy, and land redistribution, pitted against the conservatives who ruled out nationalization of the economy and wished to maintain the pre-independence status quo for their own self-aggrandizement. Within UNIP at the same time, the political groups that competed for the control of the party and government policies were generally ethno-regional groups, which responded to their constituents in the provinces, regions, and localities. In both countries, this party factionalism and sectionalism became apparent in 1966. In Zambia it climaxed in the formation of the UP by dissidents from UNIP led by Nalumino Mundia. The UP was a result of growing disenchantment and relative deprivation felt by many political leaders of Lozi origin within UNIP over what they regarded as the neglect of Barotseland (now Western Province) in terms of system distributive outputs. It was also in view of what they regarded as Bemba domination of the party. In Kenya, on the other hand, party factionalism culminated in the resignation of Vice President Oginga Odinga and his formation of the KPU following an orchestrated move to marginalize him and his fellow radicals from the center of power.

In Kenya, immediate steps were taken soon after independence to nip the nascent opposition in the bud and this was achieved a year into independence when the opposition KADU was forced to dissolve itself. Although the formation of the KPU in 1966 returned the country to a two-party system, this was a short lived interregnum as the new opposition party was banned in 1966 making Kenya a de facto one party state until 1982 when it became a single-party state by law. For their part, the Zambian political elite entertained the idea that the opposition would die a natural death at the ballot box. This expectation was fueled by the decisive victories that UNIP registered in a series of local government elections in the immediate post-independence period. Political developments in 1966 coupled with the resignation of Vice President Simon Kapwepwe and his formation of the UPP that posed a formidable challenge to UNIP necessitated the social engineering of a one-party state. This was attained via amendments to the UNIP and state constitutions in 1972. Once the single-party system was established in both Kenya and Zambia, as elsewhere in Africa, provision was made for the supremacy of the party organs over state organs and the notion of single-party rule was objectified and elevated to the level of a hegemonic ideology. This was done by attributing political independence to the dominant party; objectifying the party as the embodiment of nationalism; projecting it as a moral community; equating the party with the state and presenting it as the agent of development; and positing the single-party system as a reflection of traditional African democracy.

Overall, by using the ideology of the one-party state, African leaders sought to transform their regimes towards actualization of political unanimity. They went about this through various ways. These included co-optation, intimidation, exile, or deportation of political opponents. Other mechanisms included modification of the electoral system to make competition impossible; transformation of the inherited constitution to centralize wide discretionary power into the executive and to restrict the role of representative institutions such as parliament. This authoritarian paradigm of governance also saw the increasing use of a criterion of political loyalty to select key administrators; administrative control over local government; reduction of the independence of the judiciary; as well as governmental control over the mass media, both print and electronic. Furthermore, it witnessed the erosion of consultation within the party and of accountability of the leadership to the members, even as the language of collective leadership was invoked. In other words, it was the antithesis of the democratic mode of governance.

Chapter Two
The Forces of Democratization

Neopatrimonial authoritarianism, the established paradigm of governance in Africa, met its opposite in the form of heightened activism for democratic governance at the close of the 1980s. By the beginning of the 1990s, as Crawford Young (1994) notes, Africa, from Capetown to Cairo, Algiers to Nairobi faced a common political conjuncture, an imperative of democratization, broadly defined. According to Young, at this juncture, the African State, battered by economic decline and weakened by political decay, faced narrowed choices. Political opening was no longer an option but an obligation: "A political economy where . . . political man ruled the economy and economic man ruled politics had finally produced an impasse whose sole exit was liberalization both political as well as economic" (Young, 1994: 230).

This eventuality was a consequence of a combination of factors. It is noteworthy that the social, economic, and political development of any given modern state is shaped both by endogenous and exogenous factors. This is a function of the interdependent nature of the international system hinged on the reality that no state has been able to achieve autarkic levels of development. Hence, the crusade for democratic governance in Africa was as much a product of a combination of domestic political forces as it was a consequence of external factors spawned by the end of the Cold War and the collapse of the Soviet Empire in Eastern Europe.

DOMESTIC POLITICAL FORCES IN KENYA

As noted in Chapter One with regard to Kenya, institutional authoritarianism marked the beginning of the 1970s following the banning of KPU in 1969. The display of force in the confrontation that led to the proscription of KPU was such that it intimidated those that might have harbored intentions of constituting an opposition party to challenge the ruling KANU. As such, though the country remained only a *de facto* one party system, no attempts were made to form another party between 1969 and 1982. It was in 1982, four years into the Moi era that attempts to form another political party by Oginga Odinga and George Anyona were nipped in the bud when a constitutional amendment was rushed through parliament, shepherded by the then Vice President and Leader of Government Business in Parliament, Mwai Kibaki, making the country a one-party state by law. Against this background, dissenting political views and opposition to the single-party authoritarianism reverted to the parliamentary backbenches, university students and intellectuals, as well as to Churches and other non-governmental organizations.

Parliamentary Voices of Political Dissent

The first source of political dissent in one-party Kenya was the parliamentary backbench. William Ochieng (1995) writes that with the banning of the KPU in 1969, radicalism reverted to the parliamentary backbenches. In particular, the most incisive critic of the Kenyatta regime at the time was Josiah Mwangi Kariuki, popularly known as JM, then Member of Parliament for Nyandarua North in the Rift Valley. Regarding himself as "a man of the people" rather than a socialist like the former KPU stalwarts, JM stood for justice and equality of individuals and championed the people's right to free medical services, education, and land. He was especially critical of the privileged status of the political elite and their lopsided policies, which, he observed, were geared toward creating a Kenya of ten millionaires and ten million beggars. On economic and social justice, he said: "A small but powerful group of greedy, self-seeking elite in the form of politicians, Civil Servants and businessmen, has steadily but surely monopolized the fruits of independence to the exclusion of the majority of the people. We do not want a Kenya of ten millionaires and ten million beggars" (Ochieng, 1995: 103). Taking cognizance of the fact that the adopted ideology of nation-building was a mere smokescreen, JM noted: "It takes more than a National Anthem, however stirring, a Coat of Arms, however distinctive, a National Flag, however appropriate, a National Flower, however beautiful, to make a nation" (Ochieng, 1995: 103).

J. M. Kariuki was supported by fellow parliamentarians Jean Marie Seroney, MP for Tinderet, Joseph Martin Shikuku, MP for Butere and self-declared "people's watchman," and George Anyona, MP for Kitutu Chache, among others. These nationalists argued that the KANU government had failed to meet the challenge given by the people when they rallied behind it. The greatest failure of KANU in their estimation, was its inability to forge the country's ethnic groups into one nation after independence (Ochieng, 1995: 103). Shikuku went so far as to claim that the Kenyatta regime was intent on "killing" parliament the same way it had killed KANU. Amid calls for substantiation or withdrawal of the remarks, the presiding Deputy Speaker, Seroney, wondered how Shikuku could substantiate the obvious! Whereas JM was brutally murdered in March 1975 for his incessant criticism of the government,[1] Shikuku and Seroney were arrested within the precincts of parliament in October 1975 and shunted to detention without trial, with Jomo Kenyatta metaphorically warning that " . . . the hawk in the sky is ready to swoop on the chickens" (Chepkwony, 1987: 167; Nasong'o, 2001a). In detention, Shikuku and Seroney joined their former colleague, Koigi wa Wamwere, the young and firebrand MP for Nakuru North who was detained in August 1975 for his stand against the self-aggrandizing activities of the political elite and his strong advocacy for the rights of the poor and landless. Thereafter, only George Anyona, MP for Kitutu Chache, remained to constitute what was popularly referred to as the "one-man backbench." However, Anyona's strong stand against oppression, corruption, and inefficiency in the high echelons of government landed him in detention in 1977.

The political murder of J. M. Kariuki saw dissention against the Kenyatta regime even from within the cabinet ranks. A parliamentary Select Committee that was constituted to probe the murder, chaired by the then fiery MP for Bungoma East (now Kimilili), Elijah Wasike Mwangale, found the government culpable. However, the then attorney general, Charles Njonjo moved an amendment motion to have the government "note" the Committee's findings, rather than adopt the same, which would have required its implementation by way of investigating and prosecuting those named. In this event, cabinet Minister Masinde Muliro, and Assistant Ministers Peter Kibisu and John Keen broke ranks with the government side and voted with the backbench against the government's motion. In so doing, the three ministers jettisoned the idea of collective responsibility that binds the cabinet in parliamentary democracies. Masinde Muliro argued that his conscience could not allow him to abide by the principle since he had no hand in the murder and, in any event, there can never be collective responsibility in murder! All the three were promptly relieved of their ministerial positions (see Gimode, forthcoming, Ochieng, 1995).

By the time Kenyatta died in August 1978, there were 26 detainees in Kenya, most of them detained on political grounds. However, on succeeding Kenyatta, Moi released all detainees including Martin Shikuku, George

Anyona, Ngugi wa Thiong'o, and Koigi wa Wamwere. In these initial years
of the Moi regime, parliamentary voices of political dissent came from a
group of seven young, radical parliamentarians, whom the then Minister
for Constitutional Affairs, Charles Mugane Njonjo, branded "the seven
bearded sisters," though only one of them—Philomena Chelagat Mutai—
was a lady. The seven who represented a radical alternative view to that of
the establishment included Lawrence Sifuna, James Orengo, George Anyona, Chibule wa Tsuma, Mashengu wa Mwachofi, Chelagat Mutai, and
Koigi wa Wamwere. However, by the end of the 1980s, parliamentary dissent was largely emasculated on account of an increasingly repressive
regime as well as its tight and centralized control of the electoral process
that ensured only KANU loyalists made it to parliament.

University Students and Intellectuals

University students and intellectuals, especially at the University of Nairobi
(UoN), represented the second source of alternative political views. Scholars
who remained independent thinkers and thus branded by the system as radicals or communist agitators included Ngugi wa Thiong'o, Micere Mugo,
Shadrack Gutto, Willy Mutunga, Alamin Mazrui, Kamoji Wachira, Mukaru
Ng'ang'a, Nicholas Nyangira, Odegi Awuondo, Edward Oyugi, Ngotho
Kariuki, Oki Ooko Ombaka, Katama Mkangi, and Peter Anyang' Nyong'o,
among others. Most of these intellectuals were hounded out of their teach-
ing positions, detained and tortured, and/or generally harassed, with some
forced into exile. Overall, the sense of betrayal and despair on the part of
the citizenry in Kenya was metaphorically captured by Ngugi wa Thiong'o
according to whom the flowers of independence had, quite ominously,
turned out to be petals of blood! The promise of independence had proved
to be a false promise.[2] For his radical views against the government, Ngugi
wa Thiong'o was the first academic to suffer detention. He was detained by
Kenyatta in 1977 and went into exile shortly after his release in 1979 following the government directive to the University of Nairobi not to rein-
state him to his former position in the Literature Department.

Among other scholars that were detained include Mukaru Ng'ang'a,
who was bundled into detention simply for stating that the introduction of
section 2 (A) to the Kenyan constitution and the crackdown on prodemocracy activists would only drive the opposition underground. Quite ominously, the government retorted that it had the capacity to go underground
after the activists. Edward Oyugi was arrested in 1983 and jailed for five
years on "sedition" charges after a police search in his house found Marxist
literature. For his part, Nicholas Nyangira was detained in 1988 for his

views, expressed in a university lecture theatre, that there can never be democracy in a one party state. Similarly, Katama Mkangi suffered detention twice for his political views. It was within this context of an increasingly intolerant state that many academics left the academy for more "secure" positions in research organizations even as many others took off into exile.

Maurice Amutabi (2002) has elaborated the role of university students in national leadership and the democratization process in Kenya. According to him, student activism in Kenya has been informed by a democratic agenda and the desire to create democratic spaces within and outside the university. From the inauguration of de facto single-party rule in 1969 to the return of multiparty politics in 1991, university students and a number of scholars constituted an enduring bastion of opposition to authoritarianism. Freedoms of speech, assembly, and association comprised part of the demands that students made of the establishment, and the checkered history of the Student Organization of the University of Nairobi (SONU) is testimony to this pursuit (see Klopp & Orina, 2002). Secondly, university students also contested policies affecting the general populace at the national level. They fought against Structural Adjustment Programs (SAPs), attendant problems such as cost sharing, unemployment, and most particularly, against the retrenchment and freezing of employment in the civil service, a situation that affected them directly.

Students also fought against corruption, tribalism, the grabbing of public land, against oppression of radical politicians and other government critics, political assassination, and police brutality by participating in popular protests, street demonstrations, rallies, and strikes to assert their position (see Amutabi, 2002: 158–159). It is against this background that Amutabi contends that the university students have bequeathed to Kenyans and to the democratization process the power to riot, to protest, and to stand up for their rights (Amutabi, 2002: 164). He concludes that "[t]he political course in Kenya would not be the same today without university students" (Amutabi, 2002: 157).

For their struggle in the quest for increased democratic space, many university student leaders were expelled and even jailed on trumped-up charges. Among those expelled for their student activism include Chelagat Mutai and Ochieng K'Onyango, expelled in 1972 following the banning of the university student paper, *University Platform* for which they were lead editors; John Munuhe, Mukhisa Kituyi, Odindo Opiata, and Saul Busolo were the first student casualties of the Moi regime when they were expelled on government instigation because of their political activism; Mwandawiro

Mghanga, Tirop arap Kitur, and Karimi Nduthu were expelled in 1985 for their anti-government activities and for being opponents of the then pro-government SONU leader, P. L. O. Lumumba. Among students who were jailed for their political activities include Tito Adungosi, Peter Oginga Ogego, David Onyango Oloo and 65 others who were detained following the 1982 abortive coup, which university students demonstrated in support of. Adungosi, then SONU chairman, was charged and convicted of "sedition" and sentenced to 10 years. He died in prison in 1988 under unexplained circumstances. For his part, Wafula Buke, arguably the most popular SONU chairman ever, was jailed for five years in 1987 for leading a student meeting on November 3, 1987 that demanded autonomy for the university, security for students on campus, and the right to speak out on national problems, especially corruption (Amutabi, 2002; Klopp & Orina, 2002: 52).[3]

Churches and other NGOs

The third source of opposition to authoritarianism and push for democratic opening was the Church and a number of other non-governmental organizations.[4] In particular, the National Council of the Churches of Kenya (NCCK), the umbrella organization of the main Protestant Churches, remained on the forefront over the years in opposition to the KANU politics of exclusion. Along with its constituent Church members, for instance, NCCK on various occasions called for the abolition of the queue voting system in elections that was introduced in 1988, which violated the principle of secret ballot. This procedure was exclusionary because only those in support of the preferred KANU candidates would venture to the polling stations. It was on account of this crusade against the regime that NCCK's newsmagazine, *Target,* was banned in 1988.

In the run-up to the multiparty era, NCCK produced civic education materials urging people to exercise their constitutional right to vote. At times NCCK did this with a demonstrated preference for the opposition to the extent that former NCCK General Secretary Rev. Samuel Kobia was threatened with bodily harm. NCCK has continued to play a significant role in channeling political demands. For instance, it organized a commission to study the causes and effects of the 1992 ethnic clashes. Its report, together with that of the parliamentary select committee, the Kiliku Report, implicated high government officials especially Local Government Minister William ole Ntimama, Energy minister Nicholas Biwott, and nominated MP Ezekiel Barng'etuny. "Thus the role of the church in the struggle for pluralism and government accountability has been an extremely important one" (Nyang'oro, 1997b: 144).

Similarly, individual members of the clergy remained vocal in articulating the need for good governance thus serving as the voice of the voiceless during the era of single-party monolithism. Following the riots of July 1990, for example, the Church of the Province of Kenya (Anglican Church) took issue with the government over the causes of the riots. The CPK clergy, especially Manases Kuria, Archbishop of Nairobi, Henry Okullu, Bishop of Maseno South, and Alexander Muge, Bishop of Eldoret, as well as Rev. Timothy Njoya of the Presbyterian Church of East Africa (PCEA) demanded that the government face up to the economic and political needs of the people. More specifically, Okullu asked the government to resign to clear the way for a new beginning. In a Sunday sermon on July 15, 1990, Okullu asked the government to convene a constitutional assembly and called for a transitional government of national unity. Justifying his position, Okullu argued, "Who has driven us to this ugly predicament; these temptations to go back to a stage of backwardness which we could never ever have thought of? The blame must lie on the KANU Government which in spite of calls to arrange for a national convention, a dialogue with all the people and a democratic form of government, has insisted on going its own way" (Nyang'oro, 1997b: 143; *Daily Nation* July 16, 1991: 1). Okullu concluded his sermon by condemning the detention without trial of former cabinet ministers Kenneth Matiba and Charles Rubia who were arrested for allegedly inciting people to riot.

Overall, internal pressure for political reform in Kenya for a decade prior to 1989 came from church leaders (see Galia, 2000), farmers' associations, old-time politicians forced out of politics by Moi, university students and intellectuals. These teamed up with such professional organizations as the Law Society of Kenya (LSK) and other social formations to push the cause for opening up political pace in the country.

DOMESTIC POLITICAL FORCES IN ZAMBIA

Jan Kees van Donge (1995) notes that after the establishment of one-party rule in Zambia, opposition only remained among intellectuals, especially at the University of Zambia (UNZA), which experienced dramatic closures in 1971 and 1976 on issues tied to the struggles in Southern Africa. Later, closures became common with bread-and-butter issues at the center of debate. Protest against party dominance was nonetheless always an element in the politics surrounding UNZA. During the 1980s intellectuals in both the Law Association of Zambia and the Economic Club voiced opposition to the Kaunda regime. The forums provided a platform for businessmen to vent critical views. Despite these voices of dissent, however, Jotham Momba (1993: 196) contends that an important feature of the one-party system in Zambia was that it was generally accepted by the major interest and social groups for the whole of the 1970s and most of the 1980s. Momba posits that what happened is that various social groups attempted to fight for their interests and to assert themselves within the context of the one-party system. In other words, domestic political forces in Zambia did not seek to directly challenge the legitimacy of the single-party system.

Acceptability of the Party System

A number of factors accounted for the general acceptance of the single-party system in Zambia during the period 1973 to mid 1980s. In the first place, the system received limited resistance from the very beginning on account of the fact that the ruling party, UNIP, sought to co-opt the leadership of existing political parties. Kaunda, for example, invited the president and vice president of the opposition ANC to the membership of the commission that was set up to prepare the constitutional instruments for the establishment of the one-party system. Although they declined and ANC took the matter to court, once the single-party system was introduced, ANC members decided to formally join UNIP as a bloc under the famous Choma Declaration of June 27, 1973. As a result, several ANC branches in Southern Province were reregistered as UNIP branches. This enabled ANC leaders to participate in both primary and general elections in 1973.

Indeed, former ANC leaders came to play prominent roles in the single party system. For instance, the former ANC vice president, Nalumino Mundia, won a by-election after his release from detention in late 1974, was made a cabinet minister in 1977, a member of the UNIP Central Committee in 1978, and in 1981, he became prime minister. The former ANC secretary general, Mungoni Liso, became a member of the UNIP Central Committee in December 1973; while Mufaya Mumbuna, a Western Province ANC veteran who won his parliamentary seat in both 1973 and 1978, was made minister in 1976. Even Harry Mwaanga Nkumbula, former ANC president was reelected to parliament on the UNIP ticket after the establishment of the single-party system, and was thus among six of the former ANC parliamentarians elected from Southern Province out of a total of 16 parliamentarians from the province (Gertzel et al, 1984: 112). On the other hand, although UPP continued to resist cooperation, it eventually decided to join ranks with UNIP and several of its former members came to play prominent political roles, though not to the level former ANC members did (Momba, 1993: 196–197). Momba (1993: 197) notes that "once the two parties ceased their opposition to the one-party system, no organized group thereafter sought to challenge the one-party system . . ."

Secondly, the one-party system in Zambia enjoyed a large measure of legitimacy on account of its promotion of free participation of citizens in parliamentary elections with limited Central Committee control. "The system was such that anybody with a UNIP membership card who wished to try his luck participated" (Momba, 1993: 197). Because of this open nature of parliamentary elections under the one-party system, recruitment into the political arena was very high during this time than at any other time. Momba argues that the open system of parliamentary elections that existed under the one-party system contrasted sharply with the one experienced during the First Republic, 1964–1972, when only trusted and well known party activists contested, and that was only one from each of the parties.

Thirdly, the one party system enjoyed much acceptability in Zambia because various social and interest groups accepted to participate within the framework of the one-party system and by so doing gave it some legitimacy. "Instead of distancing themselves from the system, important social groups such as the labour movement and the business community fought to protect their class and corporate interests within the one party system" (Momba, 1993: 198). Momba asserts that the one-party state thus successfully managed the many conflicts, especially between the various interest groups and the state until UNIP lost its working class and peasant political support.

The general acceptability of the single party system notwithstanding, however, a number of crucial factors worked to create problems for the system. One such factor was the constitutional provision that provided for the supremacy of the party organs over state organs as well as the methods employed by agents of the party. The idea of party supremacy had several implications. First, members of the National Assembly were the most democratically recruited, yet they enjoyed less political power compared to the UNIP National Council. Although parliamentarians were also members of the National Council, the council had a large number of party officials who were not popularly elected. Secondly, whereas members of the cabinet could legitimately claim to have more popular mandate from the electorate than members of the UNIP Central Committee, the committee, rather than the cabinet, was the most powerful body. According to Momba, it was the method of recruiting members of the Central Committee that received most adverse commentary. As Bornwell Chikulo notes, between 1972 and 1978 no election for members of the Central Committee took place; while in 1977 a Select Parliamentary Committee Report pointed out that "the present method of electing members of the Central Committee is unsatisfactory. Available evidence supported the view that members of the Central Committee should be elected by a popular vote" (Chikulo, 1980: 108–109).

The expansion of the party bureaucracy was another factor that contributed to the collapse of the one-party system. A number of party positions were created with doubtful productivity. The 1977 Select Parliamentary Committee Report commented on the drain the huge bureaucracy was placing on the economy. According to the Report, the bureaucracy was not only a drain on the economy but was also a serious constraint on efficiency (Momba 1993: 198–199). Momba argues, however, that even with these serious shortcomings of the one-party system, the various social groups never sought to challenge the legitimacy of the party system. Instead the various groups, especially the labor movement and the property-owning group, fought to protect their corporate and class interests within the one-party system. Nevertheless, the labor movement and the business community constituted the most potent political forces within the rubric of one-party Zambia.

The Role of the Labor Movement

Of all organized groups in Zambia, the labor movement gave the UNIP government the most difficult time in its attempt to protect its corporate interests:

> In essence, what happened was that during the period of the one-party system the labour movement continued to resist any form of subordination of the labour movement to the party. This had been its traditional position since the beginning of the 1950s. Secondly, the major area of conflict between the labour movement and the government was over the struggle for the control of the wage-earners. (Momba, 1993: 199)

Momba notes that the control of the wage earners was perhaps the most important area of difference between the Zambia Congress of Trade Unions (ZCTU) and the UNIP government. ZCTU felt that it was its responsibility to speak for wage earners and that the party and its government should have kept away from labor matters. For instance, in 1979 the ZCTU chairman, Frederick Chiluba, urged workers to stop directing their industrial disputes and complaints to politicians who, Chiluba said, had no right to deal with their cases. The crunch in this struggle for the control of workers came in 1978 when the labor leaders were prevented from speaking at Labor Day rallies. Thereafter, labor leaders refused to have anything to do with Labor

Day rallies. The relationship between labor and the government deteriorated and confrontation between the two became a common feature.

In mid 1970s, the Zambian government was engaged in an attempt to enunciate a wages and incomes policy that took into account the country's growing problem of unemployment and changing economic conditions, as well as provide a basic strategy for the Third National Development Plan. Towards this end, the government invited an International Labor Organization mission to carry out a Basic Needs Survey, and in 1978, it engaged a Professor Turner to make a second wages, incomes and prices report (Gertzel, 1984: 93). At the same time, the government pursued other contradictory policies. Throughout the 1970s, it enforced a five percent limit on wage increases; and the 1978 IMF agreement with the government resulted in a total freeze on wage increment in the public sector. In addition, other than the Mwanakatwe Report in 1975 which provided the most generous wage increases to the lowest paid government employees, little had been done to reduce income inequality in the country (Gertzel, 1984: 93).

Consequently, controversy over the implementation of wage increase recommendations emerging from the Turner Report became a source of conflict between the UNIP government and the labor movement. In early October 1979 ZCTU chairman, Chiluba and secretary general, Newstead Zimba gave the government until month's end to solve the issue of the Turner Report or "face unspecified consequences." Although the K156 wage increase was endorsed as agreed upon between the government and ZCTU, the ZCTU chairman warned in September 1980 of a countrywide strike before the end of the year because, he said, the party and its government had failed to respond to the workers' demands to improve the standard of living. He called on workers throughout the country to brace themselves for industrial action, asserting that he was ready to press the strike button (Momba, 1993: 199). The mood of labor, especially on the Copperbelt, was thus uneasy at the beginning of 1980 (Gertzel, 1984: 93).

At the same time, the labor movement challenged the state over the 1980 administrative reforms. The administrative reforms emanated from a bill introduced in parliament in August 1980 to provide for a new structure of decentralized administration. According to Cherry Gertzel (1984), the proposals had far-reaching implications for political participation in the one-party state as well as for government administration. They thus came under severe scrutiny by parliamentarians. The legislators in particular criticized the method of election of the new District Councilors, which was confined to party members. Critics justifiably argued that this infringed the constitutional rights of Zambians to vote. With regard to workers, especially on the Copperbelt, the implications of decentralization included integration of the mine townships into the urban local authorities and thus the merger of the mines' social and welfare services with those of the urban authorities. The miners' services were, however, superior to those provided by the local authorities and as such miners had consistently rejected earlier proposals for integration.

The Mineworkers Union of Zambia (MUZ) thus opposed the decentralization proposals and threatened to go on strike if they were implemented. The ZCTU supported MUZ in this regard on account of three reasons. First, on the basis of the adverse effects the new structure would have on the miners; second, on account of the fact that the proposed decentralization would result in a costly and cumbersome bureaucracy that the country could ill afford; and finally on the grounds that the proposed changes had not been discussed at the party's general conference (see Gertzel, 1984: 93–95). On the basis of these arguments, ZCTU Chairman Chiluba announced, at a press conference, that he had sent a petition to the Prime Minister meant for the secretary general of the party rejecting the new local government system.

The government rejected the ZCTU argument and proceeded with party elections in preparation for the implementation of the new local government administration structure. ZCTU and MUZ reacted by prohibiting their members from participating in the elections and subsequently suspended the few who participated. This labor action saw an acrimonious exchange between the party and union leaders with the UNIP National Council strongly criticizing ZCTU and MUZ leaders for their "indiscipline" and Central Committee members vowing that the party would "crush its enemies as it had done in the past" (Gertzel, 1984: 94). President Kaunda went further to launch a personal attack on the ZCTU chairman and accused the ZCTU of subversion. He alleged that there was a subversive plot against the government and observed: "Zambia intelligence services early this year learnt of a plot by subversive elements backed by South Africa to use the labor movement to paralyze the country through a strike to topple the government . . . of late the nation has been puzzled to hear labor leaders call a nationwide strike before the end of the year" (Momba, 1993: 200). Naturally, ZCTU denied these allegations. In spite of the seeming intransigence of the government, it relented on the local government reforms. When the legislation was finally enacted in December 1980, it was substantially amended and the threat to the miners' loss of services was removed.

Nevertheless, in reaction to the labor movement's action, the UNIP Central Committee first suspended then expelled 17 MUZ and ZCTU leaders from the party in January 1980. At Konkola Mines in Chililabombwe, 5,000 miners reacted by work stoppage on January 20. The rest of the mine labor force on the Copperbelt followed suit. The threat of a general strike became apparent when postal workers stopped work in support of the miners and bank employees also went on strike when their union chairman was assaulted by local UNIP officials in an incident at the Lusaka party offices. According to Cherry Gertzel (1984), the ensuing strike constituted the most serious industrial action that had faced the country since 1966. Gertzel writes that the strike took place at a time not only of acute economic difficulty but also great political uncertainty in the wake of an alleged coup plot uncovered in early 1980 (see Mwanakatwe, 1994) and about which a treason trial was pending.[5] The strike lasted eight days, was marked by considerable violence, and resulted in police action and loss of one life in Kitwe and serious injuries to three miners in Mufulira. The party was unable to handle the conflict, which, in the final analysis, was resolved by the combined efforts of Ministry of Labor officials and leaders of the trade union movement themselves. The latter were keen to effect reconciliation and their readmission into the party at a special meeting of the UNIP National Council in April 1980 helped to stem the tide of tension between the labor movement and the party.

What is to be noted from the strike, as Gertzel rightly observes, is that the strike reflected not only the protest by miners at the expulsion of their leaders from UNIP, but also their concern for their own livelihood at a time of great difficulty within the mining industry. It is noteworthy that at the time of their expulsion, MUZ leaders were engaged in negotiations with mining companies over incentive bonuses and their expulsion had serious implications for these negotiations (see *Times of Zambia,* January 24, 1981). In political terms, the significance of the strike went beyond the determination of miners to maintain their independence from the party. It demonstrated a new cohesiveness within the labor movement in its confrontation with the party exemplified by the firm unity between MUZ and ZCTU in their mutual defense. At the end of the day, the strike and the role of labor leaders in its defusion clearly underscored the power of the labor movement in the one-party state and simultaneously demonstrated the weakness of the party at the local level (see Gertzel, 1984: 95).

The vulnerability and jitteriness of the party was once again manifested in July 1981 following three wildcat strikes that paralyzed the copper mining industry. The strikes were a culmination of the incessant friction between labor and the UNIP government. The government reacted by rounding up labor leaders, Fredrick Chiluba, Newstead Zimba, Chitalu Zamba and Timothy Walamba. These ZCTU leaders were detained at Mumbwa Remand Prison " . . . for inciting workers to disrupt industrial peace and eventually overthrow the government" (Kamwambe, 1991: 43). The reaction of ZCTU was that the movement stood for correcting government, not replacing it. It was while in detention that Chiluba avidly read the bible and came out of detention a more ardent Christian than he went in.[6] His political speeches now contained biblical references (see Mwanakatwe, 1994).

The ZCTU leadership also differed with several other UNIP government policies and after mid 1970s became very critical of what they saw as UNIP's socialist and nationalization policies. For instance, at a labor symposium in 1980, ZCTU exhorted the government to scale down nationalization of industries and instead encourage private investments. Defending the alliance between the labor movement and international capital, ZCTU commented: "our concern is not who owns what but who develops the country . . . The labor movement in Zambia is not against nationalization of private companies but is concerned about the poor performance of these institutions that have been taken over" (Momba, 1993: 200). In general, ZCTU favored a capitalist strategy of development as well as establishing strong links with capitalist countries. It thus was critical of the government's strong leanings to socialist countries and its unwillingness to undertake trade with countries that were not its political friends. In December 1977, Chiluba called on the government to introduce what he called bold economic and foreign policy which entailed removing economic bottlenecks that literally tied Zambia's trade links to one area thus blocking the country's entry into more profitable areas. Chiluba reiterated his position in September 1978: "[t]he best political ally was not essentially a mere trading partner but trade must be seen to be carried out primarily for the economic and financial benefits of the country . . . Political friends and good neighborliness which followed should not be the basis of the Government instituting bilateral or multilateral trade links" (Momba, 1993: 200).

Jotham Momba notes that in all its conflicts with the government, the labor movement never publicly challenged the legitimacy of the one-party system until 1989. Instead, it sought, and successfully articulated its grievances within the one-party structure. Labor leaders consistently denied any suggestions that they constituted some kind of pressure group or any hint of disloyalty to the party.[7] For instance, in July 1977, Chiluba noted that the need for closer links between the party (UNIP) and the Congress

(ZCTU) could not be questioned as "they were aimed at serving people in developing the country" (Momba, 1993: 201). Then in July 1980, he called upon labor leaders to help the party recruit more members: "Unions would be partly to blame if the party membership declined because it was their responsibility to deliver the benefits of the party to the people" (Momba, 1993: 201). Thus labor leaders remained members of the party up to 1990 and only ceased to be members when they were expelled. Furthermore, ZCTU leaders participated actively in party organs under the one-party system. Chiluba and Zimba were members of the UNIP National Council and took their membership seriously. For instance, in March 1977 Zimba appealed to the party to consider having the Zambia Federation of Employers (ZFE) represented in the UNIP National Council because, he said, ZFE and ZCTU worked together as sister organizations. In addition, Chiluba was a member of several party committees, including the Legal and Political sub-Committees.

In spite of the fact that the labor movement sought to participate in the one-party system without challenging its legitimacy as Momba posits, it is arguable that the labor movement in Zambia represented a potent political force that constituted some form of opposition from within, as the foregoing exposition illustrates. ZCTU sought to participate in the parliamentary system as a separate group. They wanted labor leaders to be treated as a group with special privileges in the one-party system. In 1979, for instance, Chiluba complained of poor representation of labor in parliament and warned that in that year's election, ZCTU would put up its own candidates. In the elections, Newstead Zimba, ZCTU secretary general, successfully contested Chifubu constituency on the Copperbelt. In the 1983 elections Chiluba once again sought preferential treatment for the labor movement. In an address to a ZCTU district seminar at the Ridgeways campus of the University of Zambia (UNZA), he stated that ZCTU wanted a number of seats to be specially reserved for the labor movement: "We do not want to be appointed but to be given a block of seats in parliament for which union members would elect their representatives" (Momba 1993: 202). He argued that it was only such a constitutional arrangement that would make workers be seen to participate at the source of law making.

Thus it was only in the late 1980s following the crisis in Eastern Europe that Zambian labor leaders began to question the wisdom of the one-party system in Africa. "And it was only after Kaunda announced that a referendum would be introduced to decide the issue that they openly and specifically declared their preference for the multiparty system in Zambia" (Momba, 1993: 202).

Zambia Industrial and Commercial Association

The property-owning social groups in Zambia also actively sought to participate within the one-party framework rather than directly challenge it. The Zambia Industrial and Commercial Association (ZINCOM)—later Zambia Confederation of Industries and Chamber of Commerce—as an organization for business avoided challenging the legitimacy of the one-party system. Instead, successive chairmen of ZINCOM sought to reassure the party and government of ZINCOM's loyalty. For instance, in 1983, Vernon Mwaanga, ZINCOM chairman, pledged "unflinching support and cooperation with the party and its government in the struggle for national development" and urged for the reelection of Dr. Kaunda because "[n]o business enterprise in Zambia could survive in the absence of political stability and we therefore have a vested interest in the continued political stability of Zambia which Dr. Kaunda has provided" (Momba 1993: 202). In 1988, another ZINCOM chairman, Alexander Chakwanda called for "intensive consultations between his organization and the party on crucial economic issues" (Ibid.). Like Mwaanga before him, Chakwanda also pledged ZINCOM's loyalty to the party: "I want to assure you, ZINCOM's stand is to work with the party. Those of us who are Zambians are not ashamed to be patriotic" (Momba, 1993: 202).

The property-owning class attempted to assert themselves through participation in parliamentary elections where they forcefully articulated their interests. Bornwell Chikulo (1980) in a study of the 1978 elections notes that over time, the property-owning class had their representation in parliament increased at the expense of other social groups. According to Chikulo, 41 percent of all members of parliament elected in 1978 had some business connection of some kind. Carolyn Baylies and Morris Szeftel also observed this trend in 1973 and 1978. They noted, in respect to the 1973 elections:

> There has been a tendency by private business to seek political contacts or an active role in the political process. This can be seen with respect to the background of nominees and elected members of Parliament in Zambia's first election under the one party state in 1973. About 40 percent of those who placed their names in nomination had business interests and of those elected, about 44 percent owned business or state land farms, or had shares in local companies. (Baylies and Szeftel, 1982: 201–202; Momba, 1993: 203)

ZINCOM consistently called for the introduction of some form of market economy. In April 1986, ZINCOM Chairman Andrew Kashita stated that

Zambia's drive towards economic recovery would be futile unless the limited economy was allowed to flow freely. He also stated that ZINCOM favored the foreign exchange auction system. Like labor, ZINCOM began to express some sentiments against several aspects of the state's political, economic, and social policies seen as unfavorable to their interests as early as the 1970s. For instance, they began to express some disquiet and criticism of what they saw as the UNIP government's socialist leanings in its economic and foreign policies.

Arthur Wina, Member of Parliament from 1973–1978 and founder Chairman of the MMD, seem to have been the main parliamentary spokesman for this social group. He said, in parliament in 1978:

> Statements have been made by His Excellency and Minister for Industry that Zambia welcomes investments from outside [and] this is the right decision, which must be followed . . . I am worried that a series of counter statements from certain other levels in our country tend to spoil this effort . . . it is not unusual to read from newspapers that some leading members of the government addressed a visiting dignitary and took almost three quarters of the time congratulating that dignitary about the achievement of their system . . . These are contradictions, which are embarrassing to anybody who is supposed to interpret Zambia's industrial policy. You cannot on one hand say you welcome investment from outside and then, on the other . . . denounce capitalists. (Momba, 1993: 203)

Wina also called for the voluntary liquidation of parastatal organizations and encouragement of private investments as, in his view, the parastatals had failed and were in a state of bankruptcy. The emerging propertied class also began to question Zambia's Southern African policy. They called for the normalization of relations between Zambia and apartheid South Africa, with one parliamentarian saying: "There is no sense in buying goods like farming tractors made in South Africa through Malawi. Why can't we buy direct from South Africa . . . I have been sent by my employers and masters, the masses, to ask the Government to reopen the border because there is too much suffering" (Momba, 1993: 204).

According to Hamalengwa (1992), Kaunda's rule was based on the support of the middle class of Zambia, which he lavishly aggrandized for most of his rule. Zambia's economy was very good in the first decade of independence during which time a strong middle class with state assistance was allowed to mushroom. The nationalization policy of the late sixties led to the further growth of the parastatal bourgeoisie, which was beholden to Kaunda. A state bourgeoisie also blossomed without restraint. However, from the mid-seventies, particularly from the early eighties, the Zambian economy hit rock bottom and the state's failure to respond effectively to the crisis began to increasingly alienate Kaunda's regime from its supporters.[8] He could no longer effectively lavish the middle class as before. The pressures of private capitalism as opposed to state capitalism further created a rupture within the alliance supporting Kaunda and his one-party state. As Kaunda's hegemonic alliance became threatened by the labor movement, he increasingly became more repressive and the use of emergency powers became more widespread. Despite this intimidation, opposition to his rule became more pronounced until the critical crises of June 1990 with student riots and the attempted military coup. This conjuncture severely weakened Kaunda's regime and prompted him to accept the notion of multiparty democracy (Hamalengwa, 1992: 161).

THE EXTERNAL CONTEXT

A conjuncture of international factors and political developments both within and outside of the Soviet Union combined to bring the Cold War to an end towards the close of the 1980s. Within the former Soviet Union, especially in Russia, Former Soviet leader, Mikhail Gorbachev is credited with having brought the Cold War to an end by abrogating the Brezhnev Doctrine and thereby facilitating the crumbling of the Communist Empire in Eastern Europe. Armed with the principles of *glasnost* (openness) and *perestroika* (reform), Gorbachev, in response to factors beyond his own control, unleashed a political process that systematically dismantled the basis upon which communism was founded and thus opened a floodgate of revolutionary changes in the former Communist states. Even the 'Iron Curtain' that divided Communist East Germany from Capitalist West Germany came tumbling down in October 1989 marking a momentous reunion of the two Germanys. By the turn of the 1990s therefore, the Communist Empire was no more.

To the Western world, the collapse of the "strongest and the best organized totalitarian systems" in Eastern Europe heralded the triumph of capitalism over communism and proved that Western socio-economic and political values were the one and only path to the progress and development of humanity. Indeed, according to Francis Fukuyama (1989: 3–12), the "death" of communism marked the end of history because, "whatever failings real-life democratic political systems might experience, the 'ideal' of liberal democracy could not be improved upon." It is, so to say, ideological development in its ultimate form and thus the highest stage of human government. Marina Ottaway (1997) points out that implicitly, the "end of history" thesis asserts that modernization theorists were right when they viewed industrialized states as the mode of civilization all other countries will have to follow. "By extension, this also meant that those [countries] which had attained the highest stage of human history—or at least embraced ideas that represented such a stage—had the right and even the duty to impose their model on the rest of the world, particularly now that the Soviet Union was no longer there to tell them otherwise" (Ottaway, 1997: 2).

The Impact of Desovietization

Although the dramatic collapse of state socialism and Soviet model economy in Eastern Europe was not in itself a direct cause of African democratization, it had greater resonance in Africa than any other region and helped energize anti-authoritarian forces. Former U.S. president, George Bush exemplified this reality in January 1989. Taking advantage of the new international political dispensation following the collapse of the Soviet Union, George Bush, as newly elected U.S. president, declared that there was a breeze blowing because of which a world refreshed by freedom seemed reborn, " . . . for in man's heart, if not in fact, the day of the dictator is over" (Munene, 1993: 88). The then Secretary of State, James Baker, perhaps taking cue from his boss, observed that after the end of the Cold War, it was time for sweeping away the old dictators and building up new democracies. With specific reference to Africa, he asserted: "I reject and I hope that America always rejects the view that democracy is for certain societies but has no place in Africa" (Adar, 1995: 100).

Similarly, International Financial Institutions (IFIs) introduced political criteria into their policy discourses, preferring the concept "good governance" as a more antiseptic substitute for "democratization." They predicated further disbursement of financial resources on demonstrated progress towards good governance. They defined governance as the exercise of political power to manage a nation's affairs and posited that this required " . . . building a pluralistic institutional structure, a determination to respect the rule of law and vigorous protection of the freedom of the press and human rights" (Young, 1994: 234, World Bank, 1991: 61). It was against this background that authoritarian leaders all over Africa were placed on the defensive by demands for political pluralism. Some, as in Mali were driven from power by street actions. Others, as in Benin were forced to concede their sovereign power to redefine the polity to national conferences that were assembling major political forces within countries. "By 1991, more than 40 states (of Africa's 54) . . . had either undertaken political liberalization or pledged implementation of such a program" (Young, 1994: 234).

The end of the Cold War thus constituted a major factor that had significant consequences for the democratization process in Africa. As Angelique Haugerud (1995: 19) argues, though few would suggest that foreign events were the main cause of Africa's 1990 political protests, political changes such as those in Eastern Europe and elsewhere shaped the politicization and timing of protests in sub-Saharan African nations. They contributed to the legitimization of calls for democratization and attacks on one-party states. The end of the Cold War, Haugerud contends, helped to reshape the fate of marginalized and submerged African discourses, conferring on some of them new attention and authority. The rhetoric of democracy and human rights became newly convenient for dissident elites vying for political power. The effectiveness of prodemocracy voices in Kenya, for instance, was strengthened by ties with the international press and with international Church and human rights organizations such as Amnesty International and Human Rights Watch (Haugerud, 1995: 20).

Similarly, Munyonzwe Hamalengwa (1992) notes that events in Zambia leading to the defeat of Kaunda in 1991 were overlaid by international, albeit attenuating demands for democratization in Africa as well as the changing international context. The latter, he posits, was triggered by events in Eastern Europe where the one-party communist systems were falling like dominoes as a result of mass protests for change. According to Hamalengwa, changes in Zambia, Africa, Eastern Europe, and elsewhere took place in the context of changing and shifting intellectual frameworks and epistemology about what kind of social forces were propelling these political changes (Hamalengwa, 1992: 160). The debate in Africa ceased to revolve around "class struggle," "working class," and "dictatorship of the proletariat," among other concepts. These were replaced by concepts of "popular movements," "popular classes," "social movements," "mass struggles," and other categories which lump people together undifferentiated by class, ideology, or social belonging. The end result of these struggles was envisaged as the attainment of democracy and guaranteed observance of human rights without any class connotation whatsoever.

SAPs and the Aid Crunch on Kenya

The second major external factor was the economics of structural adjustment programs (SAPs) introduced in Africa beginning the early 1980s in response to the worsening economic conditions. Towards the close of the 1980s, it was obvious that the SAPs had had limited impact in redressing the economic crisis on the continent. Against this background, multilateral aid donors, the World Bank and International Monetary Fund (IMF), joined the U.S. in calling for political reform as a companion to the economics of structural adjustment. "Good governance—including such polyarchic features as citizen influence and oversight, responsible and responsive leadership, and meaningful accountability and transparency—became a regular theme on the discourse of structural adjustment" (Young, 1996: 59). This "Washington consensus" as Crawford Young calls it, favored making external economic assistance conditional not only on economic reform, but also on implementation of a democratic agenda. Soon, economic reform and political pluralism became "the only game in town." Aid donors hoped that political liberalization would improve economic management, debt repayment, and political legitimacy. The language of good governance, transparency, and accountability emerged (Haugerud, 1995: 20).

The predication of aid by both bilateral and multilateral donors on political conditionality had significant impact in Kenya. In May 1990, Smith Hempstone, the U.S. Ambassador to Kenya stated: "The U.S. would give preference in its grants of foreign aid to those countries which nourished democratic institutions, defended human rights, and practiced multiparty democracy" (Murunga, 2002: 103). In the same year, the U.S. Congress asked the Bush administration to delay the transmission of U.S.$ 7 million in economic aid and U.S.$ 8 million in military assistance to Kenya. In the same vein, in November 1991, the Paris Club, which includes most of the donor countries and Kenya's traditional benefactors, deferred for six months, aid commitments to Kenya for the 1992 fiscal year, "pending progress on political and economic reforms in the country" (Murunga, 2002: 104; Muigai, 1993: 28). This external aid crunch against Kenya coupled with internal demands for political pluralism to force president Moi in December 1991 to repeal section 2(A) of the country's constitution that legalized one party rule. The decision was made by President Moi in spite of the fact that a KANU National Delegates meeting was overwhelmingly in favor of continuing with the single-party state.[9] It is noteworthy that the announcement by President Moi of the legalization of multipartyism came just two weeks after the Western donor meeting in Paris decided to suspend U.S.$ 328 million in new commitments of fast disbursing aid until Kenya adopted political and economic liberalization measures.

IMF/World Bank SAPs and Zambia

With regard to Zambia, SAPs as a conditionality for aid lending on the part of the IMF and World Bank had devastating effects on the lives of

Zambians and, ipso facto, on the impetus for political change. Although the IMF and World Bank were involved in Zambia's economy in the 1970s, it was in the 1980s, with increasing economic problems facing the country that the two institutions began to play a politically significant role. Zambia's foreign debt rose from U.S.$ 108 million in 1975 to U.S.$ 7.5 billion in 1990. After 1984, IMF/World Bank insisted that credit facilities to Zambia be conditioned upon the government's acceptance of extensive economic structural adjustment. The two institutions insisted on a flexible exchange rate; improved foreign exchange budgeting and import licensing system; acceptance that there should be no arrears under debt rescheduling agreements and reduction in commercial payment arrears; reduction on government personal emoluments and a freeze on employment levels for ministries except health, agriculture, and education; limits on the increase of internal government and non-government borrowing and money supply; and decontrolling of prices and interest rates (Momba, 1993: 204). These measures, coupled with the introduction of the Kwacha[10] auction system saw a steep rise in the prices of essential commodities, in spite of the state's attempt to control prices of some essentials. Inflation for low-income groups jumped from 20.1 percent in 1984 to 39.9 percent in 1985 and to 41.9 percent in 1986 (Momba, 1993: 205).

On June 30, 1989, the Zambian government was forced again into taking other measures, which negatively impacted upon consumers. It decontrolled prices on all items it had decided to control in May 1986, including cooking oil, salt, baby foods, stock-feed, and did away with government subsidy on maize meal, the staple food in Zambia. As a result, inflation shot up from 55.7 percent in 1988 to 120.2 percent in 1989 and 129.9 percent in 1990 (Momba 1993: 205). The direct consequence of these measures was the spontaneous uprising of urban populations in 1986 and 1990. The rise of maize meal prices as a result of removal of subsidies in 1986 (reinstated after the riots) led to the first food riots and looting, the worst urban unrest in post-colonial Zambia, which begun on the Copperbelt and spread to Lusaka leading to 15 deaths. In this case, the government invoked the state of emergency to deal with the crisis and compulsorily acquired privately owned milling companies located in various parts of Zambia to the chagrin and consternation of owners who received public sympathy (see Mwanakatwe, 1994).

The riots of 1990 again followed implementation of IMF austerity measures that saw the doubling of maize meal prices to levels people could no longer bear. The first on the streets were University of Zambia (UNZA) students, triggering a wave of protests in Lusaka, Ndola, Kitwe, Kafue, and

Kabwe in which 29 people were killed and more than 100 suffered gunshot wounds. The rioters targeted government shops and looted more than 70 shops and, in the process, brought business in Lusaka almost to a standstill. The political dimension of the protests was such that President Kaunda was squarely blamed for the debilitating economic conditions in which most Zambians found themselves. As such, student protesters carried placards that read: "The struggle continues unless Kaunda resigns," "Your time is up, KK resign now," and "Power-hungry Kaunda must go" (Mwanakatwe, 1994: 173).

In the midst of the crisis over maize meal prices, Lieutenant Mwamba Luchembe went on national radio at 3:15 A.M. on June 30, 1990 to announce that the army had overthrown the government, prompting much jubilation in Lusaka and elsewhere. Lusaka residents poured onto the streets joyfully shouting "Kaunda no more," "Kaunda *walala*"— Bemba for Kaunda is dead—(Mwanakatwe, 1994: 148). Although the coup lasted only about four hours, it underscored most dramatically, unlike anything before, the unpopularity of the Kaunda regime. The attempted military coup further fueled the advocates for a multiparty system. Because of internal and external pressure, the political leadership promised a referendum on this issue to be held in October 1990, but then postponed it to August 1991. Later, partly as a result of the support MMD was enjoying, demonstrated by huge rallies, President Kaunda decided to forego a referendum on the reintroduction of multipartyism. Consequently, multiparty politics was permitted in 1990 by an amendment to article 4 of the Constitution of Zambia, which had forbidden the formation of political parties other than UNIP.

CONCLUSION

This chapter has explored the forces of political dissent and opposition to single-party authoritarianism in Kenya and Zambia and the emergence of democratization. The foregoing analysis shows that there was greater opposition to the single-party state in Kenya than in Zambia where the system was generally accepted once it was put in place. This reality was a function of the promotion of free participation and inclusive politics in the Zambian one-party state where former opposition leaders such as Harry Nkumbula, Nalumino Mundia, and Mufaya Mumbuna were co-opted into UNIP, with Mundia even rising to become prime minister. In Kenya, on the other hand, the tendency was one of practicing the politics of exclusion with the tightening of political control to ensure only regime loyalists participated. As such, former KPU oppositionists such Oginga Odinga, Bildad Kaggia, and Wasonga Sijeyo, among others were to remain in political limbo throughout the single-party era.

The chapter has demonstrated that the push for the opening up of political space in the two countries in particular, and indeed in Africa generally, was a consequence of both internal and external forces. Internal political forces in Kenya were constituted by radical politicians, university students and intellectuals, as well as the Church and other NGOs. Intellectuals and university students in Zambia also constituted significant opposition to the single-party state, but of critical importance was the role of the labor movement as well as the business community. These internal political forces were augmented by external factors to force the incumbent regimes in both countries to adopt multipartyism. The first external factor was the collapse of the totalitarian communist regimes of Eastern Europe, an eventuality that served to energize the pro-democracy forces in Africa and to legitimize demands for political change. The second key factor was the economics of SAPs. This had its greatest impact in Zambia where implementation of IMF/World Bank austerity measures led to riots in major cities that essentially marked the beginning of the end of the Kaunda regime. Third was the aid crunch especially against Kenya by both the country's bilateral and multilateral lenders, all of whom predicated further lending on political liberalization.

In the face of the above forces, the incumbent regimes in Kenya and Zambia faced narrowed choices. In Zambia, President Kaunda opted for a referendum to decide on whether to adopt multiparty politics. He then postponed it, and ultimately opted for multipartyism without the referendum. In so doing, Kaunda sought to steal the initiative for political change from the MMD, which, gauging from the popular turnouts at its rallies, was sure to win the referendum. In addition, by acceding to multipartyism much earlier than the referendum would have allowed, Kaunda acted in his own self-interest. He thereby afforded himself a whole year to repackage his party and political agenda in readiness for the electoral showdown in October 1991. Kenya's President Moi faced similar options. First, he constituted a committee to collect views from Kenyans on the future of the party system. Whereas the committee reported that majority Kenyans were for the continuity of the system and a KANU National Delegates conference gathered in 1991 at Kasarani, Nairobi was ready to rubber-stamp the committee's "findings," Moi announced, to the surprise of the delegates, that it was time for political pluralism. In so doing he, like Kaunda sought to stem the tide of agitation for political change and to placate external aid donors, as well as to control the momentum for political change to his own advantage.

Overall, Kaunda was overwhelmingly vanquished in the first multi-party elections of October 1991. Indeed, the tide against Kaunda was such that Zambians averred that, "If a frog stands against Kaunda, we will elect the frog!" For his part, Moi emerged victorious in the 1992 elections in spite of the popular slogan "Moi must go!" and even went on to win again with an improved tally of votes in 1997. This study argues that the contrast with regard to regime change in Zambia and regime continuity in Kenya in the face of democratization may be explained in terms of three key variables. These include the role of civil society, ethnicity, and electoral system design. These variables, in addition, have serious implications for the prospects of democratic consolidation in the two countries. It is on the analysis of these variables in the politics of transition in Kenya and Zambia that the subsequent chapters focus.

Chapter Three
The Centrality of Civil Society

Since the second half of the 1980s, Africa has undergone a period of sustained political activism towards democratization. A plethora of social formations have emerged and thrust themselves into the political arena to help push the agenda of what is regarded as the continent's second liberation. According to John Harbeson (1994: 1), "[t]oday, grassroots movements have arisen in nearly every sub-Saharan country to remove autocratic, repressive governments and empower African peoples to reclaim control over their political destinies." In this regard, 'civil society' is assigned the central place in the process of democratizing Africa. Harbeson, for instance, argues that civil society is the hitherto missing key to sustained political reform, legitimate states and governments, improved governance, viable state-society and state-economy relationships, and prevention of political decay. Scholars taking this view argue that the structural adjustment programs initiated in Africa in the early 1980s have not succeeded largely because they failed to emphasize the political role of civil society. Instead, they consigned civil society to the realm of market economics and private enterprise. The idea here is that civil society's political role is indispensable to political transformation towards greater democracy in Africa.

THE CONCEPTUALIZATION PROBLEMATIC

The contemporary currency of the concept of civil society in the discourse on African democratization is a recent phenomenon. However, the concept has a long pedigree dating back to the social contract theorizations of Thomas Hobbes and John Locke, through to Hegel, and Karl Marx and his followers. In their postulation of the social contractual shift from the "state of nature" to "civil society," the Hobbesian and Lockean perspectives viewed civil society as coterminous with the state. These pre-eighteenth century conceptions of civil society drew inspiration from Aristotle for whom civil society simply equaled the polis, " . . . a type of political association which placed its members under the influence of laws and ensured peaceful order and good government" (Mamdani, 1995: 603). It was Hegel, according to Chabal and Daloz (1999), who first used the concept of civil society to philosophically distinguish between state and civil society. Whereas Marx argued that the state is, in fact, an instrument of the dominant classes in society for the domination and oppression of civil society, Hegel conceived of the state as the regulating institution that made the separate operation of civil society possible. In contrast to the view of civil society as the realm of freedom against the state as institutional despotism, as Mamdani observes, Hegel conceptualized civil society as a contradictory construct. For him, the state does not arise against civil society, but in continuous conflict with it. Instead of the picture of a harmonious and non-contradictory sphere, civil society is posited as a contradictory combination, replete with conflict between classes and groups. The implication, according to Mamdani (1995: 604), is clear: "neither civil society nor movements that arise from it can be idealized. In contrast, movements within civil society demand concrete analysis to be understood, for they harbour contradictory possibilities."

The eighteenth century marked a shift toward an understanding of civil society and state in a diametric and one-sided opposition. Citing Thomas Paine, who saw civil society as a natural condition of freedom, a legitimate arena of defense against the state, Mamdani (1995: 603) argues:

> This point of view is reflected in what is today the dominant tendency in Africanist thought, one which considers the process of democratisation as synonymous with the coming to life of civil society. In turn, civil society is conceptualized as existing against the state. This tendency involves nothing less than a one-sided anti-state romanticisation of civil society.

Taking Mamdani's argument even further, Björn Beckman (1998) contends that the current emphasis on the state-civil society dichotomy is an ideological strategy of the current neoliberal offensive. Beckman argues:

> In an effort to delegitimise the principal ideological rival—economic nationalism—neoliberals seek to delegitimise the state, the main locus of nationalist aspirations and resistance to the neoliberal project. In order to undercut the claims by the state to represent the nation, its alien nature is emphasized. Its retrogressiveness is explained in terms of its separation from civil society . . . [its] rent-seeking, patrimonialism and . . . autonomy. (Beckman, 1998: 46)

Nevertheless, it is clear that for the pre-eighteenth century social theorists, civil society was coterminous with the state. The Hegelian postulation marked a shift in this regard, utilizing the concept of civil society to philosophically distinguish between state and society. Subsequently, the concept has been politically and ideologically applied in various ways depending on the dictates of the moment. It has variously been conceived of as a bulwark against anarchy, against the Church, the Leviathan State, and most recently, as a bulwark against the hegemonic and predatory authoritarian state. On the basis of this, Chabal and Daloz point out that there is no accepted genealogy of the concept that would provide an analytically useful framework for the study of African politics. The two scholars contend that, as is often the case with notions that become widely practiced and analytically fashionable, it becomes difficult to know whether their heuristic value matches their common currency.

Indeed, there is a great deal of contestation over the meaning of the concept of civil society. There is disagreement over whether it is a relational or locational concept; whether it is a truly organically constituted actor, or its corporeal being is a mirage of distant perception that dissolves as one approaches. Some scholars celebrate what they posit as the actual and potential capacity of civil society to transform African politics towards greater democracy. They elevate the phenomenon of civil society to the position of a providential spirit dispatched to redeem a political world gone awry (see Diamond, 1999; Harbeson, 1994; Callaghy, 1994). Other scholars, on the other hand, view the notion of civil society as a mere metaphor masquerading as a political player. They deny the concept concrete reality and contend that it is, in actuality, a child of the anthropomorphic fertility of the social scientific mind. It is, in this view, a theoretical construct lacking empirical locus (see Nasong'o, forthcoming, 2001b, 2004b). For instance, while noting that civil society forcefully entered the African political arena following the end of the Cold War, Crawford Young (1994: 43) asks:

> But precisely what has ventured upon the stage? Is this truly an actor, organically constituted? Is its corporeal being only an illusion of distant perception, dissolving as one approaches? Is it merely a metaphor masquerading as player? Is it yet another child of the anthropomorphic fertility of the social scientific imagination? Or do we spy a redemptive spirit, providentially dispatched to right a political world gone awry?

In essence, there are two basic perspectives on civil society. The first views civil society as a relational concept, and defines it as "society in its relation to the state . . . in so far as it is in confrontation with the state . . .

[it is] the process by which society seeks to 'breach' and counteract the simultaneous 'totalization' unleashed by the state" (Young 1994: 44). Similarly, viewing civil society as a theoretical construct devoid of empirical locus, Michael Bratton (1994: 56) argues that though civil society and the state are conceptually distinct, they are best considered together. In other words, the concept of civil society is a relational rather than a locational concept. It points to society's relations with the state whether such relations are confrontational or cooperative.

The second conceptualization views civil society as a locational concept, that is, in terms of the position that groups constituting civil society occupy in the polity. Taking this approach, Naomi Chazan (1994) argues that the notion of civil society in regard to Africa occupies a middle ground between the state-society dichotomy. It is a linkage concept and an all-encompassing term referring to social phenomena putatively beyond formal state structures, but not necessarily free of all contact with the state. She posits that the conceptual vision that either pits society against the state or allows for cooperation or collusion with the state inevitably yields a mechanistic view of the political domain, which neglects both the web-like structure of the human landscape and the fluid nature of social exchanges (Chazan, 1994: 256). The advantage of the locational conception of civil society, therefore, is that it takes into account the interpenetrations between civil and political societies, the straddling of one over the other, and vice versa.

Victor Azarya (1994) provides a most comprehensive definition of civil society. He conceptualizes civil society in terms of three components. First, he says that civil society is a part of society comprising a set of autonomous institutions that are distinct from the family, the class, the locality and the state. Secondly, he sees civil society as a part of society that conducts a particular set of relationships between itself and the state, possesses mechanisms that safeguard the separation of state and civil society, and maintains effective ties between them. Thirdly, Azarya contends that it is a widespread pattern of refined and civil manners, which may also be called "civility" (Azarya, 1994: 89). Azarya writes that the implications of civility go much deeper than simple courtesy and good manners. Such manners mean respect for the dignity of fellow members of society. It is:

> . . . an acknowledgment of consideration toward 'the other,' beyond one's family, a recognition of dignity derived from the individual's humanity or membership in a given community. It recognizes that all people have similar rights and obligations and hence implies a readiness to moderate particular individual or parochial interests in consideration of some common good, through which others' basic rights and

interests would be protected as well as one's own. Acceptance of such collective responsibility to the common good and the positive value of activities meant to safeguard it are at the core of civility and form the fundamental virtue of civil society. (Azarya, 1994: 90)

Overall, therefore, civil society is the realm of organized social life that is open, voluntary, self-generating, at least partially self-supporting, autonomous from the state, and bound by a legal order or set of shared rules. According to Larry Diamond (1999: 221), it is different from "society" in general in that it involves citizens acting collectively in a public sphere to express their interests, passions, preferences, and ideas; to exchange information; achieve collective goals; make demands on the state; improve the structure and functioning of the state; and hold state officials accountable. On the basis of this definition, Diamond provides a succinct elaboration of the centrality of civil society to democratic transition. In his estimation, civil society helps to generate a transition from authoritarian rule to democracy and to deepen and consolidate democracy in four main ways. First, being an intermediary phenomenon standing between the private sphere and the state, it provides the basis for the limitation of state power, for the control of state by society, and thus for democratic political institutions as the most effective means of exercising that control.

Second, it supplements the role of political parties in stimulating political participation, increasing the political efficacy and skill of citizens, promoting an appreciation of the obligations and rights of democratic citizenship, and articulating, aggregating, and representing interests. Third, civil society promotes civic awareness through civic education for democracy and recruits and trains new political leaders. And fourth, it disseminates information widely and so empowers citizens in the collective pursuit and defense of their interests and values hence strengthening the social foundation of democracy. Civil society thus enhances the accountability, responsiveness, inclusiveness, effectiveness, and hence legitimacy of the political system, and, ipso facto, gives citizens respect for the state and positive engagement with it (see Diamond, 1999: 239-250). Essentially therefore, in the grand scheme of Africa's democratization, civil society is assigned the role of Lenin's strong vanguard Communist Party—that of political mobilization and education (indoctrination, in the case of Lenin's party)—of the masses.

Civil Society in Africa

Conceptualized in the above pristine and idealized form, the question then becomes whether such forms of civil society exist in Africa. According to

Chabal and Daloz (1999: 17), "[a]lthough until the nineteenth century the notion of civil society was virtually synonymous with that of the state, it is commonly taken today to refer to the opposite—namely that which is outside the state." The two scholars argue that though the state-civil society dichotomy is taken for granted in discourses on African politics, it does not reflect reality on the ground. They argue:

> The notion of civil society would only apply if it could be shown that there were meaningful institutional separations between a well-organized civil society and a relatively autonomous bureaucratic state. Instead, what we observe in Black Africa is the constant interpenetration, or straddling, of the one by the other. Those who emphasize the role of civil society are thus forced to identify it very largely as a residual category, including as it were all the individuals and groups who express dissent. (Chabal and Daloz, 1999: 17)

The two scholars hold that in Africa there is no genuine disconnection between a structurally differentiated state and a civil society composed of properly organized and politically distinct interest groups. They contend that the common view is that

> . . . civil society refers to those intermediary associations, which are capable both of representing the country's various groups and of countering the state's hegemonic ambitions. As a result, it is commonly assumed that the political reform of the continent may depend on the extent to which civil society is able to counteract the stultifying weight of the oppressive state. It is often argued that the most vibrant and innovative sections of society are those linked with Non-Governmental Organizations (or NGOs), associations of active citizens speaking for ordinary people and small-scale but dynamic business groups. (Chabal and Daloz, 1999: 19)

Chabal and Daloz thus pose the question as to whether one should restrict the notion of civil society in Africa to 'high' elite associations such as those of lawyers, journalists, businessmen, academics, or to 'low' popular groupings like village associations, squatter defense committees, market traders, and the unemployed.

In the same vein, Peter Wanbali (2001) argues, with specific reference to Kenya, that the concept of civil society is a misnomer extracted from the liberal tradition. In his view, this concept of civil society has been used by opportunistic traders masquerading as principled civil society activists to cheat millions of dollars out of the gullible wallets of well-funded groups in Western countries. Wanbali contends:

> The claim that [civil society] can transform Kenyans through civic education is a brazen NGOs lie . . . The bifurcated nature of the state . . . rubbishes any claim these 'civil society' crusaders may have to legitimacy. Their very existence as the better-off, affluent, urban dwellers, somewhat spared the tyranny and poverty of rural . . . existence, undermines their posture as knights bringing the liberating philosophy of 'civicness' to the rural masses. (Wanbali, 2001, ct. in Orvis, 2003: 247)

In spite of this pessimistic prognosis that tends to dismiss the very idea of civil society in Africa, the fact that there exists a civil society in Africa is beyond denial. As Stephen Orvis (2001) contends, optimists and pessimists in the civil society debate tend to define civil society too narrowly and ask too much of it. By " . . . insisting on a definition of civil society that is an idealized and rather narrow vision of civil society in the West, neither optimists nor pessimists have portrayed African civil society accurately" (Orvis, 2001: 17). Orvis defines civil society as "a public sphere of formal or informal collective activity autonomous from the state and the family" and argues that much of African civil society is guided by what John Lonsdale (1994) has termed "moral ethnicity" and what Stephen Ndegwa (1998) has analyzed in terms of "civic republican citizenship." Indeed, interviews with a cross-section of African personalities on the continent reveal an unmistakable appreciation of the role civil society organizations have played in pushing forward the democratic agenda.[1]

As for the perspective that juxtaposes Western and African political experiences and denies the existence of an African civil society, Mahmood Mamdani (1995) accuses it of engaging in mythology and caricature. Mamdani (1995) argues that the state-civil society perspective was not originally formulated to compare the West and the rest yet it has been treated in Africanist scholarship as a turnkey project instead of being modified as an appropriate technology. As such, according to Mamdani, the perspective is guilty of the double maneuver of mythology and caricature. Given its unilinear evolutionist orientation that equates the rise of civil society with that of democracy and eschews struggles that inform the historical development of African societies, the state-civil society perspective mythologizes European experience and caricatures African experience, in the process mutilating both (Mamdani, 1995: 609).

Indeed, Naomi Chazan's (1994) postulation obviates Chabal and Daloz's concerns. As noted above, Chazan posits that the notion of civil society in regard to Africa occupies a middle ground between the state-society dichotomy. It is a linkage concept and an all-encompassing term referring to social phenomena putatively beyond formal state structures, but not necessarily free of all contact with the state. She observes:

> When the term is not used loosely as a synonym for society, it has been conceptualized in the African context, alternately, as a necessary pre-condition for state consolidation, as the key brake on state power,[2] as a benign broker between state interests and local concerns, or as a medley of social institutions that interact with each other and with formal structures in ways that may either facilitate or impede governance and economic development. (Chazan, 1994: 255)

Chazan's conceptualization is thus most appropriate for our purposes. It dovetails very well with the Hegelian perspective, which views civil society as a contradictory construct. As Mamdani (1995: 604) contends, an analysis anchored in a view of civil society as a realm of contradictory possibilities is not content with highlighting demands of social movements, like those for democracy and human rights, as the general demands of civil society against the state. It calls for reaching beyond every general formulation to fathom and clarify the concrete meaning of a general demand like that of democracy, from different and particular viewpoints. It demands raising fundamental questions: what, for instance is the meaning of democracy from the point of view of different classes and groups? What specific interests are organizing behind the general demand for democracy? What is the political significance of different types of democratic transitions, such as those from above as in Senegal where the tendency has been to freeze class and property relations, as opposed to transitions effected through struggles from below, as was the case in South Africa?

To some scholars, the question as to whether there exists a civil society in Africa as conceptualized above is, in fact, axiomatic. For instance, in Thomas Callaghy's (1994) view, the triumph of trade unionist Frederick Chiluba over the long-serving President Kenneth Kaunda in the first Zambian multiparty elections of 1991 symbolized the victory of civil society over authoritarianism. He enthusiastically declares that civil society overthrew a corrupt and authoritarian state leading to high expectations about economic rebirth and a return to the politics of distribution. Extrapolated to the African continent therefore, the concept of civil society has come to mean the emergence of a conjuncture in which societal groups assert their autonomy from the post-colonial authoritarian state and challenge its political hegemony. "Teleologically, civil society comes to stand for reinvigorated forms of participatory politics, for forces pushing toward some type of democracy. Society strikes back against oppression in the form of 'civil' society" (Callaghy, 1994: 233).

It is this kind of enthusiasm that facilitated placement of great emphasis on the role of civil society in the new political conjuncture of democratization in Africa. Indeed, the emergence of civil society organizations onto the African political arena in countries as diverse as Gabon, Cameroon, Congo, Kenya, and Tanzania immensely contributed to what has been described as a veritable explosion of associational life. It also injected an explicitly political dimension into the associational arena, pressing for guarantees for basic human rights and advocating democratic reforms (see Chazan, 1994). It is this conception of civil society as a vanguard of African democratization that has facilitated the emergence of a plethora of NGOs in Africa as representatives of "civil society" in the battle of democratizing the hitherto authoritarian African State. The situation has further been helped by the policy shift on the part of Western development financiers away from channeling development resources through state institutions to channeling the same via these emergent social formations.[3] For instance, in an article aptly entitled *What are NGOs Doing Here?* Sue Wheat (2000: 55) points out that more than 19 million people are currently working for NGOs worldwide and that NGOs are dealing in at least US$ 1.1 trillion annually. The idea of strengthening civil society through these NGOs as a way of making democracy work has become a major factor in the dealings between the Global North and the Global South in the emergent international political milieu following the end of the Cold War. However conceptualized therefore, the centrality accorded "civil society" in the African democratization project cannot be belabored.

CIVIL SOCIETY AS AGENT OF POLITICAL CHANGE

Michael Pietrowski (1994) underscores the centrality of civil society as political norm setter and agent of political change. He argues that whether in a one-party state or in a multiparty one, if human rights are to be protected, not only in theory but also in practice, "there must be a strong, democratized civil society independent of the ruling government" (Pietrowski, 1994: 132). He contends that government plans for regime transformation in Africa have been mostly reactionary hence true change and reform is not likely to come from above. "Thus civil society has a key role to play in the political liberation of a state, and a pluralized society is crucial to the respect for human rights" (Ibid., p. 141). Pietrowski contends that in order to achieve this goal, the first task of civil institutions is to gain autonomy from the state because " . . . an effective civil society only exists to the extent that it is self-conscious of its existence and of its opposition to the state" (Ibid., p. 142). For his part, Julius Nyang'oro contends that,

> [t]he more the members of society organize themselves into groups to advance their particular interests, the less likely the state can function in an autonomous and unaccountable manner . . . the proliferation of organized interests is a bulwark against unbridled state power. This autonomy may be one of the key principles in the building of democracy. (Nyang'oro, 2000: 98)

The Zambian case illustrates this argument with particular clarity.

Civil Society and the Zambian Transition

The clearest manifestation of the role of civil society in democratization is the transition from the Kaunda regime to that of Chiluba in Zambia in 1991. Whereas other civil society organizations in Zambia such as the Law Association of Zambia, the Economic Club, and Churches among others were important in the politics of transition in the country, the trade union movement played the key role. Munyonze Hamalengwa (1992) notes that by 1987, it could not be foreseen that Zambia's one-party political system would be fundamentally changed within a few years' time. However, in October 1991, Kaunda's regime was defeated in a landslide victory by the Movement for Multiparty Democracy (MMD) led by Frederick Chiluba, the Chairman-General of the Zambia Congress of Trade Unions (ZCTU). According to Hamalengwa (1992: 159), " . . . the events that hoisted Chiluba to the helm started germinating a long time ago from the time the labor movement gravitated towards political engagement in the late seventies to the time it began to constitute itself as an unofficial opposition in the early eighties."

In seeking to explain the transition from the long-serving President Kaunda, Michael Bratton (1994: 103) argues that one-party regimes submit to competitive elections only where there are sources of countervailing political power. These include a mobilized citizenry, a free press, civic watchdog groups, a unified political party, a professional civil service, and an independent judiciary. Bratton focuses on the first factor in regard to Zambia and posits that the independent ZCTU and MMD provided channels through which economic grievances could be expressed and organized into an electoral bid for state power. The existence of powerful interest groups in Zambia, especially organized labor, which enjoyed an unusual degree of autonomy, meant that economic grievances could be translated into political action. According to Bratton, the trade union confederation played a catalytic role in directing mass opposition against the perceived incompetence and dishonesty of the ruling United National Independence Party (UNIP) leaders and the authoritarian strictures of the single-party state. The emergence of MMD as a cohesive opposition party, what Jan Donge (1995) calls a "maximum coalition," both reflected and enabled a fundamental political realignment among Zambian voters, in which urban wage earners changed from supporters to opponents of the UNIP government.

Of crucial importance also, was the integrity of Trade Union leaders, especially ZCTU's leader Frederick Chiluba and his deputy, Newstead Zimba both of whom represented long-standing opposition to Kaunda and UNIP, suffering detention in the early 1980s but, unlike other union leaders, refused to be co-opted by Kaunda. According to Donge (1995), Chiluba's popularity stemmed in the first place from the fact that, unlike the others, he had never accepted high office under Kaunda and, again unlike the others, he was not an intellectual. He had risen in the trade union movement through grassroots organizing. Donge writes that there was a widespread, almost eschatological, expectation that multipartyism would cure Zambia's economic ills. "This arose not because of concrete policy measures, but because of a resurgence of belief in integrity in politics personified by Chiluba. Chiluba occupied the moral high ground in Zambian politics as he had never in the past been tempted by political office, which was associated with economic failure" (Donge, 1995: 205). Many supporters of the MMD were simply captivated by Frederick Chiluba's sincerity and courage (Ihonvbere, 1996: 113). Larry Diamond's exposition that civil society helps identify and train leaders is thus exemplified by the emergence of Chiluba in Zambia. As Munyonze Hamalengwa (1992) asserts, Chiluba was rooted in the labor movement whose platform was social democracy whereby the labor movement would play its role as the protector of working class interests and divorced from state and party politics and the role of the state was to be answerable to the needs of the entire society including the working class. Because of the economic crisis and increasing repression in Zambia, the working class was increasingly forced to enter the political arena, forming the bedrock of support for their leader.

Once the ZCTU declared its support for the MMD, its organizational structure served a significant role in mobilizing support for the new party across the country. "All trade union offices all over the country immediately became recruiting centers . . . Towns served by railroads, provincial and district capitals, and all public institutions with trade-union branches became major organizing centers for MMD" (Ihonvbere, 1996: 117). The unions, assisted by schools, Churches, and businesses, helped to spread the

MMD's political message to the remotest parts of Zambia thereby mobilizing support for the party.

MMD's organizational advantage was coupled with the resource base of the trade union movement, based as it is on membership dues, to afford the movement autonomy and the crucial support of the subscribed membership. In this regard, members of the trade union movement had a direct stake in the Zambian politics of transition because of the worsening economic situation and the self-aggrandizement of the Kaunda regime. Hamalengwa (1992) notes that trade unions in Zambia had been campaigning for political and economic accountability for a very long time. Chiluba, in particular, was a very popular union leader who was on record as having frequently challenged the government to clean up the system in the interests of non-bourgeois forces. As noted in Chapter Two, the crisis in Eastern Europe gave them new impetus and they started to organize openly. The struggle was further energized by the externalities wrought by the implementation of IMF/World Bank austerity measures by the Kaunda regime to stem the economic crisis in Zambia.

Against this background, Julius Ihonvbere (1996) observes that UNIP knew for a long time that the day of reckoning would dawn sooner or later. The 1980s had seen consistent challenges to Kaunda, UNIP, and the ideology of Humanism. As shown in Chapter Two, in every confrontation with the state, through the 1980s, the labor movement came out victorious, or at least, losing nothing. But each victory also meant the demystification of Kaunda and his ideology. "It meant a delegitimation of his rule and his government. It meant an explosion of the invincibility and popular support his party was supposed to be enjoying. It also meant erosion of the legitimacy and invincibility of the one party" (Ihonvbere, 1996: 104). Ihonvbere rightly notes that Labor was able to lead the struggle because of its organizational advantages, its resource base, the character of its leadership, and the fact that its members were often the first victims of the state's economic policies of adjustment and stabilization.

Indeed, on account of the fact that workers and urban residents who bore the brunt of inflation, unemployment, crime, and deteriorating social services had turned to the MMD, Kaunda concentrated his campaigns in the rural areas. Relying on traditional chiefs, making promises and hoping rural dwellers had remained insulated from MMD's campaigns and the paths of a failed adjustment program. "With this, the reports from his security forces, and the scores of sycophants surrounding him and his personal confidence that there was no way a person like him could lose the election in Zambia, Kaunda predicted several times, even on election day, that

UNIP would not only sweep the polls but will continue winning any polls" (Ihonvbere, 1996a: 121). Unfortunately for Kaunda, as Ihonvbere writes, such predictions were completely out of tune with reality. Bitter ethnic and regional divisions and badly eroded legitimacy had pushed most Zambians in and beyond the urban areas to the MMD's camp, except perhaps in the Eastern Province, Kaunda's home base. UNIP was shocked to be confronted in villages by shouts of "the hour has come" (MMD's slogan). Villagers had felt the brunt of the government's failed economic policies. They were still neglected and had seen a drastic fall in the monetary remittances from urban relatives who had been forced out of cities by poverty, unemployment and other pressures.

Furthermore, Chiluba's popularity meant that he also had the capacity of keeping the opposition coalition together. His control of the well-structured labor movement meant that no other opposition party could emerge to attract a sufficient following to split the vote.[4] From the very outset therefore, it was clear that the electoral battle was going to be between UNIP and MMD. "The few fringe political parties that emerged on the national scene lacked the organizational structure, resources, credible leadership and programs as well as the experience and ability to mount effective political campaigns" (Ihonvbere, 1996a: 119). For instance, the Movement for Democratic Process (MDP) paid the Kwacha 20,000 candidacy deposit but failed to raise the requisite 200 signatures from registered voters in support of Chama Chakomboka's presidential ambition. Similarly, the Christian Alliance for the Kingdom of Africa (CHAKA) led by James Kalisirila withdrew from the electoral race on "technical grounds." For his part, Emanuel Mubunga Mwamba of the National Alliance for Democracy (NADA) never even bothered to file his nomination (Ibid.).

It was against this background that the victory of Chiluba over Kaunda was hailed as a victory of civil society over an entrenched authoritarian regime. As Victor Azarya (1994) enthusiastically declares, civil society overthrew a corrupt and authoritarian state leading to high expectations about economic rebirth and a return to the politics of distribution. Emerging fresh from within the ranks of civil society onto the national political stage, and untainted by the corrupt politics of the single-party state, it is no wonder that Chiluba generated the kind of enthusiasm he did about the possibilities of Zambia's economic rebirth.

Civil Society and the Kenyan Transition

In his analysis of the role of civil society in political transition, Michael Pietrowski (1994) glorifies the role of the Church in Kenya, especially the

National Council of the Churches of Kenya (NCCK); and the legal profession (Law Society of Kenya). He particularly gives pride of place to NGOs, both local and international, in the key role of strengthening civil society and empowering the ordinary people. He argues: "NGOs, churches, and professional organizations all represent potential counters to centralized power" (Pietrowski, 1994: 143). Julius Nyang'oro (2000: 92), however, argues that Kenyan civil society is relatively weak and fractured, a weakness that arises from its being based on rising ethnic divisions. He argues nonetheless that in spite of this weakness, civil society has played an important role in the struggle for political liberalization. According to Nyang'oro, throughout the post-independence period, there has been no consensus in Kenya on the desirability of a one-party system. He argues:

> Indeed, foreign pressure on the Moi government on the question of human rights has always been in reaction to internal struggles—by students, lawyers, politicians, clergy, etc. Thus the massive riots by various segments of the population, which took place in July 1990 . . . in response to the banning of public meetings called to advocate political pluralism, must be seen as reflecting this long-standing tradition of opposition to one-partyism. (Nyang'oro 2000: 94)

Nyang'oro asserts that the call by Smith Hempstone, U.S. Ambassador to Kenya, in 1990 for the release of political prisoners was based on evidence provided by the Law Society of Kenya, among other groups.

Nyang'oro stresses first, the role of university student associations, which focused their political activities on demonstrations, class boycotts, and issuing of leaflets in support of underground pro-democracy groups such as *Mwakenya*.[5] Second, he highlights the role of Church leaders, most of whom took to condemning the Kenya African National Union (KANU) regime on corruption, undemocratic practices, and openly called for political pluralism. And third, he singles out the National Council of the Churches of Kenya (NCCK) and its political role, especially in holding seminars and joint meetings with other pro-democracy groups and providing political education, channeling political demands, and calling for good governance.

Although civil society organizations contributed significantly to the push towards multipartyism and the opening of the Kenyan political space, compared to the Zambian case, they fell far short especially in regard to political mobilization for regime change once political pluralism was instituted in 1991. The first explanation for this difference is provided by Nyang'oro's argument that Kenyan civil society is weak and fractured along ethnic lines. The Forum for the Restoration of Democracy (FORD) formed to fight for the return to multipartyism in Kenya was, in its orientation and objective, reminiscent of the Movement for Multiparty Democracy (MMD) in Zambia. The Zambian opposition alliance was broad, spawning the politically relevant cleavages in society. It included both urban and rural dwellers, mine workers and the unemployed, businessmen and civil servants, plus representatives from most regions of the country, and remained intact after transforming itself into a political party in December 1990. This inclusive coalition contrasts with narrower opposition movements in other African countries, which for instance, are predominantly urban in Côte d'Ivoire, ethnic in Kenya, and Islamic in Algeria (see Bratton 1994). Indeed, in contrast to the MMD, FORD in Kenya disintegrated into two factions—FORD-A and FORD-K—along ethnic lines once multipartyism was allowed and elections became imminent in 1992.[6] Hence whereas MMD went on to vanquish Kaunda's UNIP in Zambia, Moi's KANU faced a fractured FORD in Kenya and thus took advantage of this weakness to retain political power in 1992.

The second factor lies in the nature and organization of the civil society organizations involved in the quest for political change. In the case of Zambia, the autonomous trade union movement was the one at the center of political mobilization for change. The movement was well structured, both in terms of the various trades, with the ZCTU at the apex, and organizationally with branches in all major Zambian towns. Of crucial importance was the integrity of the ZCTU top leadership, which refused to be co-opted by the Kaunda regime, even after harassment and detention. As Mwanakatwe (1994) notes, Chiluba enhanced the reputation of trade unions and ZCTU by his uncompromising stand on the question of co-optation, thus maintaining the independence of the labor movement from control by the party and its government. "The more he resisted threats from Kaunda and senior party officials, the more popular Chiluba became among the rank and file of the labor movement and ordinary folk, ordinary men and women in Zambia who saw him as the protector of the underprivileged people" (Mwanakatwe, 1994: 186). The leadership remained steadfast in championing the cause of the working class especially in the face of the debilitating effects of the structural adjustment programs implemented in Zambia in the mid 1980s. Julius Ihonvbere (1996: 119) underscores this factor by noting that the labor movement's organizational structure, resources, credible leadership, and programs were crucial in facilitating the mounting of effective political campaigns.

In contrast, the top leadership of the labor movement in Kenya had long been co-opted into the ruling party by the turn of the 1990s. Indeed,

ZCTU's counterpart in Kenya, the Central Organization of Trade Unions (COTU) was affiliated to KANU and renamed COTU-KANU. The COTU leadership thus lacked incentive to politically engage the Kenyan State within the context of activism for political change and as such, the labor movement in Kenya remained politically obtuse. Consequently, political activism in Kenya remained the preserve of non-governmental organizations (NGOs) such as the National Convention Executive Council (NCEC), Catholic Justice and Peace Commission (CJPC), NCCK, and Education Center for Women in Democracy (ECWD) among others (see Orvis, 2003). In this event, most NGOs lacked the advantage of a countrywide network of branches to serve as mobilization centers. Hence although some of them, like NCEC, engaged in heightened activism for political change including use of mass action (see Nasong'o, forthcoming), this remained largely an urban phenomenon concentrated mainly in Nairobi and thus had limited impact.

The third explanation lies in the emergence of a new leader from the ranks of civil society to challenge the incumbent in Zambia and the lack of such a leader in the case of Kenya. Frederick Chiluba emerged from the ranks of the trade union movement to become the Chairman-General of ZCTU. He was politically untested, a man of integrity who had stuck to the fight for the rights of workers and refused to be compromised by Kaunda. As noted above, Chiluba's popularity stemmed in the first place from the fact that, unlike the others, he had never accepted high office under Kaunda and, again unlike the others, he was not an intellectual. He had risen in the trade union movement through grassroots organizing. Hence at the MMD convention to nominate the presidential candidate, he garnered 683 votes against Arthur Wina's 208, Humphrey Mulemba's 186, and Edward Shamwana's 24, all of whom were experienced politicians who had fallen out with Kaunda. Chiluba and like-minded leaders in MMD such as Newstead Zimba thus represented a genuine alternative to the incumbent leadership and raised hopes for a new political dispensation in the new Zambia that was envisaged to emerge out of the 1991 election. The opposite was the case in Kenya. The three opposition leaders who faced President Moi in the 1992 election—Oginga Odinga, Kenneth Matiba and Mwai Kibaki—were all old timers in politics, two of whom (Odinga and Kibaki) had previously served as vice president. Indeed, whereas Odinga fell out with President Kenyatta way back in 1966 and remained in opposition since then, Matiba resigned from Moi's cabinet only in 1990, while Kibaki did so on Christmas eve in 1991 after multipartyism was legalized. There was thus no genuine alternative presented to the electorate in the 1992 Kenyan presidential election.

Table 3.1: Presidential Vote Distribution in Kenya's 1992 Election

Name/Party	Votes	% of Total Vote
Moi/KANU	1,927,640	36.91%
Matiba/Ford-A	1,354,856	25.95%
Kibaki/DP	1,035,507	19.83%
Odinga/Ford-K	903,886	17.31%
Total	5,221,889	100%

Source: compiled from Electoral Commission of Kenya figures

Nevertheless, the old guard opposition presidential candidates would have managed to upstage the incumbent KANU regime in the 1992 had they united and presented a common front as the opposition did in the case of Zambia. As the 1992 election results in Table 3.1 above indicate, the combined opposition garnered 63 percent of the total valid votes cast to the incumbent President Moi's 37 percent. Opposition unity a la MMD would thus have facilitated a transition of power in Kenya in 1992, as indeed it did in 2002 (see Chapter Five).

The fourth factor lay in the high levels of urbanization in Zambia, which is the highest in Africa. As Michael Bratton (1994: 124) argues, the case of Zambia draws attention to high levels of urbanization and industrialization as a significant characteristic of civil society that facilitates electoral transitions. This fact meant that Zambia had an unusually well educated, well-paid, and class-conscious population. The extent and rapidity of contraction in the national economy, among the most precipitous in Africa according to Bratton, provoked a particularly keen grievance among urban wage earners. Economic contraction and austerity policies had a profound social impact, in which poverty "trickled up" to most social classes in Zambia. But, whereas UNIP's patronage machine had always protected its key constituency of urban wage earners, by 1985, it had exhausted its resources. Previously privileged elements in society came to bear a share of the adjustment burden once the government committed itself to a serious reform effort. The urban wage earners thus shifted their loyalty and support to MMD. Recognizing this shift, the ruling party sought reelection by bidding for the rural vote, only to discover that after years of neglect by government, peasant farmers had also defected to the opposition.

The fifth factor was the resource base of the politically active civil society organizations in the two countries. As Larry Diamond observes, civil society makes its deepest, most organic, and most sustainable contribution to democracy when it cultivates a significant base of financial support among a broad and indigenous constituency. This confers autonomy to a civil organization and promotes identity and a sense of ownership on the part of individual donors. When such financial donations are combined with broad grassroots organization, Diamond contends further, "they are likely to produce a particularly strong membership commitment and demand for democratic control" (Diamond, 1999: 257). This situation obtained in the case of Zambia with its politically active labor movement relying on membership dues, and whose membership interests were its very raison d'être. In Kenya on the other hand, the labor movement remained politically averse leaving the arena to NGOs, which are largely urban-based non-membership organizations that rely heavily on donor funding from international benefactors to whom they remain accountable. Their political activism thus remained suspended from the rest of the populace and did not meet with the kind of popular support necessary to effect political change.

The NGO dependency on donor finances is something of an Achilles heel for these organizations as it compromises their independence and renders them incapable of being effective policy actors and agenda setters in their own right since they are forced to defer to the priorities of their foreign benefactors. Indeed, as Abubacar Momoh (1999: 38) argues, some of these organizations start off as specialists but over time become generalists for purposes of attracting funding from all quarters. This leads to underperformance as a result of the NGOs spreading themselves too thin. In this sense, these organizations are incapable of effectively countering claims, made by incumbent governments, to the effect that they are in the service of foreign rather than local interests.

From the foregoing analysis, it is evident that the differential roles played by civil society in the transition politics in Kenya and Zambia is a function of the nature, organization, and resource base of the politically active civil organizations. At the time of the Zambian transition elections of 1991, politically active civil society organizations included Churches, the Law Association of Zambia, The Economic Club, and the Trade Union Movement. Of these, the most politically engaged was the trade union movement. On the other hand, at the time of Kenya's transition elections of 1992, the politically active civil organizations included the Law Society of Kenya, Churches (under the auspices of the NCCK and the CJPC), Non-Governmental Organizations (NGOs), and student associations. Of these,

NGOs were the most politically engaged. These differences and their implications for regime change in Zambia and regime endurance in Kenya are captured in Table 3.2 below.

It is important to note, nevertheless, that whatever contribution made by civil society organizations in African democratization has been a direct result of what Stephen Ndegwa (1996) calls the window of political

Table 3.2: Accounting for the Difference in the Role of Civil Organizations in Political Transition in Zambia (1991) and Kenya (1992)

Zambia	Kenya
1. The key political actor within civil society ranks was the labor movement led by the ZCTU.	1. The key political player on the part of civil society organizations was the NGO movement.
2. The autonomous ZCTU provided channels through which economic grievances were expressed and organized into an electoral bid for state power.	2. By 1991, COTU had been affiliated to the ruling party, KANU and its leaders co-opted; hence the labor movement remained politically obtuse.
3. ZCTU's organizational structures served a significant role of mobilizing support for MMD, with trade union offices all over the country serving as recruiting centers for the new party.	3. NGOs are non-membership organizations, largely urban based, whose activities remained sporadic, disconnected, and largely suspended from the mass publics.
4. The ZCTU had a relatively sound resource base based on membership dues; hence members had a stake in transition politics and remained politically mobilized.	4. NGOs are highly donor dependent, are accountable to their benefactors, and lack collaborative synergy even among themselves, hence they failed to marshal the support necessary to effect political change.
5. The MMD remained intact as a "maximum coalition" and sole opponent to UNIP and no other viable party emerged to compete with MMD for the opposition vote.	5. FORD disintegrated into two factions and was joined in the opposition by the DP, further splintering the opposition.
6. New leaders of high integrity and honesty emerged within the ranks of civil society who represented a genuine alternative to the incumbent regime.	6. The three politicians who contested against Moi were old time politicos, two of whom defected from Moi's cabinet only when multipartyism became imminent, Moi's former vice president, Mwai Kibaki, being one of the two.

Source: Author's own tabulation

opportunity afforded them by the general movement for "good governance" following the end of the Cold War. The emergence and vibrancy
of these organizations, be they in the realm of relief work and welfare,
health and the environment, development and institution building, or
advocacy and democratization, is explicable in the context of this emergent reality of an international system governed by liberal political and
economic values. As pointed out above, these organizations have made a
modest contribution to democratization in Africa and much of the available literature celebrates their role and potential in democratizing the
hitherto authoritarian African State. Arguably however, there is a flip side
to these civil society organizations that has not been adequately interrogated and that thus remains untheorized.

Furthermore, the political role and limitations of NGOs warrant
closer attention as they speak not only to the Kenyan reality, but to most
African countries, as well as all democratizing countries of the Global
South in general. The increasing role of NGOs as agents of civil society in
the process of African democratization is a phenomenon that assumed
prominence at the close of the 1980s. The situation was helped by the policy shift on the part of Western development financiers away from channeling development resources through state institutions to channeling the
same via these newly emergent social formations. The idea of strengthening
civil society through these NGOs as a way of making democracy work has
become a major factor in the dealings between the Global North and
Global South in the emergent international political milieu following the
end of the Cold War. As mentioned above, however, there is a flip side to
these NGOs as embodiments of civil society that has not been adequately
interrogated, yet it has significant implications for the role of civil society
organizations as political norm setters and agents of social change.

THE FLIP SIDE OF AFRICAN CIVIL SOCIETY

The most erstwhile and enduring critique of the state in Africa is that over
time, it has mainly been used for the self-aggrandizing activities of the political elite and their associates to the detriment of the mass of citizens. Jackson and Rosberg (1982) for example, have observed that the state in Africa
in the late twentieth century was an arena in which individuals could
obtain great power. The two scholars argue that what the Church was for
ambitious men in medieval Europe or the business corporation in nineteenth and twentieth century America, the state in the late twentieth century was their equivalent for ambitious Africans with skill and fortune

because it remained the major arena of privilege. In this context, the African political class simply adapted colonial based political structures and processes to a form of personal rule that Richard Sandbrook (1987: 89) calls "neopatrimonialism." This conjuncture led to overwhelming dominance of the state in the African political economy. As Neocosmos (1993) argues, this phenomenon of statism simultaneously provided a vehicle of accumulation from above by large sections of the ruling class as well as the systematic economic plunder and political oppression of the masses of the people of Africa. Within this framework, the relations between the state and the mass of citizens in Africa have remained directly oppressive. It is this oppressive, coercive, and exploitative relationship between the state and the people that civil society organizations in Africa are supposed to moderate and ameliorate.

Conceived of as an intermediary phenomenon between the state and the individual, civil society organizations are assumed to mediate, cushion, and ameliorate the oppressive, coercive, and exploitative relationship between the state and the people in Africa. The problem, however, is that the nature and structure of the leadership of most of these organizations mirror that of the authoritarian state. As Stephen Ndegwa (1996) observes, the organizations operate under a highly personalized leadership, which, though largely benevolent, nonetheless remains unaccountable. The organizations seek to democratize the African State yet they are themselves undemocratic and unaccountable. They seek to deconstruct personal rule in Africa yet at the same time, they are themselves embodiments of personal rule albeit at a microcosmic level. This reality has serious implications for the capacity of civil society organizations, especially NGOs, to alter the fundamental relations between the state and the people in Africa.

It is important to note that the enthusiasm with the political role of civil society eschews discussion of the requisite conditions for the social differentiation between civil society, political society, economic society, and parochial society. As a result, hastily constituted NGOs are funded to undertake political projects in the name of civic education, political mobilization, and shielding individuals from oppressive states. Furthermore, the democratic nature and orientation of civil society organizations in Africa is taken for granted. Yet, as Godwin Murunga (2000: 101) argues, in respect of Kenya, this movement is neither democratic in nature nor in orientation. Its leadership is self-appointed and largely wanting in democratic conscience and credentials. It would seem that authoritarianism has been so entrenched in most of Africa's body politic that anyone purporting to be anti-establishment is regarded as a democrat. Arguably, most leaders of "civil society" in Africa have rationalistically seized the opportunity spawned by the evangelism for democracy and are there not necessarily to serve the purpose of democratization, but their own selfish primitive accumulation interests. This attitude is fostered by the current shift among Western donors away from dealing with states to channeling their development resources through NGOs.

A corollary to the above is the fact that most of the civil society organizations, especially as manifested in NGOs, share the alignment and project of the state-based elite in the form of self-advancement and personal accumulation. The emergence of what have come to be termed "MONGOs" (my own NGO) that are run as personal or family outfits points to this eventuality. Against this background, it is the chief executives of the NGOs who, in the process, get "empowered" partly vis-à-vis the state but mainly vis-à-vis rank and file members of civil society. The speed with which some NGO executives have transformed themselves from modest living standards to bourgeois lifestyles complete with state-of-the-art limousines and palace-like residences is a glaring pointer to the fact that some of these outfits are largely avenues for accumulation within civil society[7] much as the state has remained an arena for self-aggrandizement with regard to the political class. In essence they are, to paraphrase Frantz Fanon, sources of "primitive advancement" within a political game of democratization (see Gibson 1994: 24).

It is further significant to note the lack of collaborative synergy amongst civil society organizations. If anything, they compete against each other as they jostle and lobby for donor funding. As Abubacar Momoh notes:

> There is often a cliquish camaraderie amongst NGOs; that is, they form a bloc in order to deter other NGOs from entering the community of NGOs. Moreover, donors often ask young and "obscure" managers of NGOs seeking donor funding to get "clearance" and letters of "recommendation" from the established and bigger NGOs. Trade-offs and perfidious activities often take place in the process. The politics of exclusion and inclusion is a very big behind-the-scene weapon used in NGO politics. (Momoh 1999: 38)

With regard to Kenya for instance, the only time that civil society organizations found common ground in opposing the state was when the NGO Act was passed in 1990 with a view to regulating the activities of these organizations. The latter saw the Act not as meant to regulate them, but as intended to rein them in and control them. Against this background, the

NGOs responded to the legislation in three ways. First, they sought to adjust to repression with the realization that given the parliamentarians' response to the Bill it was highly unlikely that it would be repealed or amended on the basis of strong NGO lobbying. A more important and practical response, it was reckoned, was to try and influence the regulations defining the actual operation of the regulating Bureau (Ndegwa, 1996: 40). Second, the NGOs mounted opposition to the legislation through lobbying and consultations with state representatives. Third, they instigated sanctions, including calling upon Western diplomats in Kenya to intercede on their behalf, to force the state to adjust.

In this regard, the NGOs succeeded in forcing the state to amend parts of the legislation and to revise the subsidiary legislation, including the already published forms. Ndegwa attributes this NGO success to four main factors. First, he posits that it was a result of the availability of political opportunity to voice dissent and to pursue oppositional action including openings that allowed access to the state to express disagreement with policy and to lobby for change. The second factor was NGO collective organization and combined resources especially the formation of the NGO Network and the election of an NGO Standing Committee to spearhead the lobbying effort and establishment of a functioning secretariat to coordinate the campaign, which gave the NGOs a strong collective voice. Thirdly, international donor agencies also played a role by consistently facilitating the NGO effort to fight the controlling legislation, including funding their activities in this regard and issuing public statements in support of the NGO struggle. The fourth factor was NGO alliance with other opposition forces in civil society especially the newly emergent opposition political parties, which also contributed significantly to the successful effort to challenge the regime.

It is noteworthy nevertheless, that Ndegwa seems to gloss over the significant implications of the role of external forces in helping the NGOs force the Kenyan State to acquiesce. In their efforts to have the legislation repealed or significantly amended, the NGOs held a series of seven workshops all funded by external donors. In fact, it was at the first of these workshops that the NGOs decided to challenge the legislation instead of adjusting to it. Furthermore, NGO reliance on these donor agencies to fund their lobbying process and their recourse to Western diplomats to put pressure on the state to alter the legislation is a manifestation of the fact that the democratization process has pretty little local impetus and is inexorably dependent on external forces for its continuity. This reality has significant implications for the civil society and African democratization thesis. As

Ndegwa (1996) observes, there is no evidence to suggest that the NGOs' oppositional actions in respect to the NGO Act were moved by grassroots sentiment. The episode was essentially an organizational effort to secure an enabling environment for NGOs. They had traditionally deferred to state control and mounted opposition only after their own existence had been threatened and only after a general wave of societal mobilization for political change was already under way. This points to the fact that civil society organizations are not necessarily inherently forces of democratization.

Stephen Ndegwa (1996) has undertaken an empirical analysis of the role of NGOs as part of civil society, their contribution to democratization in Africa, and what conditions facilitate or inhibit their contributions. He proceeds by focusing on a comparative analysis of two local NGOs in Kenya—the Green Belt Movement and the Undugu Society of Kenya—with a view to explicating the interface between NGOs and the state in the process of democratization, how the process unfolds, and its determinants and limitations. Ndegwa argues that for NGOs and other civil society organizations to advance democratization, four conditions must obtain. These include organization, resources, alliances, and political opportunity. He adds however that these four conditions are not enough because, of the two NGOs he examines, a discrepancy emerges between their actions, one actively advocating political pluralism and the other remaining politically obtuse, in spite of the similarity of the NGOs and their circumstances.

This reality is what Ndegwa calls the "two faces of civil society" which, according to him, strikes at the heart of the thesis that civil society organizations such as NGOs necessarily invest their resources in support of democratization efforts. He hypothesizes that an important determinant of whether a well-endowed NGO is transformed into an activist organization is whether the organization's leadership chooses to commit its resources to a progressive political agenda. In this case, Undugu Society of Kenya has a well-structured and institutionalized leadership and well-developed mechanisms for generating its own resources, but remains politically uncommitted to activism for good governance. On the other hand, the Green Belt Movement has a highly personalized leadership in the form of its founder and Coordinator, Wangari Maathai and is highly donor dependent, yet it is the most vocal on issues of governance and human rights. This reality is quite troubling in democratic terms and, in Ndegwa's estimation, calls for the need to reexamine present assumptions about the real and potential contribution of organizations in civil society to democratization in Africa.

Juxtaposing Ndegwa's exposition to the case of Zambia, one notes that though the Green Belt Movement has remained politically active, it has only one branch or two outside Nairobi. It thus lacks the requisite organizational structure for political mobilization reminiscent of ZCTU's branch network in Zambia. It does seem plausible to argue that for civil society to effect political change from authoritarian regimes in Africa, it is imperative first, to constitute a grand coalition along lines of the MMD in Zambia and the original FORD in Kenya. Secondly, chances for success are enhanced where a new leader emerges to challenge the incumbent rather than leaders who simply defect from the old authoritarian party to the opposition as was the case in Kenya in 1992 and in 1997. Finally, membership civil organizations enjoying a wide branch network hold the key to effective political mobilization for change, especially where they remain autonomous and independent of state manipulation.

CONCLUSION

Given the foregoing analysis, the question of the implications of the civil society promise in regard to championing democratization remains open to debate. Noting that civil society in politics has become the corollary or equivalent of the market in economics as the answer to Africa's problems, Julius Nyang'oro (1997a: 119) observes that the 1990s discourse is one of unbridled enthusiasm regarding the capacity of civil society to build democratic institutions, and to serve as a bulwark against the state and its authoritarian tendencies. Nyang'oro cautions, however, that there is a danger in the over-celebration of civil society as the principal midwife of democracy in Africa. He quotes Fatton Jr. who states that civil society is not always civil, it is replete with anomalies. While in periods of acute scarcity and deprivation, it mitigates some of the most deleterious effects of the economic crisis and offers subordinate classes a fragile refuge from predatory rulers; it is incapable of generating collective welfare and of supplanting the state in the provision of public goods. Embedded in the coercive social discipline of the market, civil society is virtually bound to come to the defense and promotion of private rights and sectional claims (Nyang'oro 1997a: 120, Fatton, 1995: 71).

According to Ndegwa, the thesis that civil society actors are important contributors to democratic change is essentially a statement on their positive contribution to altering power relations in Africa. He argues that analysts should raise fundamental questions regarding where civil society actors derive their power to oppose the state and, even more importantly, where this power resides. To Ndegwa, if this power derives from grassroots mobilization and participation and if it resides with citizens at the local level or in representative and accountable elites, then, and only then, can civil society be said to hold a promise of democratizing African states. Otherwise he posits, on the basis of the findings of his study, that it is a mistake for analysts to view civil society organizations as steadfast supporters of democratization. Evidence suggests that the only interests such organizations are likely to represent forcefully are those that are intimately tied to their own institutional survival. Available evidence does point to the fact that grassroots empowerment through NGO development activities is crucial and this is where civil society's promise of contributing to democratic development in Africa should be rooted. Such grassroots empowerment, as Ndegwa has noted, presents the possibility of civil society organizations not only contributing to the reform process but also enabling local communities to participate in, and preserve evolving democratic political processes. Fortunately, this process of grassroots empowerment is possible even when the civil society organization itself remains aloof toward direct political engagement, the way Undugu Society of Kenya has remained over the years.

With regard to non-membership civil society organizations including NGOs, it is important for purposes of promoting a sense of probity and self-efficacy that they operate in a democratic and accountable manner. Most of these organizations receive money from donors in the name of the people. They must, therefore, maintain a scrupulous level of accountability as a counter-position to the opaque manner in which states in Africa have been run. This does not mean the short-term formalistic and functional accountability whereby at the end of a project or program, an organization files a report to the donor detailing how project/program objectives have been accomplished and emphasizing the honesty and efficiency with which donor resources have been utilized. It means, to borrow a phrase, strategic accountability, which not only stresses probity in financial management and use, but also requires accounting for the impact that an organization's activities have on other social formations and the entire social realm in which it operates. It is only in this way that the contribution of civil society organizations to the process of socio-economic and political empowerment can be taken stock of and thus fortified.

Overall, it is noteworthy that whatever contribution so far made by civil society organizations in African democratization has been a direct result of the window of political opportunity afforded them by the general movement for good governance following the end of the Cold War. The emergence and vibrancy of these organizations, be they in the realm of relief work and welfare, health and the environment, development and institution building, or advocacy and democratization, is explicable in the context of this emergent reality of an international system governed by liberal political and economic ideals. These organizations have made a modest contribution to democratization in Africa as a result of which much of the available literature celebrates their role and potential in democratizing the hitherto authoritarian African State. Arguably however, as the foregoing exposition elaborates, there is a flip side to these civil society organizations that needs to be addressed if only for purposes of strengthening and enhancing the contribution of civil society organizations to African democratization.

In the final analysis, this chapter has demonstrated that the nature, organization, and resource base of the politically active civil society organizations is an essential variable in explaining incumbent regime change and/or regime continuity in the face of democratization. With regard to Zambia, The key political actor within civil society ranks was the labor movement led by the ZCTU. The autonomous ZCTU provided channels through which economic grievances were expressed and organized into an electoral bid for state power. ZCTU's organizational structures served an imperative role of mobilizing support for MMD, with trade union offices all over the country serving as recruiting centers for the new party. The ZCTU had a relatively sound resource base based on membership dues; hence members had a stake in transition politics and remained politically mobilized. In Kenya on the other hand, COTU had been affiliated to the ruling party, KANU by 1991, and its leaders co-opted; hence the labor movement remained politically obtuse. The key political player on the part of civil society organizations was the NGO movement. The limitation of this eventuality is that NGOs are non-membership organizations, largely urban-based, whose activities remained sporadic, disconnected, and largely suspended from the mass publics. Furthermore, NGOs are highly donor dependent, are accountable to their benefactors, and lack collaborative synergy even among themselves, hence unlike the labor movement in Zambia, they failed to marshal the support necessary to effect political change in Kenya.

Chapter Four

The Role of Ethnicity

Ethnicity as a social category is an important, perhaps the most important, variable not only in African politics, but also in the politics of every society across the space of time and place. Yet there is no such thing as a pure ethnic group as each and every one of them comprises varying degrees of miscegenation. Ethnic groups are thus maintained and differentiated via a deliberate process of social construction and cultural objectification of group values and boundaries. It is this process of cultural objectification that facilitates the maintenance of ethnic groups even as they develop and change in their cultural form and substance over time. Artificial as these social categories may be, however, their analysis is crucial to our understanding of the politics of democratic transition in Africa.

CONCEPTUALIZING ETHNICITY AND ETHNIC DIFFERENTIATION

Whereas in the Marxist perspective, ethnic groups are viewed as products of shared material interests that are rooted in particular historical circumstances, according to Benedict Anderson (1983), ethnic groups, or nations as he calls them, are "imagined political communities," imagined as both inherently limited and sovereign. To Anderson, a nation is imagined because the members of even the smallest nation will never know most of their fellow-members, meet them, or even hear of them, yet in the mind of each lives the image of their communion. The nation is imagined as limited because even the largest of them has finite albeit elastic boundaries beyond which lie other nations. No nation, Anderson asserts, imagines itself to be coterminous with mankind. A nation is imagined as sovereign in the sense that each one of them imagines itself to be free from all the others. Finally, a nation is imagined as a community because, regardless of the actual inequality and exploitation that may prevail in each, the nation, or ethnic group for that matter, is always conceived as a deep, horizontal comradeship. In the same vein, Walker Conner (1994) posits that the essence of a nation is intangible. It is a psychological bond that joins a national group and differentiates it, in the subconscious conviction of its members, from all other groups in a most vital way. Connor argues that when analyzing socio-political situations, what ultimately matters is not what is, but what people believe is. As such, a subconscious belief in the group's separate origin and evolution is an important ingredient of national psychology. He argues that "[s]ince the nation is a self-defined rather than an other-defined grouping, the broadly held conviction concerning the group's singular origin need not and seldom will accord with factual data" (Conner, 1994: 94).

Central to the differentiation of national groups once they have been created in whatever form is the notion of group boundaries. Thomas Eriksen (1993) has analyzed this issue and points out that the first fact of a national group, or ethnicity as he calls it, is the application of systematic distinctions between insiders and outsiders; between "us and them." If no such principle exists, he asserts, there can be no ethnicity, since ethnicity presupposes an institutionalized relationship between delineated categories whose members consider each other to be culturally distinctive (Eriksen, 1993: 18). For his part, Frederick Barth (1969) contends that when defined as an ascriptive and exclusive group, the nature of continuity of an ethnic unit or national group is clear. It depends on the maintenance of a social boundary, which may at times have a territorial counterpart. The cultural features that signal such a boundary may change, and the cultural characteristics of the members as well as the group's organizational form may likewise be transformed. But the fact of continuing dichotomization between members and outsiders remains a permanent feature. It is this fact of perpetuity of dichotomization, in Barth's view, that allows us to specify a national group's nature of continuity, and to investigate its changing cultural form and content. Barth writes that if a group maintains its identity when members interact with others, this entails criteria for determining membership and ways of signaling membership and exclusion. According to him, ethnic groups are not merely or necessarily based on the occupation of exclusive territories; and the different ways in which they are maintained, not only by a once-and-for-all recruitment, but also by continual expression and validation. He posits that ethnic boundary canalizes social life as it entails complex organization of behavior and social relations (see Barth, 1969: 9–38).

Barth elaborates further that the identification of a person as a fellow member of an ethnic group implies a sharing of criteria for evaluation and judgment. It entails the assumption that the two are fundamentally 'playing the same game,' and this means that there is between them a potential for diversification and expansion of their social relationships to cover eventually all sectors and domains of activity. On the other hand, a dichotomization of others as strangers, as members of another ethnic or national group, implies a recognition of limitations on shared understandings, differences in criteria for judgment of value and performance, and restriction of interaction to sectors of assumed common understanding and mutual interest. Entailed in ethnic boundary maintenance according to Barth, are also situations of social contact between persons of different cultures. In this regard, ethnic groups only persist as significant units if they imply marked difference in behavior and persisting cultural differences.

Group differentiation is also attained by application of social sanctions against errant members in order to keep them in line with what is expected of them as national group members. There thus exist sanctions within national groups for producing adherence to group-specific values. It is argued that where social identities are organized and allocated by such principles, there will consequently be a tendency toward canalization and standardization of interaction and the emergence of boundaries, which maintain and generate ethnic diversity even within polyethnic social systems. For instance, the boundaries of an Indian caste system are defined by such effective criteria that individual failures in performance lead to outcasting rather than down casting (Barth, 1969: 27).

Thomas Eriksen (1993) identifies another effective mechanism by which national groups are differentiated. This involves use of stereotyping. Eriksen defines stereotyping as the creation and consistent application of standardized notions of the cultural distinctiveness of a given group. The essential role of this process is that it makes it possible to divide the social world into kinds of people, and provides simple criteria for such a classification. It gives the individual the impression that he understands society. Stereotypes also justify privileges and differences in access to society's resources. They are crucial in defining the boundaries of one's group as they inform the individual of the virtues of his own group and the vices of other groups. It is important to note that self-applied stereotyping always emphasizes the superiority of one's group vis-à-vis the others. Group stereotyping, and the articulation of competition or conflict, according to Eriksen, confirm and strengthen group membership. Stereotyping is a manifestation of the subjective form of nationalism. Whereas the objective form of nationalism merely stops at the practice, defense and promotion of national values and beliefs, this subjective form aims at denigrating other national groups as a way of boosting the loyalty of members to their own 'superior' group. It is largely attitudinal in form and perceptual in content but quite effective in galvanizing people's loyalties to their own groups by creating social boundaries between them and others.

Overall, an ethnic group may be defined as a social group distinguished by a claim to a common descent and the assertion of a history or a presence of shared culture. At the heart of ethnic identity is the perception that "we are different from them." What people share within a particular ethnic boundary varies along three dimensions. These include interests, institutions, and culture (see Cornell, 1996; Connor, 1994; Anderson, 1983). The question of ethnicity and its role in politics is a dominant issue on the African political scene. It is noteworthy that the colonial imperialists divided up Africa amongst themselves without regard to ethnic or cultural boundaries. It is argued for instance, that of the fifty-four continental African states, only Ethiopia, Liberia and Sierra Leone correspond to historical states. Algeria, Botswana, and Western Sahara on the other hand, have a clearly defined cultural identity (Nzongola-Ntalaja, 1985), which, in the case of Algeria, omits the Berber minority. The remaining majority of African countries comprise a mixture of disparate peoples some of whom find themselves divided between two or more states (see Nasong'o, 2003). For example, Nigeria, the most populous African country, with a population estimated at 120 million has about 250 ethnic groups. Zambia, with a population of 10 million has 73 ethnic groups. For her part, Kenya, with a population of 30 million, has 41 ethnic groups. Indeed, globally, ethnically homogenous state borders are extremely rare. Against this background, the problem of politicized ethnicity, or, conversely, ethnicized politics is the political norm rather than the exception in Africa.

ETHNICITY AND AFRICAN POLITICS

According to available evidence, Africa is the continent with the highest number of ethnically diverse countries (Miguel, 2004; Easterly & Levine, 1997). Accordingly, the popular image of Africa is one of a continent with countries that are incessantly rent by ancient ethnic enmities that retard and complicate the development of national consciousness. In this regard, Nzongola-Ntalaja (1985) posits that attachment to one's ethnic group still remains a more relevant unit of identification than attachment to the country as a whole. The concept of ethnicity is associated with interactions between members of different ethnic groups. The latter are social formations that are distinguished by the communal character of their boundaries with the relevant communal character being lineage, language, culture, religion, or a combination of all or any of these factors. There is positive and negative ethnicity. Positive ethnicity is restricted to the practice and defense of an ethnic group's traditional integrity, traditional beliefs, and traditional customs. Negative ethnicity on the other hand emerges when ethnicity becomes the major determinant of one's behavior especially in the allocation of society's scarce resources where this is done not on the basis of merit and achievement but on ascription based on kinship and ethnic ties. Such subjective dimensions of ethnicity are said to be behaviorally attitudinal in form and perceptual in content (see Mazrui, 1972). In essence, therefore, the objective discourse of tradition has been stranger than its subjective rival at the state level.

Ethnicity has not always played a negative role in the African sociopolitical setting. There are a number of key positive functions of ethnicity. In the first place, ethnicity provided a basis for the organization of resistance against colonial domination, especially at the cultural level. Examples here include the Maji Maji war in Tanzania; Mau Mau rebellion and the Chetambe war in Kenya; and the Chimurenga wars in Zambia among others. Second, ethnicity provided a basis for adaptation to the uncertainty and insecurity caused by the rapid changes introduced by colonialism. In particular, the activities of ethnic welfare associations in urban areas across colonial Africa ameliorated these uncertainties and insecurities. Third, ethnicity played an important function in the anti-imperialist struggle for independence in Africa. It provided the basis for mobilization of the massive rural populations of the continent behind the nationalist movements thus increasing the credibility of the movements in the eyes of both colonialists and world public opinion.

Fourth, and in more contemporary terms, ethnicity provides a sense of belonging as part of an interdependent layer of social relations between the individual and the state, which cushions the former against the negative effects of alienation inherent in a complex modern mass society. In so doing, ethnicity facilitates appreciation of one's social roots in a community and cultural group, which is essential for the stability of the individual, communal group, and the country at large. Fifth, it is noteworthy that most ethnic movements demand justice and liberty, express fears about oppression and nepotism in the distribution of national resources and social services and thereby contribute to democratic practice by emphasizing equity and justice in socio-political relations. Sixth, ethnic identity has played an instrumental role in the promotion of community development in Africa, especially in rural areas. For instance, the Harambee movement in Kenya that has remained the cornerstone of community development projects is hinged on ethnic solidarity of various communities. Finally, the mobilization of populations of various ethnic groups behind various factions of a nation's political elite contributes to the decentralization of power that is healthy for the institutionalization of democratic freedoms (see Ajulu, 2002; Nnoli, 1998: 7–8).

In spite of the above positive functionality of ethnicity, politicized ethnicity has had devastating political consequences for the continent as manifested in the many civil wars on the continent and the ubiquitous crisis of political instability. On account of this, some scholars define the concept of ethnicity simply in terms of its negative dimension. According to Walter Oyugi (1998: 287), for instance, ethnicity emerges when individuals acting in groups attempt to use their supposed common origin as a basis for their relations with others. He posits that ethnicity involves a common consciousness of being one in relation to the other interacting groups; and connotes group antipathy against others, including suspicion, hatred, and envy. "In that sense it is not a neutral concept merely depicting and signifying the act of inter-ethnic relations that are expected to take place in a multiethnic society. To speak of ethnicity is to speak of inter-group interactive situations characterized by rivalry, competition, and often conflict" (Oyugi, 1998: 288).

Overall, ethnic identity is conducive to severe conflict on account of one major factor. This is the fact that ethnic identity has a symbolic dimension, which makes conflict arising from it more intense than otherwise. As Okwudiba Nnoli (1998) points out, ethnicity, like religion, has the symbolic capability of defining for the individual the totality of his existence, including embodying his hopes, fears, and sense of the future. While symbolism in religion explains the hereafter, ethnic symbolism explains the here and now. Hence individuals are very sensitive to matters of ethnic and religious symbolism. Any action or thought that is perceived to undermine the religious faith or the ethnic group evokes very hostile and sometimes violent response. For ethnicity, the actions likely to undermine the ethnic group include those that diminish its status in the eyes of its members. Since status is a relative concept, such subversive activities include those that prevent the ethnic group from its perceived due in the inter-ethnic scheme of things. By undermining the group, such actions strike at the very (symbolic) existence of the individual members of the reference group, even though the action may not be directed to them personally (Nnoli, 1998: 5). This is what explains the tendency of members of the group to identify with the fortunes of their co-ethnics. An epitome of this reality is the poor villager who believes that a co-ethnic cabinet minister represents his share of the national cake even though the said villager may never receive any personal material gain as a result of the appointment.

Against this background, ethnicity has remained the most portend political force in contemporary Africa. This is mainly because at independence, ethnic nationalism was a phenomenon that emerged forcefully in the political arena on account of the fact that whereas ethnic loyalty was an accomplished and ingrained fact, loyalty to the postcolonial state was only in the making. Ali Mazrui (1972) has argued that the behavior of an ethnic group that was led by successful political elite and entrepreneurs was to tighten its ranks in order to safeguard its gains while those less favored sought to press their own case by organizing their own communities for concerted self-defense.[1] He contends that most African elites, political and otherwise, have, in spite of their training and specialization, only been de-traditionalized but not de-ethnicized. The process of Westernization that they have undergone, according to Mazrui, has led to the weakening of their cultural affiliation but not their ethnic loyalty. This perspective dovetails with Eric Hobsbawm's differentiation between "tradition and custom." According to Hobsbawm, the object and characteristic of 'traditions,' including invented ones, is invariance. The past, real or invented, to which they refer imposes fixed—and normally formalized—practices such as repetition. On the other hand, 'custom' in traditional societies " . . . has the double function of motor and fly-wheel. It does not preclude innovation and change up to a point . . ." (Hobsbawm, 1993: 2). In essence therefore, the African political elite may have been "de-customized" by the process of Westernization, but their loyalty to their "imagined communities" remains intact.

Examples of the deleterious consequences of politicized ethnicity include the Biafran civil war in Nigeria of 1967–1970; the Sudanese civil war that has continued intermittently since 1955; the civil wars in Angola and Mozambique occasioned after the two countries' independence from Portugal in 1975; as well as the perennial crisis of instability in Sierra Leone and Liberia, among others. Since the advent of democratization at the beginning of the 1990s, ethnic conflicts in Africa have taken a turn for the worse. Eritrea seceded from Ethiopia in 1993 under conditions that have increased ethnic consciousness in Ethiopia, and created new poles of ethnic conflict including violent and non-violent opposition from Oromo, Amhara, and Ogadenian ethnicity (see Nnoli, 1998). Protracted fights between the Issa and Afar in Djibouti have continued unabated; while ethnic-like conflicts among Somali clans have fractured the Somali nation and dismembered the Somali state.

Similarly, Kwazulu-Natal, Burundi, and Rwanda experienced the worst forms of ethnic conflict between 1989 and 1995: "Although in Kwazulu-Natal the killings involved different factions of the Zulu ethnic group, and not other ethnic groups, the demands of the Inkatha political party were decidedly ethnic in character. Those demands and the slaughter that backed them up nearly ruined the process of transition from apartheid to black majority rule" (Nnoli, 1998: 3). In Burundi, the carefully orchestrated transition from the Pierre Buyoya military regime to multiparty democracy was destroyed by a Tutsi-led abortive coup in which the elected president, Melchior Ndadaye was killed. "Ever since his death there has been a free-for-all massacre of ethnic and political opponents which has continued to drain the energy and manpower resources of the country, and emasculated governance" (Ibid.). For its part, Rwanda has been the victim of the most macabre and horrifying genocide in the history of post-colonial Africa in which an estimated 800,000 Tutsis and moderate Hutus were massacred within a period of three months in 1994 (see Nasong'o, 2003b; Chege, 1996).

Donald Horowitz (2000) examines the phenomenon of ethnic groups in conflict and raises a number of questions that are pertinent to the role of ethnicity in the electoral politics of democratizing countries. Some of these questions are; what makes for political conflict and cooperation in multiethnic societies? Are such political conflicts fundamentally a function of the mere existence of these parochial identities? What can be done to maximize the likelihood of inter-ethnic cooperation and the eventuality of democratic multiethnic polities? For instance, fragmentation of the opposition in Kenya along ethnic lines has been cited as one of the factors that facilitated incumbent regime victory in 1992 and 1997 (see Barkan & Ng'ethe, 1998; Oyugi, 1997; Muigai, 1995; Chege, 1993; Barkan, 1993). A perusal of the literature on Zambia, however, reveals no such phenomenon of divisions along ethnic lines in the 1991 poll yet, whereas Kenya has 41 ethnic groups, Zambia has 73 of them. A delineation of the factors that account for the seemingly higher rates of politicized ethnicity in Kenya than in Zambia should be important in shedding more light on our understanding of Africa's politics of transition and theorization about the practice of democracy in multiethnic societies.

MAXIMUM COALITION IN ZAMBIA VS. ETHNIC FRAGMENTATION IN KENYA

The four largest ethnic groups in Zambia include the Lozi in the West; Tonga in the South; Bemba in the North; and Nyanja in the East. The four are supplemented by the Lunda, Kaonde and Luvale in Northwestern Province; Ile, Lenje, Sali, Sala, Toka-Leya, who are considered to be part of the Tonga; Inamwanga, Mambwe, Lala, Bisa, Tabwa, Lunda, Unga, Lima, and Lungu are associated with the Bemba. "Thus Zambia does share the ethnic structure of countries such as Nigeria, Kenya, Uganda and Mozambique" (Momba, 1993: 184). Overall, sectionalism in Zambia is mostly expressed in terms of the language groups, which are dominant in particular provinces. The most significant divisions are between (1) Bemba speakers in Northern Province, Luapula Province, and the urban areas of the Copperbelt. (2) Nyanja speakers in Eastern Province and in the capital, Lusaka. (3) Lozi speakers in Western Province. (4) Tonga speakers in Southern Province (Donge, 1995:196–197). Jotham Momba (1993) writes that there is very high regional differentiation in development between provinces on the line of the old rail and those outside this corridor. Copperbelt, Lusaka, Central, and Southern Provinces are far more developed than Northern, Luapula, Eastern, Northwestern, and Western Provinces. For instance, three of the line-of-rail provinces contribute most of the marketed maize, they produce most of the tobacco, Soya beans, cotton, and sunflower, and most of the livestock is in these provinces.

On the other hand, the Southern, Central, and Lusaka Provinces had a long tradition of peasant and commercial farming with relatively highly developed infrastructure erected by the colonial authorities compared to other provinces. Almost all the industries are based in the line of rail provinces, especially Copperbelt and Lusaka Provinces. The discrepancies between the provinces on the development front to a great extent also mean discrepancies in the level of development of various ethnic groups. For instance, the Lozi of Western Province and the Kaonde, Lunda, and Luvale peoples of Northwestern Province at times feel neglected because their provinces are among the least developed in Zambia (Momba, 1993).

On the other hand, of the 41 ethnic groups in Kenya, the leading ones are the Kikuyu in Central Province who constitute 21 percent of the total population; the Luhyia of Western Province—14 percent; Luo in Nyanza Province—13 percent; Kamba of Eastern—11 percent; Kalenjin in the Rift Valley—11 percent; Kisii in Nyanza—6 percent; and Meru of Eastern—5.5 percent (Human Rights Watch, 1993: 5). The remaining 35 ethnic groups account for 18.5 percent of the total Kenyan population. Just as is the case in Zambia, there are great disparities in regional development and public resource allocation in Kenya. It is noted, for instance, that during the Kenyatta regime (1963–1978), national resources were allocated in a manner that clearly favored Kenyatta's ethnoregion. " . . . more than half of the country's development resources were being channeled specifically to Kiambu, President Kenyatta's own home district, as a result of which even Kikuyu parliamentary backbenchers from other districts . . . voted and spoke in favor of motions that specifically urged support for poorer districts, because they feared uneven development in the Central Province as elsewhere" (Nasong'o, 2000: 50; Gertzel 1974: 44). Githu Muigai notes, further that:

> . . . the dominance of the Kikuyu within the [Kenyatta] regime was beyond question . . . the 1969, 1974, and even the 1979 cabinets were. 30 percent Kikuyu.[2] Concomitantly, the Kikuyu enjoyed tremendous state support in commerce and agriculture and were soon the only indigenous rivals to Asian and European capital. (Muigai, 1995: 173)

Similarly, the Moi era in Kenya (1978–2002) saw the redirection of state resources toward the Kalenjin. However, since state resources were dwindling, the Moi regime resorted to what Rok Ajulu (2000) refers to as "looting from the original [Kikuyu] looters" of state resources, thereby exacerbating the emerging tense relations between the Kikuyu and Kalenjin.

Ethnicity has thus always been a factor in the politics of Kenya and Zambia since independence. For example, in the run-up to independence in Kenya, the Kikuyu and Luo, the two largest ethnic groups in the country at the time, dominated KANU. Fearing domination of the post-independence national political dispensation by the two ethnic groups, other smaller ethnic groups formed KADU to push for a *Majimbo* (quasi federal) constitution. Even the parting of ways between President Kenyatta and his vice president, Oginga Odinga in 1966 leading to the emergence of the KPU, though based on ideological differences between the two leaders, was nevertheless cast in ethnic terms.[3] Kenyatta described the opposition KPU as "tribal malcontents concerned mainly with sectional interests, who would also drag Kenya into communism" (Haugerud, 1995: 39; Barkan, 1987: 225). In the same vein, according to Donge (1995), the breakaway Zambian parties, United Party (UP) that emerged in 1966 and United Progressive Party (UPP) that was formed in 1972 (see Chapter One) were strongly associated with particular regional and ethnic groups, the Lozi in Western Province and the Bemba speakers in Northern Zambia and on the Copperbelt, respectively who felt disadvantaged over the political dispensation of the moment.

Be it as it may, however, available evidence indicates that the question of ethnicity was not a major factor in the electoral process in the watershed 1991 multiparty elections in Zambia and even in the 1996 elections as Karolina Hulterström (2002, 2004) ably shows. Hulterström has developed four parameters for analyzing ethnic politics. The first measurable component of ethnic politics, according to her, is a formula for distribution of both resources and positions in a given polity. The second parameter of measurement is ethnic bloc voting. Third is the party system, or more specifically, the exclusiveness of political interest. Fourth and finally are the actions of the political elite in regard both to elite collaboration in the party system and mobilization strategy. The last three parameters are particularly relevant to the analysis of the role of ethnicity in the Kenyan and Zambian transition politics.

In the first place, Hulterström argues that the extent of ethnic bloc voting reflects the extent to which people identify politically with their ethnic groups and thus underscores the nature of ethnic politics in a given society. She operationalizes ethnic bloc voting as " . . . a certain percentage of ethnic affiliates voting for the same political party" (Hulterström, 2002: 7).[4] Hulterström uses a 33 per cent (one third) threshold in her regression analysis of the cases of Kenya and Zambia and establishes that three (4.10%) of the 73 ethnic groups in Zambia bloc voted in 1991 compared to five (11.90%) of the 41 communities in Kenya in 1992 as Table 4.1 below shows.

Table 4.1: Effect of Ethnicity on Party Support in Zambia and Kenya

Ethnic Group Zambia	Effect on 1991 Party Support	Ethnic Group Kenya	Effect on 1992 Party Support
Inamwanga	-.48 MMD; .42 UNIP	Kikuyu	-.47 KANU; .42 DP
Nyanja	-.49 MMD; .50 UNIP	Kalenjin	.49 KANU
Tumbuka	-.68 MMD; .66 UNIP	Luhyia	.89 FORD-K
		Luo	-.52 KANU; .97 FORD-K
		Turkana	.54 KANU
N = 73		N = 41	

Source: adapted from Hulterström, 2002: 9

The above figures indicate, in the case of Zambia, that:

1.   A one percent increase in the number of the Inamwanga led to a .48 percent decrease in the support for MMD while simultaneously leading to a .50 percent increase in the support for UNIP.

2.   A one percent increase in the number of the Nyanja led to a .49 percent decrease in the support for MMD while at the same time leading to a .50 percent increase in the support for UNIP.

3.   A one percent increase in the number of the Tumbuka led to a .68 percent decrease in the support for MMD while at the same time leading to a .66 percent increase in the support for UNIP.

In the case of Kenya, the regression coefficients indicate that:

1.   A one percent increase in the number of the Kikuyu led to a .47 percent decrease in the support for KANU while increasing the support for DP by .42 percent.

2.   A one percent increase in the number of the Kalenjin led to a .49 percent increase in the support for KANU.

3.   A one percent increase in the number of the Luhyia led to a .89 percent increase in the support for FORD-K.

4.   A one percent increase in the number of the Luo led to a .97 percent increase in the support for FORD-K while at the same time leading to a .52 percent decrease in the support for KANU.

5.   A one percent increase in the number of the Turkana led to a .52 percent increase in the support for KANU.

Hulterström finds all the coefficients, except in the case of the Turkana in Kenya, to be statistically significant at .05 confidence level. The Turkana coefficient is statistically significant at .10 confidence level. What the statistics illustrate is the fact that more ethnic groups in Kenya vote cohesively for particular parties than in Zambia. This scenario obtained in the first multiparty general elections in 1991 and 1992 in Zambia and Kenya respectively, and was replicated in the second multiparty elections in the two countries in 1996 and 1997. In the case of Zambia, three communities, the Inamwanga, Kaonde, and Lunda-Luvale, bloc-voted in 1996. For Kenya, five communities once again bloc-voted in 1997—the Kikuyu, Kalenjin, Luo, Luhyia, and Turkana. It is important to note that whereas the largest ethnic group in Kenya, the Kikuyu, bloc-voted both in 1992 and 1997, the largest ethnic group in Zambia, the Bemba did not bloc-vote in both the 1991 and 1996 elections.

The second parameter is the party system, or the cohesiveness of political interest. In this regard, if ethnicity is so salient in society that each ethnic group identifies with distinct political interests, the consequence is a party system with parties that command their support from specific ethnic groups. As such, " . . . a party will be regarded as ethnic if two-thirds of its supporters share the same ethnic affiliation" (Hulterström, 2002: 13; Rose & Unwin, 1969: 10–11). On the basis of this, Hulterström finds that none of the two parties that seriously contested the 1991 Zambian election—UNIP and MMD—had cohesive enough support to qualify them as ethnic parties. She argues, nonetheless, that there is " . . . good reason to believe that at least the UNIP should be regarded as multiethnic rather than non-ethnic in character" (Hulterström, 2002: 14). This is on account of the fact that UNIP got a very large share of support from the Tumbuka and Nyanja-speaking communities of Eastern Province.

For Kenya, five opposition parties contested against the incumbent KANU in 1992. However, all the five opposition parties gained ethnically cohesive support. Three parties with Kikuyu presidential candidates, the DP, FORD-A, and KNC garnered more than 74 percent of their votes from the Kikuyu. FORD-K, then led by Jaramogi Oginga Odinga obtained 68.4 percent of its support from the Luo; while the Kenya Social Congress (KSC), led by George Anyona, received virtually all its support from his own Gusii community. It was only KANU, in spite of a clear bias toward certain regions that did not qualify as an ethnic party. "Once again one might suspect that Kanu would be categorised as multiethnic rather than non-ethnic, as it got such large portions of its support from the Kalenjin groups and other smaller pastoralist communities" (Hulterström, 2002: 14; see also, Adar, 1998).

The same scenario was once again replayed in the second multiparty elections in Kenya and Zambia.[5] Although the MMD support in 1996 was biased in favor of the Bemba (58.4 percent of the total votes cast), its support was clearly cross-regional and multiethnic, or even non-ethnic according to Hulterström. Similarly, though the Zambia Democratic Congress (ZDC), formed by disillusioned MMD parliamentarians, received the bulk of its support (13.2 percent of all votes cast) from the Bemba, its support was distributed across all ethnic groups. The same applies to the National Party (NP) and the National Lima Party (NLP), which received between six and seven percent of the national vote. Indeed, support for the NLP was so evenly distributed that in spite of winning over six percent of the national vote, it failed to gain any representation in the National Assembly. Of the five parties that contested the 1996 Zambian elections therefore, only the Agenda for Zambia (AZ) led by Mbikusita-Lewanika qualifies as an ethnic party. The AZ garnered 1.4 percent of the national vote, 85.5 percent of which came from the Lozi community of Western Zambia.

For Kenya's 1997 elections, only two parties, KANU and FORD-K qualified as non-ethnic parties. However, FORD-K, led by Michael Wamalwa Kijana, was more of a borderline case. The party obtained 64.3 percent (only slightly less than the two-thirds threshold) of its total support from the Luhyia who constituted 12.6 percent of the electorate. Eight parties, ranging from the largest opposition party, DP to the smallest inconsequential ones like KNC and KENDA garnered more than two-thirds of their total support from the Kikuyu. The National Development Party (NDP) obtained 82 percent of its total support from the Luo as the KSC retained its Gusii character by garnering 89 percent of its support from the community. Similarly, the Shirikisho Party of Kenya (SPK) drew 98.9 percent of its support from the Mijikenda community of Coast Province. It is thus evident that the vast majority of political parties in Kenya are ethnically cohesive while the opposite is the case in regard to Zambia.

Table 4.2: Presidential Vote Distribution in Kenya's 1992 and 1997 Elections

Name/Party	1992	% of Total Vote	1997	% of Total Vote
Moi/KANU	1,927,640	36.91%	2,500,320	41.21%
Matiba/Ford-A	1,354,856	25.95%	—	—
Kibaki/DP	1,035,507	19.83%	1,905,640	31.41%
Odinga/Ford-K	903,886	17.31%	—	—
Raila/NDP	—	—	667,825	11.00%
Wamalwa/Ford-K	—	—	505,713	8.34%
Ngilu/SDP	—	—	487,538	8.04%
Total	5,221,889	100%	6,067,036	100%

Source: compiled from Electoral Commission of Kenya figures[6]

With regard to the third parameter of analyzing ethnic politics, the idea of elite collaboration and mobilization strategy, it is apparent from the foregoing that the Kenyan political elite exhibit a high inability or unwillingness to collaborate with one another and thus mobilize support across ethnic divides. It is this reality that immensely contributed to the opposition's electoral defeat in Kenya in both the 1992 and 1997 elections. For instance, in the presidential elections, KANU received 36.9 percent and 41.2 percent of the total votes cast in 1992 and 1997 respectively, while the combined opposition garnered 63.1 percent and 58.8 percent of the total votes in 1992 and 1997 respectively (see Table 4.2 above). However, the opposition vote was so ethnically fragmented that the incumbent KANU emerged victorious on both occasions. As Harvey Glickman (1997: 46) rightly observes in regard to Kenya and Congo Brazzaville, "[p]ragmatism, leading to cooperation among the opposition parties, would have defeated the incumbents."

The above findings in regard to ethnic bloc voting, ethnic parties, and lack of political elite collaboration, are buttressed by conclusions by other scholars on the same subject. Harvey Glickman (1997), for one, observes that in Zambia, there was little open campaigning on the basis of ethnic politics. The opposition Movement for Multiparty Democracy (MMD) was a maximum coalition that comprised all the elements opposed to the regime of President Kenneth Kaunda. The MMD, according to Karolina Hulterström (2002), clearly cut across ethnic, socio-economic and professional cleavages. Glickman stresses that the rivalry between UNIP and MMD was largely between Kenneth Kaunda and Frederick Chiluba. It was never cast in ethnic terms. Indeed, results of the 1991 elections in Zambia revealed a remarkable consistency in voting behavior, with Zambians in every part of the country except Eastern Province strongly favoring MMD over UNIP (see Table 4.3 below). As Michael Bratton shows, there was no discernible difference in the pattern of party preference between urban and rural areas. MMD won over 89 percent of the parliamentary votes in the industrial Copperbelt Province, and also attained more than 84 percent in the rural constituencies of Luapula, Northern, and Southern Provinces. "Nor, for the most part, did voters express ethnic preferences through the ballot, with MMD running well in Bemba-, Tonga-, and Lozi-speaking areas. The only exception to MMD's countrywide ascendancy was UNIP's strong showing at the polls in Eastern Province [Kaunda's home province]" (Bratton, 1994: 102).

Indeed, an interesting post-1991 election challenge in Zambia was maintaining the inclusiveness of the MMD coalition. The victorious MMD

Table 4.3: Results of 1991 Zambian Parliamentary Elections by Province
(Percentage of Valid Total)

Province	Dominant Group	MMD	UNIP
Central	Nyanja	73.07%	26.93%
Copperbelt	Bemba	89.77%	10.23%
Eastern	Nyanja	26.08%	73.92%
Luapula	Bemba	86.27%	13.73%
Lusaka	Bemba	77.03%	23.03%
Northern	Bemba	85.97%	14.03%
Northwestern	Kaonde	70.33%	29.67%
Southern	Tonga	84.10%	15.91%
Western	Lozi	80.56%	19.44%
Total		75.31%	24.69%

Source: adapted from Bratton, 1994:102.

may have been too inclusive in that previously excluded groups could not
share in the rewards of victory proportionate to their perceived deprivation, thus leading to splinter opposition parties that reflected disappoint-
ments cast occasionally in terms of ethnic groups.

The emergence of the original FORD in Kenya was reminiscent of the
MMD in Zambia and for some time, it was almost a foregone conclusion
that KANU would be routed from power by FORD. The popularity of
FORD, gauged from the crowds it attracted at its political rallies, was a
waking nightmare for the incumbent KANU for some time. The problem,
however, is that once the first multiparty elections became imminent in
1992, FORD split as ethnic factions within the party began to jostle for
power. The Kikuyu, Luo, and to some extent Luhyia factions began to
emerge centering around Kenneth Matiba (still recuperating in London),
Oginga Odinga, and Masinde Muliro respectively. "Increasingly, the
jostling for power assumed ethnic character with Kikuyu delegations made
of prominent personalities in FORD reportedly visiting Matiba regularly in
London to impress on him that a leadership vacuum existed in the party"
(Oyugi, 1998: 302). With Matiba's return in May 1992, the struggle for
power culminated in the split of FORD into FORD-Kenya led by Oginga
Odinga (Luo) and FORD-Asili, led by Matiba (Kikuyu).

The situation in the Kenyan opposition was further compounded by the formation of the Democratic Party (DP) in December 1991, further splintering it. The party was formed by a section of wealthy Kikuyu associated with the former GEMA on realization that the GEMA community lacked credible representation in the then interim FORD leadership. A prominent DP supporter told his listeners while on a recruitment mission in a social club in Nairobi: "Who is Gachoka to represent Kikuyu interest?[7] Does he measure up to Odinga, Muliro and Shikuku?" (Oyugi, 1998: 303). When it appeared during the May-November 1992 period that Matiba might not be a serious candidate on account of the state of his health[8] and wrangling within FORD-A, it was to the DP that most of the Kikuyu defecting from KANU turned following the dissolution of parliament. The formation of the DP, led by Mwai Kibaki, a Kikuyu like FORD-A's Matiba, reflected the rivalry and differences in sectional interests between the Kikuyu of Kiambu, Murang'a, and Nyeri. It is this split in the opposition, as observed above, that cost them victory. Indeed, it is arguable that had there been only one Kikuyu opposition candidate in 1992, it is likely that he would have won. This is borne out by the fact that the combined vote for the two Kikuyu candidates, Mwai Kibaki and Kenneth Matiba, was 45.78 percent of the total votes cast, compared to the eventual winner's (President Moi's) 36.91 percent.

Writing on the role of ethnicity in multiparty politics in Africa generally, Marina Ottaway (1999) notes that the most visible manifestation of politicized ethnicity in new multiparty political systems has been the overt or covert ethnic character of the majority of emerging political parties. According to Ottaway, this trend toward the formation of ethnic political parties was accentuated in the 1990s by the discrediting of socialism following the collapse of the communist empire in Eastern Europe. She argues that the discrediting of socialism at the end of the 1980s made it difficult for political parties to define themselves in ideological terms and thus attract multiethnic cross-sections of the population on the basis of their programmatic appeal. Furthermore, the swiftness of the transition to multipartyism left new parties with little time to develop their programs with most promising little more than change of leadership. "The absence of ideological and programmatic differences left ethnicity as the major characteristic by which the various parties could differentiate themselves" (Ottaway, 1999: 311).

Against this background, Robert Bates (1999) argues that Africa's middle class failed to form a coherent opposition to governments because it is readily divided along ethnic lines. He points out that socially elites often exchange their material wealth for social standing in their communities by contributing to local causes such as building schools, clinics, and other public works. As such, politically motivated appeals to ethnic loyalty divide Africa's elites. "Led by ministers, lawyers, and other professionals, the middle class of Kenya, for example, organized in opposition to the incumbent Daniel arap Moi. However, regional ties and ethnic loyalties facilitated the division of the opposition, and Moi prevailed" (Bates, 1999: 91). Bates argues that the story of Kenya finds its parallel throughout Africa, where the splintered ranks of the opposition reflect the internal divisions of the bourgeoisie, enabling inept governments to remain in power. However, as the foregoing exposition illustrates, whereas this eventuality is true of Kenya, it does not reflect the situation in Zambia.

EXPLAINING THE DIFFERENCE

What makes for the difference between the nature of ethnic politics in Kenya and Zambia, especially in regard to the transition politics of the 1990s? Available evidence point to about four sets of explanations. First is the politics of inclusion in Zambia as contrasted with the politics of exclusion in Kenya especially following the introduction of single-party rule in the two countries. As pointed out in Chapter One, the introduction of single party rule in Zambia was orderly done. A commission was formed for purposes of working out the modalities of establishing a one-party state that would ensure all-inclusive participation. Kaunda even went so far as inviting the leading opposition figures in Zambia at the time, Nalumino Mundia and Harry Nkumbula, to join the commission. Although the two politicians declined the invitation, once a one-party state was put in place, Kaunda once again made a deliberate effort to incorporate the opposition of the moment. In this event, both Mundia and Nkumbula were co-opted into UNIP and the government, with Mundia even rising to the position of prime minister. This brand of accommodative politics on the part of Kaunda laid the foundation for inclusive politics that helps explain the propensity for maximum coalitions across ethnic divides as well as for multiethnic political parties in Zambia.

On the other hand, the dominant political elite in Kenya tended towards exclusionary politics that overplayed ethnicity and capitalized on ethnic divisions. Similarly, unlike in Zambia, the establishment of one-party rule in Kenya was not an orderly, well-thought out process. It emerged via the politics of intrigue and arm-twisting, which saw the dissolution of the opposition KADU in 1964 (see Chapter One), as well as through presidential fiat that saw the banning of the KPU in 1969 and the detention of its leaders, including Oginga Odinga who was put under house arrest. The Kenyatta regime characterized KPU as a Luo party and portrayed the party's Kikuyu backers such as Bildad Kaggia as traitors and sell-outs of the Kikuyu cause. In the emerging political conjuncture, just like colonialism had promoted ethnicity in its unequal development approach in governance, the Kenyatta regime further politicized ethnicity. "The state was constructed as an exclusive entity whose structures were utilized by various class and ethnic interests to enrich themselves at the expense of the greater Kenyan society" (Murunga, 2002: 91). The lopsided nature of the allocation of state resources that followed favored the president's ethno-region so much so that it raised a lot of concern among parliamentarians.

In the final analysis, the masses came to believe that to enjoy a share of state resources required state house tenure for a co-ethnic. It is this belief that led former cabinet minister, Elijah Mwangale to advise the Kikuyu to keep off the contest for the presidency in the 1997 elections. He argued that the community had its share of leadership during Kenyatta's time and that others had to have a chance. Mwangale contended that the Kalenjin, from whom the then President Moi hailed, would complete their turn in 2002 and usher in the Luhyia's turn to rule. He quipped: " . . . when we talk of the presidency, the Luhyia community should not be underrated since we have political heavyweights like me" (Nasong'o, 2000: 52). It is against this background that the high rate of ethnic bloc voting in Kenya can be explained.

The second major factor that explains the contrast in ethnic politics between Kenya and Zambia is the rate of urbanization in Zambia compared to Kenya, and the role of the labor movement in the politics of transition in Zambia. Zambia is the most urbanized country in Africa. Whereas over 80 percent of the Kenyan population is rural, Zambia's urban population was estimated at 51.3 percent of the total population in 1990 up from a mere 18.5 percent at independence in 1964 and 30 percent in 1969 (Momba, 1993: 185). Over 70 percent of the urban population is on the Copperbelt and Lusaka. The case of Zambia in this regard, according to Michael Bratton (1994: 124), draws attention to high levels of urbanization and industrialization as a significant characteristic of civil society that facilitates electoral transitions. This fact meant that Zambia had an unusually well-educated, well-paid, and class-conscious population. The extent and rapidity of contraction in the national economy, among the most precipitous in Africa according to Bratton, provoked a particularly keen grievance among urban wage earners. Economic contraction and austerity policies had a profound social impact, in which poverty "trickled up" to most social classes in Zambia. But, whereas UNIP's patronage machine had always protected its key constituency of urban wage earners, by 1985, it had exhausted its resources. Previously privileged elements in society came to bear a share of the adjustment burden once the government committed itself to a serious reform effort. The urban wage earners thus shifted their loyalty and support to MMD. Recognizing this shift, the ruling party sought reelection by bidding for the rural vote, only to discover that after years of neglect by government, peasant farmers had also defected to the opposition.

Third, and related to the second factor was the economic malaise in Zambia and the deleterious effects of SAPs on Zambians and their association with the regime of President Kaunda. Bratton argues that Kaunda was broadly defeated on account of a national economic crisis that led to political realignment as a ruling coalition of diverse classes and regions emerged to oppose the incumbent regime. A severe economic downturn in Zambia after 1985 seriously affected a wide range of social groups, including, most critically, urban wage earners, who had previously benefited from UNIP's patronage and welfare policies. UNIP's statist development strategy created a monumental national debt and drastically undermined living standards. "When UNIP supporters could no longer afford the price of maize meal and were reduced to eating a single meal a day, they blamed Kaunda" (Bratton, 1994: 102). The government's loss of legitimacy was marked by a series of urban food riots, which by 1990 had turned political. MMD, a loose alliance centered on the labor movement but including business and professional leaders, took advantage of the popular upsurge by blaming the economic distress on UNIP's mismanagement and corruption. Unlike the case in Kenya, Zambia's social forces possessed an organizational framework upon which to build a bid for state power, namely the labor unions.

In most African countries independent national associations do not exist, or, as in the case of the Christian Churches in Kenya and Zaire, are very wary of partisan involvement in electoral politics. "The cohesion of social forces behind MMD meant that Zambia was able to avoid the fragmentation of the opposition into multiple parties that is so characteristic of other liberalizing African countries" (Ibid.). Bratton's explanation centers on domestic rather than international factors, on civil society, rather than the state. Although Zambia's desperate need for financial credits made it pliable to pressures from external donors, Bratton argues that:

[i]n marked contrast to the case of Kenya, however, Zambia's international development partners never attached explicit political conditions to their assistance and hence were not major players in the transition to multiparty politics. Nor was the transition driven primarily by divisions within the ruling elite or by leadership defections to the opposition. Most UNIP defectors joined MMD well before the political transition began in April 1990, and once the transition was underway, the top hierarchy of the ruling party closed ranks. (Bratton 1994:103)

Fourth, and finally, was ethnic violence in Kenya manifested in politically instigated ethnic clashes intended to serve a strategic function for the incumbent KANU regime of President Moi. Harvey Glickman (1997) notes that in Kenya, Moi's KANU government instigated a campaign of ethnic cleansing of "foreigners" in the Kalenjin region before the 1992 presidential and parliamentary elections. It is significant to note that the ethnic cleansing was undertaken after registration of voters. In effect, therefore, the tens of thousands that were displaced, all of them opposition sympathizers, were disenfranchised. The government thus depended on Kalenjin support to win, although it drew support from 21 ethnic groups. It was further helped by personal conflicts among opposition leaders, which split Kikuyu and separated the Luo from a previous alliance with one Kikuyu element. The specter of ethnic clashes in Kenya in the run-up to the 1992 and 1997 elections, as a strategic weapon of the incumbent regime, warrants detailed treatment here.

ETHNIC CLASHES IN KENYA

The emergence of FORD as a mass movement for multiparty democracy seriously threatened the Moi regime in Kenya. The regime began to mobilize support from the groups likely to be affected most by the shift of power—the Kalenjin. Kalenjin politicians began to organize meetings in the Rift Valley at which they called for the revival of *Majimboism* (regionalism). At the first such meeting held at Kapsabet in Nandi district, the notion of multipartyism was condemned and portrayed as an anti-Moi and anti-Kalenjin movement, with the Kikuyu isolated by ministers Timothy Mibei and John Cheruiyot as the main opposition to KANU. Speakers at these Rift Valley meetings delivered threats that if *Majimboism* were reintroduced, all the Kikuyu who had settled in the Rift Valley would have to pack up and leave. Willy Kamuren, MP for Baringo North, was more inclusive in his warning. He asked all government critics to move out of Kalenjin areas and go back to their "motherlands." These Rift Valley politicians also declared the province to be an opposition-free KANU zone. The targets of the ethnic onslaught included the Kikuyu, Luhyia, Luo, and Kisii (see Oyugi, 1998: 30; *Weekly Review,* 13 September, 1991; *The East African Standard,* 29 September, 1991).

In the face of political opposition, therefore, the Kalenjin reacted the same way the Kikuyu had reacted before them—by organizing public rallies to mobilize ethnic support. President Moi had predicted that multipartyism would bring ethnic conflict and chaos. His opponents in 1992 argued that such conflict did not emerge until the ruling party engineered it from above in order to undermine advocates of a shift to political pluralism. Moi and his outspoken allies in the early 1990s attempted to discredit government critics and opponents by accusing them of "tribalism," of seeking power in order to benefit themselves and their own ethnoregional bases. It was against this background that the 1991–92 ethnic clashes occurred in which 779 lives perished, about 50,000 rendered homeless, and millions of shillings worth of property destroyed (Oyugi, 1998: 302; Nyang'oro, 1997b: 144; Kiliku Report, 1992).

According to Edward Mogire (2000: 137), the ethnic clashes that engulfed Kenya at the introduction of multipartyism were instigated by the state and in some cases tolerated by the same. "These clashes were designed to punish opposition supporters residing in President Moi's home region, the Rift Valley Province." The argument that multipartyism would lead to ethnic clashes was a self-fulfilling prophecy. As Mogire notes, between December 1991 and March 1992 bands of armed Kalenjins attacked Luhyia, Luo, Kisii, and Kikuyu farmers within and just beyond the borders of the Rift Valley. He observes:

> The police seemed in no hurry to intervene or charge the perpetrators of this mayhem and there have been open accusations of collusion between authorities and the killer-bands . . . By October 1993, upwards of 1,500 people had died in these ethnic clashes. In addition, an estimated 6,000 farmhouses were burnt and between 250,000 and 300,000 people displaced. (Mogire 2000:137)

In a pastoral letter read in all Catholic Churches on Sunday April 22, 1992, the Catholic bishops charged the state with complicity in these atrocities. The charges were subsequently confirmed by independent investigations by the NCCK and by a Parliamentary Commission of Inquiry chaired by Kennedy Kiliku. Mogire concludes that ethnicity played a double role in Kenya's political conflict. First, ethnic politics excluded other people from participating in the political process. Second, ethnicity was used as a political resource for mobilization by the state to instigate violence against those who were in the opposition. "Thus the ethnic clashes in Kenya were essentially political conflicts in which the state played a central role" (Ibid., p. 138).

Indeed, the 1993 report by a Parliamentary Select Committee that investigated the conflict (the Kiliku Report) concluded that some provincial administration officers " . . . had directly participated [in] or encouraged the clashes [through] public utterances" (Haugerud, 1995: 38); that slow and half-hearted responses by the provincial administration and security personnel allowed the fighting to escalate; that arrested suspects were released before being charged in court; and that youthful "warriors" were hired and transported to clash areas from outside to reinforce the local ones (Kenya Government, 1992: 81). The Committee found "root causes of the clashes to include political motivations fueled by some officers in the Provincial Administration, and the misconception that some ethnic communities could chase away other ethnic communities in order to acquire their land" (Kenya Government, 1992: 82).

Politically motivated ethnic clashes erupted once again in Kenya in the run-up to the 1997 elections, particularly in Coast Province where those targeted were up-country people settled in the province. Over 60 people were killed and an estimated 100,000 fled the province (*The East African*, Sept. 29-Oct. 5 1997, p. 3). The clashes were seen as a strategy by the KANU regime to ensure President Moi garnered 25 percent of the votes in the province. This was particularly so given the emergence of formidable opposition presidential candidates including Mwai Kibaki from Central Province, Michael Wamalwa from Western, Raila Odinga from Nyanza, and Charity Ngilu from Eastern vis-à-vis the new requirement that a winning presidential candidate must garner 25 percent of the votes cast in at least five of the country's eight provinces. As argued elsewhere:

> . . . it was the presence of up-country people [in Coast Province] that facilitated [the] election of such opposition MPs as Rashid Mzee of Kisauni, Salim Mwavumo of Likoni (both of FORD-K) and Kennedy Kiliku (DP) in Changamwe; hence the necessity to disenfranchise them by evicting them after registering as voters at the Coast and thereby tilt the political balance in favor of KANU. (Nasong'o 2000: 52)

Overall, though elections provide a vehicle for the expression of both formal and informal opposition, and may even have the effect of reducing tensions and accommodating opposition as Harvey Glickman (1998: 41) argues, the problem is not in elections per se, but rather in the politicization and mobilization of ethnicity. In situations where democratic pluralism and competition is generally perceived as a zero-sum game with definite winners and losers among a country's ethnoregional communities as is the case in Kenya, those who stand to lose organize ethnically in order to defend their positions, in the process engendering a conjuncture of highly ethnicized politics.

CONCLUSION

This chapter has analyzed the role of ethnicity in African politics of transition with particular reference to the cases of Kenya and Zambia. It has noted that ethnicity is both functional and dysfunctional relative to the purposes for which it is mobilized. On the positive side, ethnicity provided a basis for organization of resistance against colonialism and for mobilization of nationalist movements in the fight for independence. Secondly, it provided the basis for adaptation to the uncertainty and insecurity caused by the rapid changes introduced by colonialism. Thirdly, ethnicity provides a sense of belonging as part of an interdependent layer of social relations between the individual and the state. It thus cushions the individual from the negative effects of alienation inherent in a modern complex society. Fourthly, ethnic movements raise issues concerning discrimination and oppression and thus contribute to democratic practice by demanding equity and justice in the distribution of public goods and services. Finally, mobilization of various ethnic populations behind various factions of a nation's elite contributes to decentralization of power, which is healthy for the institutionalization of democratic freedoms.

On the downside, however, ethnicized politics is anathema to democratic transition in a continent partitioned into dozens of ethnically heterogeneous states. The chapter has shown that compared to Zambia, Kenya has a very high rate of ethnic politics that manifests itself in ethnic bloc-voting and ethnically exclusive political parties. This ethnicization of the political arena in Kenya has served to accentuate suspicion and rivalry and thus heightened the perception of political engagement as a zero-sum game. Overall, the high rate of politicized ethnicity in Kenya is caused by the unwillingness of elite actors to collaborate across ethnic divides. Yet it is incumbent upon the elite to establish credible multiethnic parties to facilitate mass support for such parties. Whereas cross-ethnic parties engendered a maximum coalition on the part of the Zambian opposition leading to their electoral victory in 1991, lack of elite collaboration is a major explanation for the ethnic fragmentation of the Kenyan party system that was a major causal variable for the defeat of the opposition in Kenya in 1992 and 1997.

Chapter Five
The Primacy of Electoral System Design

An electoral system may be defined as the rules and procedures under which votes are translated into seats in parliament, or into the selection of executives. Harvey Glickman (1998) posits that elections provide a vehicle for the expression of both formal and informal opposition, and may even have the effect of reducing tensions and accommodating opposition: " . . . the problem is not in elections per se, but rather in the politicization and mobilization of ethnicity" (Glickman, 1998: 41). In this regard, Sisk and Reynolds (1998: 4) argue, "[e]lectoral systems are critically important for promoting democratization and conflict management because they are highly manipulable instruments of constitutional engineering." The premise of constitutional engineering, according to the two scholars, is that rules can be established to provide structural incentives for moderate conflict-mitigating behavior on the part of politicians. They hold that the rules under which elections are held have a strong bearing on whether they will have conflict-exacerbating or conflict-mitigating effects. Accordingly, Reynolds and Sisk (1998) contend that within the constitution-making process, few choices are as important as which electoral system is to be used, because this single institution will help determine what parties look like, who is represented in parliament, and ultimately, who governs. "This is why electoral system design has been seized upon by many scholars . . . as one of the chief levers of constitutional engineering to be used in mitigating conflict within divided societies" (Reynolds & Sisk, 1998: 19).

In order to be able to mitigate conflict, the process of election of leaders and representatives must be based on genuine choice between alternative political parties. In other words, the basic measure of democratic advancement, especially for emergent democracies, is the capacity of a political system to effect alternation of power between different governing groups in the form of political parties via electoral competition. Based on this premise, this chapter contends, and seeks to demonstrate that the basic design of the electoral system has serious implications for the outcome of electoral contests because it determines the competitiveness of the electoral process and hence the chances for alternation of power between political parties. The chapter proceeds from an exposition of types of electoral systems, examines the electoral outcomes of the first multiparty elections in selected countries in Africa, and then focuses on the cases of Kenya and Zambia with a view to gauging their democratic advance. The significance of the two cases lie in the contradictory scenarios they present in regard to democratic advancement. In Zambia in 1991, as shown in Chapters Three and Four, the opposition united against the incumbent to score the first opposition electoral victory in the 1990s wave of multiparty elections in Africa. In Kenya, on the other hand, the opposition was fragmented, an eventuality that facilitated the incumbent party to retain power twice, in 1992 and 1997. In the third multiparty elections in the two countries, the situation was reversed, in Zambia in 2001, opposition fragmentation facilitated victory for the new incumbent while in Kenya in 2002 the opposition united to edge out the incumbent. These contradictory scenarios are a function of the electoral system design in the two countries. Electoral system type is thus a crucial determinant of political competitiveness and, ipso facto, of electoral outcomes.

TYPES OF ELECTORAL SYSTEMS

An electoral system is designed to do three things. First, it serves to translate votes cast into seats won in a legislative chamber. The system may give more weight to proportionality so that the disparity between a political party's share of votes and its share of seats is not great. Alternatively, it may funnel votes (however fragmented among parties) into a parliament that contains two large parties representing polarized views. According to Arend Lijphart (1998) for instance, presidential systems can have an important effect on legislative elections if presidential elections are based on a plurality or first-past-the-post (FPTP) electoral system and if legislative elections are held at the same time. In such circumstances, large parties have an advantage in presidential elections since small parties do not have much of a chance to have one of their candidates elected. This advantage tends to carry over into legislative elections. Hence presidentialism tends to discourage multipartyism as illustrated by the cases of the U.S. and Costa Rica. Second, an electoral system serves as a conduit through which the people can hold their representatives accountable. In this regard, the electorate reserves the right to renew or revoke the mandate given to their representatives at regular electoral intervals. Third, electoral systems serve the normative function of structuring the boundaries of "acceptable" political discourse and giving incentives for those competing for power, especially political parties, to couch their appeal to the electorate in distinct ways (Reynolds & Sisk, 1998: 19).

The main electoral system choices are between plurality-majority systems and proportional representation (PR) systems. Plurality-majority systems often use single-member districts (SMD). In a plurality, or first-past-the-post (FPTP) system, the winner is the candidate with the most votes, not necessarily an absolute majority of the votes. In a majoritarian system, the winner must garner an absolute majority (50% + 1). The underlying rationale for PR, on the other hand, is to reduce the disparity between a party's share of national votes and its share of parliamentary seats. For instance, 40 percent of the votes should translate into 40 percent of the legislative seats (see Lijphart, 1998: 10). In addition, PR systems enhance the representation of minority groups. Pure FPTP or plurality SMD systems are mainly found in the UK and the countries it influenced. In Africa, Botswana, Gambia, Ghana, Kenya, Lesotho, Malawi, São Tome and Principe, Zambia, and Zimbabwe all use SMD plurality systems. List PR is the electoral system most frequently used in democracies and is increasingly becoming common. More than 20 established democracies use some variant of list PR with seats allocated within a number of regionally based districts. Germany, Israel, and the Netherlands allocate seats on the basis of a single nationwide district. In Africa, Benin, Burkina Faso, Burundi, Madagascar, Mozambique, and Niger follow the district-based List PR model; while Angola, Namibia, Senegal and South Africa calculate seats at the national level (Reynolds & Sisk, 1998: 21).

According to Joel Barkan et al (1987), SMD, FPTP winner-take-all electoral systems are best suited to African societies. This is because, they argue, these systems offer a direct constituency-representative link and can promote integrative, modernizing effects across ethnic group lines (see also Barkan et al, 2001). However, the major shortcoming of the winner-take-all FPTP systems is that they induce more competitive, confrontational, and exclusionary politics. Accordingly, Andrew Reynolds (1998) posits that the PR systems are better as they produce inclusive, consensual governments. It must be noted, nevertheless, that PR systems that calculate representation at the national level have the disadvantage of creating "suspended legislatures" whose members have no direct link with the electorate and who owe their parliamentary seats largely to the party bosses.

There are a number of electoral system dimensions that have important consequences for the proportionality of election outcomes and for party systems. First is the electoral formula, including the majoritarian-plurality, PR, and semi-PR formulas. The second key factor is the district magnitude, by which is meant the number of representatives elected per district. " . . . the greater the number of members it [constituency] elects, the more closely will the result approximate to proportionality" (Lijphart, 1998: 11). This, however, applies to multi-member electoral districts. With regard to SMDs, which are the norm in most African countries, the relevant factor is constituency size in terms of population. The more equal the demarcation of constituencies in terms of population, the greater the proportionality of representation. The third dimension is electoral threshold, which applies to PR electoral systems. This refers to the minimum level of support that a party needs in order to gain representation. It is usually expressed in terms of percentage of votes garnered. For instance, a party needs to garner at least five percent of the votes cast in order to gain parliamentary representation in the case of South Africa. Finally, assembly size is the fourth dimension that has a strong influence on proportionality and on the degree of multipartyism. Lijphart (1998) notes that the smaller the assembly, the less proportional and the less the number of parties it promotes.

Available evidence indicates that of the four factors above, the first two—electoral formula and district magnitude—have the most significant impact on proportionality of electoral representation and the nature of the party system (see Nasong'o, 2004; Lijphart, 1998). Against this background, Reynolds and Sisk (1998) place analytical premium on the role of institutional design, especially on the role of elections and the systems under which they are contested in the democratization and conflict management processes. They posit that the choices about the basic rules of the game affect its outcomes. Indeed, the electoral system design determines the competitiveness of elections and hence the possibilities of either alternation of power between different parties or the entrenchment of one particular party in power. Electoral outcomes of multiparty transitional elections in a cross-section of African countries largely vindicate this contention.

DEMOCRACY AND RULES OF THE GAME

The aspiration to democratic rule is an almost universal phenomenon. This is illustrated by the ubiquitous wave of democratization across the world at the close of the last century. Indeed, the honorific nature of the concept of democracy is such that all manner of political systems claim to be democracies. Even countries that have never held an election in decades such as the former Zaire are conveniently baptized "democratic republic" while countries in which political parties are banned such as Uganda, are named "no-party democracy." However, the prerequisite for the concrete realization of representative or republican democracy which most of the democratizing countries in Africa aspire to, lies in a number of institutional guarantees. First, political authority must be based on a limited mandate with citizens reserving the right to renew it periodically in free and fair elections. Second, elections must be based on universal adult suffrage and on genuine choices between alternative political parties. Third, citizens must be guaranteed the right and freedom of association, expression, and the eligibility, in principle, of any citizen to seek public office. Fourth, aspiring political leaders must be afforded the right to compete freely for support and votes, buttressed by multiple channels of political communication. Fifth and finally is the imperative need for democratically accountable governmental decision-making institutions, with elected officials free from overriding opposition from unelected officials (see Danziger, 2004; Walle, 2003; Harbeson, 1999; Gitonga, 1987; Dahl, 1982).

In short, the realization of democracy is contingent upon rules of the game that provide for alternative political parties competing against one another for the chance to govern within institutional systems that guarantee fairness and a genuine opportunity for alternation of power between parties. The significance of such institutional design and adequate rules of the game is particularly borne out by the case of Mexico. In spite of the existence of multiple political parties in Mexico and regular electoral contests among them, it took over seven decades for Mexicans to be able to elect a president from one of the opposition parties [1] (National Action Party's [PAN] Vicente Fox) in 2000. But, as Anyang' Nyong'o (2002) points out, Fox could not have been elected had not his predecessor, President Ernesto Zedillo changed the country's electoral laws to facilitate democratic elections. In so doing, Zedillo defied his own ruling party—Institutional Revolutionary Party (PRI)—and went ahead, first, to make the national electoral commission independent of the executive and ruling party. Second, he introduced laws that guarded against election rigging. Third, he made representation fairer. Fourth and finally, he pegged presidential election on a majority rather than a plurality of the popular vote.

Similarly, as John Harbeson (1999: 43) argues, African circumstances, just like those of Mexico and other democratizing countries of Asia and Eastern Europe, make it more likely that multiparty electoral transitions will result in democratic progress to the extent that they commence with comprehensive multiparty agreements on the fundamental rules of the game, either through constitutional reform or by constitution-like pact-making. Harbeson explains that such pacts may (1) include only a narrow range of actors or be formed by constituent assemblies elected on the basis of universal suffrage. (2) They may cover only the terms for the exercise of power on the basis of mutual guarantees for the "vital interests" of those entering into the pacts, or extend more broadly to the terms of electoral competition for power and/or the reconstitution of the state as a whole. (3) They may be temporary and contingent upon ongoing consent, or be constructed so as to be enduring and inviolable. Harbeson concludes that experience dictates that pacts that are broadly constructed in terms of participants, scope, and duration *prior* to the holding of initial multiparty elections are more conducive to enduring democratization than are narrowly constructed pacts or the absence of such pacts.

Evidence from initial multiparty elections in Africa in the 1990s point to the fact that incumbent regime defeat occurred largely in cases where the elections were held following a negotiated redesigning of the rules of the political game intended to open up political space to fair competition. One case example is Benin where long-serving President Mathieu Kérékou was defeated in the first multiparty elections of 1991. This political milestone was a direct result of a new political pact that established new rules of the political game and codified these into a new constitution. As Bruce Magnusson (1999) writes, a national conference was convened in Benin on February 19, 1990, which lasted for 10 days. It brought together representatives of many socio-economic and professional groups including teachers, students, the military, government officials, religious authorities, non-governmental organizations, and more than 50 political parties. The conference, which declared itself sovereign, was chaired by the Catholic prelate, Archbishop De Souza. The National Conference elected Nicéphore Soglo Prime Minister for the transition period with Mathieu Kérékou continuing to serve as president though his powers were to remain ceremonial until elections were held. The Conference appointed a Constitutional Commission, which drafted a new constitution for a multiparty system of separated powers. The Constitutional Commission's challenge, according to Magnusson, was to design a system that could avoid the ethnoregional paralysis of the 1960s with its specter of military intervention; minimize the authoritarian ambitions of a president; and discourage the repression of political and economic freedoms that had characterized the Kérékou regime.

The result of this process saw power in Benin divided between the president, the National Assembly, which was based on proportional representation, and the constitutional court. The constitutional court was given absolute power of review. It was to determine the constitutionality of all laws, regulations, and government actions; and was also charged with enforcing the human rights provisions of Benin's constitution, which alone, among African constitutions, according to Magnusson, incorporates as law the African Charter on Human and People's Rights. In the transition period, the strategic considerations of the politically ambitious were shaped by the near-absolute uncertainty about future electoral outcomes, leading to agreement on constitutional checks and balances that would make it difficult for one political institution or individual to control the entire apparatus of state (Magnusson, 1999: 222–223). It is within this context that the Kérékou regime was defeated in the ensuing elections and replaced by one led by Nicéphore Soglo.

The second example is Malawi, where self-declared "President-for-Life" Kamuzu Banda was defeated in 1994 under circumstances similar to those of Benin. In the run-up to the first multiparty elections in 1994, the process of negotiating for new rules between the Public Affairs Committee (PAC) and the Presidential Committee on Dialogue (PCD) culminated in Malawi's transitional National Consultative Council (NCC). The PAC was composed of representatives from the Alliance for Democracy (AFORD) led by Chakufwa Chihana, Bakili Muluzi's United Democratic Front (UDF), Churches, and Malawi Law Society. The PCD on the other hand, was composed of cabinet ministers and members of the ruling Malawi Congress Party's (MCP) National Executive Committee. The NCC was held up as the "supreme body" and its decisions were followed by parliament. Three subcommittees were formed, one on new electoral laws and procedures; the other on constituency boundaries; and the third on reviewing the constitution and drafting a new one before the 1994 multiparty elections.

An electoral commission on which all parties contesting the elections were represented oversaw the May 17, 1994 elections. In addition, a transitional National Executive Council (NEC) oversaw the security services, the central bank, and other key institutions; and agreed to increase the number of parliamentary seats to more accurately reflect population densities, that is, to even out constituency sizes and thus enhance the proportionality of representation. In essence, these arrangements amounted to a diluted form of a transitional government that had been demanded by the emergent opposition in Malawi (Dijk, 2000; Venter, 1995). Like in Benin, therefore, the incumbent regime in Malawi was removed from control of the electoral process and the state apparatus in the transitional period thus facilitating some semblance of fair competition resulting in the defeat of the entrenched MCP regime of Kamuzu Banda.

Third, Mali was fortunate in being able to write a new constitution and hold multiparty elections without the burden of continued participation by an incumbent party and head of state (Vengroff & Kone, 1995: 45). Long serving military ruler Moussa Traoré was toppled on March 24, 1991 by Lt. Col. Amadou Toumani Touré on account of his intransigence and highhanded clamp down on prodemocracy demonstrators. The new regime pledged a return to civilian rule within a year, and constituted the Comité de Transition pour le Salut du Peuple (CTSP) composed of both military and civilian representatives. The CTSP set up a transitional government that organized a national conference to write a new constitution, a new electoral code, and a legal framework for establishing political parties—*La Charte des Partis*. The new constitution was approved in a referendum on January 12, 1992. It provided for a semi-presidential political system with a president elected directly by universal suffrage, a government responsible to the national assembly headed by a prime minister appointed by the president, and an independent judiciary overseen by both a supreme court and a constitutional court. The inauguration of a new constitution in Mali was followed by municipal elections on January 19, 1992, national assembly elections in two rounds on February 24 and March 9, 1992, and presidential elections in two rounds on April 13 and 27. Both the parliamentary and presidential elections were organized on a majoritarian electoral system. According to Vengroff and Kone (1995: 48), "[m]uch of this was possible because the entrenched economic and political interests identified with the Traoré regime were effectively out of power and thus unable to skew the process as has happened in some other African countries."

Fourth, and arguably the most significant transition to democracy in Africa in the 1990s, was the case of South Africa's transition from the abominable apartheid system to majority rule in 1994. Here also, the transition was facilitated by detailed negotiations on an interim constitution, which preceded the holding of the first post-apartheid national elections. These negotiations also produced an interim government of national unity that reinforced the stability of the transition through the first year of African National Congress (ANC) leadership. The interim constitution was subsequently replaced by a permanent one that was ratified by the combined houses of the South African parliament serving as a constituent assembly. In comparison with the situation elsewhere in Africa, John Harbeson (1999) notes that threats to the viability of the South African polity have been somewhat subdued. Participants in the post-transition struggles have not dared, by deed or by word, to oppose or seek to undermine the democratic rules of the game. Neither the ANC government nor any faction within it has tried to resort to extra-constitutional means to sustain its power, nor have they been accused of doing so by the opposition. All parties accepted the results of the 1994, 1999, and 2004 national elections and democratization has further been strengthened and extended by the successful conduct of local elections.

Fifth and finally, Mozambique similarly conducted successful free and fair elections in 1994 that served to institutionalize the country's peace after sixteen years of civil war. Although a number of factors contributed to the success of the election including donor financial and logistical support, gifted and dedicated Mozambicans in key positions, Harbeson argues that these powerful influences could not have been brought to bear had it not been for the *prior* comprehensive and detailed agreements among the parties—Mozambique Liberation Front (FRELIMO) and Mozambique National Resistance (RENAMO):

> Agreements on the peace and on the electoral rules did not include constitutional reform . . . but these two agreements covered the basic rules of the game for the initial period of Mozambique's democratization in comprehensive detail. These agreements were less broad than those in South Africa were, but they did extend to the period of the initial national elections. Further, although they were conducted by party elites, they were covered extensively by the press . . . (Harbeson, 1999: 47)

Harbeson's position is vindicated by Carrie Manning's (2002) findings in her empirical study of the politics of peace and democratization in Mozambique. Manning notes that though the socio-economic context seemed inauspicious in the extreme[2] at the time of the signing of the 1992 General Peace Accord, more than a decade down the road, Mozambique stood out as one of the more stable and peaceful countries in the region. There had been no return to armed conflict, there was virtually no significant political violence, and neither of the two principal parties, FRELIMO and RENAMO, had questioned the essential terms of the political settlement. Perhaps even more remarkable, according to Manning (2002: 5), " . . . Mozambique's settlement proved durable even in the absence of formal power-sharing arrangements at cabinet level and with only rather limited concessions to proportionality in the allocation of political power." In the absence of socio-economic variables deemed to be prerequisites for democratic consolidation, Manning explains this eventuality in terms of contingent factors, especially the interaction, marked by bargaining and compromise, of domestic political actors within the new institutions they are building, what Manning calls elite habituation to the new rules of the game.

Table 5.1 below illustrates with particular clarity the significance of the electoral system design—the rules of the electoral game—to electoral outcomes in regard to the first multiparty elections in selected African countries. In Table 5.1 below, of the 16 cases under review, change of regime in the first multiparty elections occurred in 50 percent of the cases. Of these eight cases, 75 percent provided for an absolute majority to win the presidency, which led to a second round of elections between the top two candidates resulting in defeat of the incumbent. Of the other eight cases that witnessed no change of regime in their first multiparty presidential contests, 87.5 percent provided for a simple plurality of votes to win the presidency. The only exceptions in the Table are Chad, which provided for an absolute majority but the incumbent won in the first round; and Zambia, with a plurality electoral system that led to incumbent defeat. Whereas the case of Chad is the exception that may prove the rule, the Zambian case is explicable in the fact that the contest was between two candidates, reminiscent of the round two elections in the other cases where change of regime occurred.

Table 5.1: Results of the First Multiparty Presidential Elections in Selected African Countries

Country	Year	No. of Parties	Presidential Candidates	Change of Regime
Angola	1992	11	11	No
Burkina Faso	1998	3	3	No
Benin	1991	12	13; 2 (runoff)	Yes
Cameroon	1992	6	6	No
C. A. Republic	1933	6	8; 2 (runoff)	Yes
Chad	1996	12	15; 2 (runoff)	No
Congo-B	1992	14	15; 2 (runoff)	Yes
Gabon	1993	17	13	No
Ghana	1992	8	5	No
Kenya	1992	9	8	No
Madagascar	1992/93	8	8; 2 (runoff)	Yes
Malawi	1994	8	4	Yes
Mali	1992	8	9; 2 (runoff)	Yes
Mozambique	1994	10	12	No
Sierra Leone	1996	12	12; 2 (runoff)	Yes
Zambia	1991	2	2	Yes

Source: Compiled from Nohlen, D. et al. 1999.

Whereas the foregoing analysis may not prove a causal relationship between electoral system design and electoral outcomes, it does underscore a correlation between the two. It demonstrates that the more competitive the system, the fairer the competition and the greater the chances for alternation of power between political parties. Barring such competitive systems for instance, Kenya's Daniel arap Moi, Cameroon's Paul Biya, and Gabon's Omar Bongo all won in 1992 with 36 percent, 40 percent, and 49 percent respectively, of the votes cast. Arguably therefore, redesigning the institutions of political engagement, both electoral and governance ones, is key to advancing the cause of democracy in Africa. In the 1992 Kenyan election, the results were such that President Moi garnered 1.9 million votes; Kenneth Matiba, 1.3 million, Mwai Kibaki, 1.0 million; and Oginga Odinga, 0.9 million (see Table 4.2). Had the electoral system been redesigned to provide for a majority to win rather than a mere plurality, it is arguable that a runoff between the top two would have resulted in a Moi defeat. Barring this, Moi emerged victorious with just below 37 percent of the votes cast. The institutional environment was not conducive to fair competition. As Hartman (1999: 477–478) argues, " . . . it was not the disagreement between the opposition leaders but the noncompetitive setting that has to be regarded as the principal reason for their defeat."

Accordingly, John Harbeson (1999), contends that African countries that commence their multiparty politics with a fundamental restructuring of the rules of the game through pacts that are broadly constructed in terms of scope and duration, like the cases of Benin, Malawi, Mali, Mozambique, and South Africa illustrated above, engender the best prospects for progress toward democratic consolidation. On the other hand, the converse is the case where such pacts are narrowly constructed or are nonexistent altogether. Under such circumstances, " . . . democratization is bound to be gradual, messy, fitful, and slow, with many imperfections along the way" (Young, 1996: 60). The cases of Zambia and Kenya illustrate with particular clarity the contention that political transition without transformation of the political institutions, especially the electoral system design, is inimical to democratic advancement.

TWO SIDES OF THE SAME COIN: KENYA AND ZAMBIA

Kenya and Zambia provide contradictory scenarios in regard to political competition and electoral outcomes. Both of these countries use the SMD plurality (FPTP) electoral system. The first multiparty elections in Zambia in 1991 saw the resounding defeat of the incumbent regime of President

Kenneth Kaunda of the United National Independence Party (UNIP) by the Movement for Multiparty Democracy (MMD) led by Frederick Chiluba. In Kenya on the other hand, the incumbent KANU regime of President Moi won the first multiparty elections in 1992 and went on to win again in 1997. It was not until 2002 that KANU was walloped in the polls by a coalition of opposition parties in the name of National Rainbow Coalition (NARC). Given the plurality basis of the electoral systems of the two countries, the opposition in Zambia was lucky in 1991 in the sense that all forces opposed to the incumbent regime coalesced into one political party, MMD thereby making the electoral contest a majoritarian one by default. In Kenya in 1992 on the other hand, the opposition splintered in a way that facilitated the incumbent to romp home with a mere 37 percent of the votes cast.

Interestingly, however, if the opposition in Zambia was lucky in 1991 and the Kenyan one was unlucky in 1992, the situation was reversed in the third multiparty elections in the two countries. In Zambia in 2001, opposition to the incumbent MMD was so divided that the MMD presidential candidate, Levy Mwanawasa, faced ten opposition candidates. This facilitated Mwanawasa's victory with a mere 28 percent of the votes cast against his closest competitor, Anderson Mazoka of the United Party for National Development (UPND) who garnered 27 per cent of the votes. In Kenya in 2002 on the other hand, having been beaten twice, the opposition parties wizened up and succumbed to popular pressure to unite, leading to the coalition, NARC. The NARC presidential candidate, Mwai Kibaki, trounced the incumbent KANU's Uhuru Kenyatta by garnering 62 per cent of the vote to Kenyatta's 31 per cent. These contradictory scenarios in the cases of Kenya and Zambia are a function of failure to redesign the electoral systems of the two countries to enhance political competition and thus advance democratic progress. A closer look at the two cases suffices to illustrate this position.

The Paradox of Regime Change in Zambia

Unlike in the illustrative cases of Benin, Malawi, Mali, Mozambique, and South Africa cited above, in Zambia, there was no major inter-party comprehensive overhaul of the electoral system, nor a restructuring of the fundamental rules of the political game prior to the first multiparty elections of October 1991. What happened was a unilateral attempt to re-write the constitution, a move that was informed by the desire on the part of incumbent President Kenneth Kaunda to enhance his democratic credentials and the political attractiveness of his party, UNIP for purposes of securing victory in the first multiparty elections. Towards this end, Kaunda established a constitutional commission, which came up with a number of proposals. These included a proposal to create the post of vice president,[3] appointment of ministers from outside parliament, expansion of the National Assembly from 135 to 150 seats, and the establishment of a constitutional court, among other proposals. These constitutional proposals constituted a major bone of contention between UNIP and MMD beginning June 1991. Whereas Kaunda accepted most of the constitutional commission's recommendations and had them submitted to the National Assembly for ratification, the MMD opposed them because they vested too much authority in the president and too little in the National Assembly. The MMD also opposed the proposal that provided for appointment of cabinet ministers from outside the National Assembly. In its view, this proposal was simply intended to create opportunity for patronage and for rewarding vested interests.

The MMD thus threatened to boycott the elections if the National Assembly ratified the recommendations and, to demonstrate their resolve, refused to attend an inter-party conference chaired by Kaunda in July 1991 to discuss the draft constitution. Later in July 1991, representatives of MMD, UNIP and other parties met to discuss the constitutional commission's proposals under the chairmanship of Deputy Chief Justice Matthew Ngulube. As a result of this meeting, President Kaunda suspended the draft constitution and agreed to further negotiations. With the intervention of Church leaders, a joint commission was set up to review the constitutional proposals following which Kaunda agreed to abandon the ideas of a constitutional court and appointment of cabinet ministers from outside the National Assembly. The power to impose marshal law previously recommended for the president was abandoned and any imposition of a state of emergency beyond seven days was to be approved by the National Assembly. The National Assembly ratified the new proposals on August 2, 1991.

The very fact of forcing President Kaunda to rescind the proposed constitutional changes was a major victory for the MMD. This fact demonstrated the vulnerability of the Kaunda regime and in a big way signaled the beginning of the end of the UNIP government even before elections were held. The powerful Kaunda had been forced to give in on practically all opposition demands. In quick succession, Kaunda agreed to allow international observers into the country to monitor the elections, a position he had previously opposed. He also agreed to grant subsidies to all registered parties (see Ihonvbere, 1996: 117–119). It is important to note, however, that though the opposition succeeded in forcing Kaunda to shelve some of his most important constitutional changes to adopt those that were favored by the opposition, these changes were largely concerned with the exercise of executive powers. They had nothing to do with the electoral system design. In this event, Zambia went to the multiparty polls in October 1991 with the same SMD-FPTP, winner-take-all system.

The greatest strength of the opposition lay in its united front, which reduced the electoral contest to one between the incumbent UNIP and the opposition MMD, with Kaunda pitted against a single opposition presidential candidate, Frederick Chiluba. Realizing his vulnerability, the jittery Kaunda introduced last minute cabinet changes in the hope of demonstrating a stronger resolve to provide a democratically credible and accountable leadership. Nonetheless, the united opposition achieved a very impressive victory over Kaunda and UNIP. John Wiseman (1995: 9) observes that although Kaunda was not averse to using his control of the state to try to create electoral advantages for UNIP, the very strength of the opposition resulted in this having limited effect and was clearly insufficient in preventing an electoral defeat of considerable magnitude. The MMD won 125 of the 150 parliamentary seats with UNIP managing a paltry 25 seats. In this event, the Zambia elections of 1991 produced the first transfer of power through the ballot box of any mainland African state.[4]

It was only after Chiluba's landslide victory over Kaunda that a process was set in motion to revise the constitution along democratic lines (see Ihonvbere, 1996; Mphaisha, 2000). Curiously, however, the MMD government resisted strong domestic and donor pressure to publish the Constitutional Commission's draft document for public debate prior to editing by the government, and it insisted that the document be ratified only by the Zambian parliament in which MMD enjoyed an 83 percent majority. Arguably, in order for a constitution to be broadly acceptable and therefore acquire the potential to endure the test of time, the constitution making process must engage all relevant population groups and seek to secure a voluntary and mutually beneficial consensual social contract (see Mbaku, 1997). In one of its most serious departures from democratic practice, the MMD revised the constitution in the run-up to the 1996 elections to restrict eligibility to run for president to third generation Zambians. This provision targeted Kaunda and explicitly curtailed his much-awaited rematch with Chiluba in the 1996 elections. As a consequence, UNIP, the main opposition party, boycotted the 1996 elections, to the great advantage of the incumbent MMD. As Chisepo Mphaisha (2000) notes, though four candidates stood against Chiluba for president in the 1996 elections, they were no match for Chiluba, who received 72.6 percent of the votes cast, with none of the four opponents managing more than 13 percent. "It is generally believed that only Kaunda, had he been allowed to contest the elections, could perhaps have posed a challenge to Chiluba" (Mphaisha, 2000: 135).

On the basis of this, John Harbeson (1999: 49–50) argues that:

> . . . [d]espite the advantages of a relatively secure state, evidence of vitality in civil society, and at least the potential for polyarchal practice within Chiluba's insurgent party, by early 1997 Zambia's democratic achievements and prospects had been severely eroded. . . . Without agreement among the parties on the basic rules of the game prior to the initial multiparty elections, no semblance of democratically legitimated constraints existed that could restrain the abuses of democratic practice by the victors. Far from strengthening and creating momentum for democracy, the 1996 elections in Zambia have had the opposite effect.

In essence, it is arguable that the resounding defeat of Kaunda was a shift from a single party state under UNIP to a single party state under MMD. The MMD controlled more than three-quarters of the seats in parliament (125 0f 150 seats), which rendered the UNIP opposition a voiceless minority that struggled with overcoming the burden of a discredited past and an unprecedented electoral humiliation.

The failure to fundamentally restructure the strategic environment of political engagement in Zambia on the part of the Chiluba regime, led Van Donge (1995: 93) to observe that though another political party (MMD) was in power under another president, major aspects of Zambian politics did not change. He observed that democratization was supposed to lead to a parliamentary system of government, but political power in Zambia remained concentrated in the presidency. Legally, after the 1991 elections, Zambia was a multiparty state, but in fact, it was ruled by one party. In its first term in office, MMD dominated in all regions of the country, except for Eastern Province, just as during its heyday, UNIP dominated in all areas except Southern Province. Although there were numerous opposition parties under the first MMD term in office, they were fragmented and, given the institutional environment in which they operated, they were largely ineffective. As a consequence, a decade after the return to multipartyism in Zambia and the defeat of the incumbent regime, it was within the ruling party rather than between contending parties, that political competition was to be found.

The inequity of the Zambian electoral system was clearly demonstrated in the country's third multiparty elections of 2001. Here, Chiluba's hand-picked successor in MMD, Levy Mwanawasa, faced ten opposition challengers for the presidency. Four of these were serious contenders, including Anderson Mazoka, Christon Tembo, Tilyenji Kaunda, and Godfrey Miyanda as shown in Table 5.2 below.

Table 5.2: 2001 Zambian Presidential Election Results

Name/Party	Votes	% of Total
Mwanawasa/MMD	506,694	28.32%
Mazoka/UPND	472,697	27.35%
Tembo/FDD	228,861	13.24%
Kaunda/UNIP	175,898	10.18%
Miyanda/HP	140,678	8.14%
Mwila/ZRP	85,472	4.95%
Zata/PF	59,172	3.42%
Mumba/NCC	38,860	2.25%
Konie/SDP	10,253	0.59%
Shamapande/NLD	9,481	0.55%
Total	1,728,066	100%

Source: Electoral Commission of Zambia

As figures in Table 5.2 above show, in spite of winning a combined total of 72 percent of the votes cast, the opposition votes were shared out among the ten opposition candidates such that MMD's Levy Mwanawasa scraped through to victory with a mere 28 percent of the votes cast. Arguably, had the electoral system required an absolute majority to win the presidency, a run-off between Mwanawasa and his closest rival, Anderson Mazoka of the UPND is likely to have produced an upset for MMD. This is particularly so given the disenchantment with the Chiluba regime and the high-handed manner in which he picked his successor within the MMD. Indeed, through the vote counting, Anderson Mazoka maintained a lead over Mwanawasa until returns from the final twenty constituencies when Mwanawasa opened a modest lead.[5] This turn of events prompted accusations of rigging and resulted in widespread opposition street demonstrations over the final result, which Mazoka unsuccessfully contested in court.

The extent of the disproportionality of the Zambian SMD-FPTP electoral system is illustrated even more clearly by the 2001 parliamentary election results as tabulated in Table 5.3 below. The figures show that MMD won a total of 28 per cent of the parliamentary vote, yet it secured 46 percent of the seats in the National Assembly. Similarly, UPND garnered 23 percent of the votes but secured 32 percent of the seats in parliament. The

Table 5.3: 2001 Zambian Parliamentary Vote and Seat Distribution

Party	Votes	% of Total Votes	Seats	% of Total Seats	Disprop. Index
MMD	490,680	28.02%	69	46.00%	18
UPND	416,236	23.77%	49	32.67%	9
UNIP	185,535	10.59%	13	8.67%	-2
FDD	272,817	15.58%	12	8.00%	-8
HP	132,311	7.55%	04	2.67%	-5
ZRP	97,010	5.54%	01	0.67%	-5
PF	49,362	2.81%	01	0.67%	-2
INDEP	59,335	3.40%	01	0.67%	-3
NCC	35,632	2.03%	00	00%	-2
Others (9)	12,435	0.71%	00	00%	-1
Total	1,751,353	100%	150	100%	-

Source: Tabulated from Electoral Commission of Zambia Figures

indices of disproportionality are 18 in favor of MMD, and 9 in favor of UPND. The rest of the parties were disadvantaged in the sense that they received a lesser proportion of the seats than their proportion of the popular vote. The most disadvantaged in this regard was the Forum for Democracy and Development (FDD), with a disproportionality index of minus 8, followed by the Heritage Party (HP) with an index of minus 5. This disproportionality is great, given that ideally, 28 per cent of the vote should result in 28 per cent of parliamentary seats as is normally the case in PR electoral systems. In such cases, the index of disproportionality would be just slightly above zero. The implication here is that there are far more electoral constituencies in areas that support MMD followed by those that support UPND. In essence, these areas are over-represented in the National Assembly, an eventuality that negates the democratic principle of equal representation and equality of the vote.

The Slow March to Regime Change in Kenya

Just like in Zambia, no pact or redesigning of the electoral system preceded the first multiparty elections in Kenya in December 1992. Faced with heightened internal demands for opening up the political space that culminated in violent riots in urban areas (see Murunga, 1999); and external pressure in the form of an aid crunch by international financial institutions, the Kenya government was forced to repeal section 2(A) of the constitution. This was the provision that made the country a one party state by law. Although at this moment the KANU government, like its UNIP counterpart in Zambia, was quite vulnerable and could have been successfully pushed into reengineering a new constitution, the forces of democratization in the country did not find it fit to push the incumbent regime towards this end. It would seem that the Moi regime had been so oppressive that the mere legalization of opposition political parties was received as a major act of political liberation. Accordingly, emergent political parties were more than willing to go to the polls within the rubric of the single party electoral system design.

The electoral system design, however, was such that the odds were stacked against the opposition. First, the opposition had no say in the appointment of the electoral commission, which was single-handedly appointed by President Moi. This reality had serious implications for electoral outcomes in the country given the role of the Electoral Commission of Kenya (ECK). The ECK is charged with the responsibility of preparation and supervision of elections, maintenance and revision of voter registers, promotion of voter education, and determination of the number and boundaries of constituencies based on the most recent census. According to Foeken and Dietz (2000), it is the determination of the number of constituencies, that is, the degree of representation that was put to effect for KANU's advantage. The Kenya constitution (1998), Chapter III section 42(3) provides that all constituencies shall contain as nearly equal numbers of inhabitants as appears to the Commission to be reasonably desirable. However, the Commission may depart from this principle in order to take account of population density, demographic trends, means of communication, geographical features, community of interest, and the boundaries of existing administrative areas. Nonetheless, the number of inhabitants is the constitutional principle for determining the size of constituencies. The other factors are exceptions that the ECK may consider to justify or depart from the principle of equality (see Mungai, 2002).

Unfortunately, as Kibe Mungai argues, since independence, particularly after 1986 when Kenya's constituencies were increased from 158 to 188, then to 210 in the run-up to the 1997 elections, ethnic considerations and boundaries of existing administrative areas have been the major considerations in constituency demarcation as opposed to the number of inhabitants. In effect, exceptions to the rule have been elevated above the

Table 5.4: Average Number of Voters in Kenya's Eight Provinces, 2002

Province	Number of voters	Number of constituencies	Ave. No. of voters per constituency
Nairobi	894,471	08	111,808
Coast	888,934	21	42,330
Northeastern	219,055	11	19,914
Eastern	1,735,169	36	48,199
Central	1,566,027	29	54,000
Rift Valley	1,293,089	49	26,389
Western	1,207,110	24	50,296
Nyanza	1,564,675	32	48,896
Total	10,495,082	210	49,976*

Source: Compiled from 2002 Electoral Commission of Kenya figures
*This figure represents the ideal number of voters per constituency

rule itself. For instance, Table 5.4 above illustrates a clear case of malapportionment whereby electoral constituencies have substantially unequal voting populations. Provinces in which KANU has traditionally the strongest support including the Rift Valley, Northeastern, and, to some extent, Coast are over-represented in the sense that they have more constituencies per capita than other provinces. Table 5.4 above indicates that whereas the ideal number of voters per constituency is 49,976, Northeastern Province has an average of 19,914 voters per constituency, the Rift Valley has an average of 26,389, and Coast an average of 42,330. This unfavorably compares with the situation in Central Province with an average of 54,000 voters per constituency, and Western Province with an average of 50,296 voters per constituency. Such malapportionment in SMD-FPTP electoral systems like the Kenyan one may systematically favor one or more political parties and thus contribute to electoral disproportionality. In this case, the situation favors KANU.

Against this background, though KANU had fewer overall votes in the 1992 parliamentary elections than those of the combined opposition, it nonetheless won 100 seats compared to 88 for the opposition. This is a result of the fact that KANU-dominated areas are over-represented in parliament, while traditionally opposition strongholds are underrepresented. It is no coincidence, for instance, that the four least populated constituencies in Kenya including Lamu East (16,794); Isiolo South (23,141); Samburu East (34,469); and Laisamis (40,976) are represented by KANU, whereas the five most populated constituencies are represented by opposition parties to KANU. These include Embakasi (434,840); Kasarani (338,925); Langata (286,739); Kisauni (278,842); and Saboti (269,197) (see Mungai, 2005). Essentially, therefore, between 1992 and 2002, KANU maintained a majority in parliament that in reality represented a minority in the national population. Arguably, therefore, without this case of malapportionment, KANU would have won less than the 64 seats it won in the 2002 parliamentary election. Since democracy is founded on the principle of equal representation and the one-person-one-vote tenet, this principle is grossly violated in situations where some constituencies have 26,389 voters and others 54,000; where some constituencies have a population of 16,794 and others have a population of 434,840, yet their respective representatives have an equal voice in the legislature. Indeed, in May 2002, two High Court judges, Justices Mbogholi Msagha and J. V. O. Juma, sitting as a constitutional court delivered a landmark ruling with the potential of having significant implications for the development of democracy in the country. In the case of *John N. Michuki vs. Attorney General and Electoral Commission of Kenya,* the justices took issue with the fact that the size of constituencies manifested serious imbalances in representation, which violated the democratic principle of equal representation. Their ruling, however, fell short of making clear orders on the issue (Mungai, 2002).

The second constraint faced by the opposition in the first multiparty election in Kenya in 1992 was the provincial administration, which was not de-linked from the electoral process and was thus used by the incumbent party to harass and intimidate the opposition. Opposition political parties found it increasingly difficult to campaign as they were denied permits for political rallies and some of their rallies were routinely disrupted and others canceled "on security grounds." Third, on account of violence, intimidation, and arrests of opposition politicians and their supporters and the declaration of so-called KANU zones in Moi's stronghold of the Rift Valley, 41 per cent (18 out of 44)[6] of the KANU candidates from the Rift Valley were returned to parliament unopposed. Fourth, opposition parties were denied equal access to state media, which alone had a national reach, in which case their campaign for change and an alternative political agenda was not received by the people and thus remained a cry in the wilderness. Edward Mogire (2000) rightly notes that the most prevalent electoral malpractice in the 1992 Kenyan elections was the establishment of a partial electoral commission and laws designed to give KANU an electoral advantage in the elections held in 1992. This included a provision requiring successful presidential candidates to win 25 percent of the votes in any five of the country's eight provinces, regardless of the population or number of voters. Mogire (2000: 133–134) argues:

> The measure was designed to minimize the chances of opposition victory as support for Forum of Restoration of Democracy (FORD) and Democratic Party (DP) opposition parties registered in 1992 was concentrated in the populous Central, Nyanza, and Nairobi Provinces. By contrast, support for KANU was concentrated in the least populated regions including Northeastern Province (with only 1 percent of the electorate).

In the same vein, Mogire observes, Moi turned a deaf ear to opposition demands to reconstitute the electoral commission to include persons acceptable to all political parties, preferring instead to stick with the commissioners he appointed prior to legalizing the opposition.

Against this background, opposition parties and civil society organizations made the issue of constitutional reform the primary focus in the run-up to the 1997 elections. Most of the activism in this regard was spearheaded by the Citizens Coalition for Constitutional Change (4Cs). The 4Cs transformed itself into the National Convention Assembly (NCA) and, with its executive arm, the National Convention Executive Council (NCEC) mobilized demonstrations and civil disobedience under the banner "No Reforms No Elections" to put pressure on the KANU regime to effect the necessary constitutional reforms. This pressure, coupled with international leverage in the form of an aid crunch, forced Moi to capitulate and initiate some token changes under the aegis of what became known as the Inter-Parties Parliamentary Group (IPPG). Under IPPG, the Members of Parliament resolved to remove and/or revise some of the draconian colonial laws such as the Chief's Authority Act, and the requirement for licenses to hold political rallies. The IPPG package also provided for the opposition representation on the ECK, providing for the first time in Kenya's history that political parties were to jointly nominate members of the Electoral Commission.[7]

The IPPG package had a number of effects. First, it paved the way for President Moi to pull the constitutional reform momentum away from the NCEC and the 4Cs. Second, it laid the foundation for further disagreements among the opposition ranks. Some of the opposition leaders rightly argued that the IPPG package did not go far enough in overhauling the constitution. Third, the pro-constitutional change advocates, particularly the 4Cs, viewed the IPPG package as an appeasement of Moi and as such rejected its spirit on the ground that it did not go far enough in dealing with the central contentious issues related to the constitution. Fourth, the donors came out in support of the agreement calling it "a step in the right direction" and in the process supporting Moi. Once again Moi solidified his grip on the direction of the political process, which meant operating under rules that greatly constrained the opposition (see Brown, 2001; Adar, 1998).

Overall, therefore, the KANU government continued to play the game of musical chairs with the much-needed constitutional reform necessary for advancing democracy. Similarly, politically motivated ethnic clashes, threats by Moi against opposition zones on withholding national development resources; harassment of private print media and arrest of its publishers and editors; the skewed nature of opposition constituency representation; and lack of independence from KANU of the judiciary and the electoral commission worked against fair political competition in Kenya. Against this reality, and given the SMD-FPTP Kenyan electoral system, the incumbent President Moi secured victory with 37 percent of the votes cast in the 1992 general elections compared to a combined opposition tally of 63 percent. Similarly, KANU won 100 of the parliamentary seats to the combined opposition's 88 seats. The same results were replicated in the 1997 general elections when President Moi once again secured victory with 41 percent of the votes cast against 59 percent for the combined opposition. The inequity of the Kenyan electoral system was further manifested in the fact that KANU received a higher proportion of parliamentary seats (51 percent) than its proportion of the popular vote (43 percent). The disproportionality index was 8 in favor of KANU (see Barkan et al, 2001).

Finally, the concerted efforts to push the government toward constitutional re-engineering bore fruit in 2000 when, through an Act of Parliament, the Constitution of Kenya Review Commission (CKRC) was constituted paving the way for the review to commence. However, as if to underscore the KANU regime's ambivalence toward the review process, the 2002 elections were called while the review process was still in progress, albeit near completion. Fortunately the key opposition politicians, namely Mwai Kibaki, Michael Wamalwa, and Charity Ngilu had found common ground and were now united under the National Alliance Party of Kenya (NAK). The position of these "Big Three," was buttressed by the fallout in KANU following President Moi's decision to single-handedly pick his successor in the party. Key politicians including Raila Odinga, Moody Awori, Kalonzo Musyoka, and George Saitoti, among others, decamped from KANU, took over the little-known Liberal Democratic Party (LPD), and joined forces with NAK in a coalition now renamed National Alliance Rainbow Coalition

(NARC). It was within this conjuncture that KANU was trounced in the December 2002 polls as shown in Table 5.5 below. It was a scenario reminiscent of the MMD victory over UNIP in Zambia in 1991.

As Table 5.5 below illustrates, the decision by the opposition to present a united front in the 2002 Kenyan elections resulted in a majoritarian electoral system by default much in the same way as the Zambian scenario in 1991. In this event, the electoral contest for the presidency was largely between NARC's Mwai Kibaki and KANU's Uhuru Kenyatta. The opposition's Mwai Kibaki garnered an impressive victory of 62 percent of the votes cast compared to KANU's Uhuru Kenyatta's 31 percent. The other three fringe candidates, Simeon Nyachae, James Orengo, and Waweru Ng'ethe, had little impact on the electoral outcome one way or the other. It should be noted, however, that the scenario presented in Table 5.5 is somewhat fallacious. This is on account of the fact that unlike the other four parties, NARC was not a single political party, but a coalition of parties. First, Mwai Kibaki's Democratic Party (DP), Michael Wamalwa's Forum for Restoration of Democracy in Kenya (FORD-K), and Charity Ngilu's National Party of Kenya (NPK) joined forces to create the National Alliance (Party) of Kenya (NAK) to which each of the parties was a corporate member. Then, following the fallout in KANU mentioned above, those who defected, led by Raila Odinga, took over the Liberal Democratic Party (LDP) and linked up with NAK, creating the new grand coalition of NARC. All the named individuals, Mwai Kibaki, Michael Wamalwa, Charity Ngilu, and Raila Odinga, contested the 1997 presidential election. Quite obviously, had each one of them led their respective parties to contest the 2002 elections, they would have splintered the opposition and without doubt, the KANU candidate would have emerged victorious with his 31 percent of the total valid votes cast.

Table 5.5: 2002 Kenyan Presidential Election Results

Name/Party	Votes	% of Total
Kibaki/NARC	3,647,658	62.21%
Kenyatta/KANU	1,836,055	31.31%
Nyachae/FORD-P	345,161	5.89%
Orengo/SDP	24,568	0.42%
Ng'ethe/CCU	10,030	0.17%
Total	5,863,472	100%

Source: Electoral Commission of Kenya

Table 5.6 below shows the results of the 2002 Kenyan parliamentary election. Compared to the rate of disproportionality in the Zambian 2001 parliamentary election (see Table 5.3), the Kenyan case illustrates some more modest disproportionality. In this case, NARC garnered 45.8 percent of the total valid votes cast in the parliamentary election, but received 59.5 percent of the seats in the National Assembly, demonstrating a disproportionality index of 14 in favor of NARC. The disproportionality indices for KANU, FORD-P, and Safina are within acceptable limits. Three other parties, FORD-A, Sisi Kwa Sisi, and Shirikisho roughly balanced the proportion of their total votes with the proportion of their seats. Nonetheless, 25 other minor political parties cumulatively received 12 percent of the total votes cast but none of them secured representation in parliament. The import of this is that the SMD-FPTP electoral system tends to encourage the proliferation of minor political parties that have the consequence of scattering votes, but without any real chances of earning representation in the National Assembly. What is interesting from Table 5.6 below is the shift in position in regard to the beneficiaries of vote disproportionality. Whereas in 1997 and 1992, it was KANU that benefited, in 2002, it was the opposition coalition, NARC. The implication here is that the disproportional nature of the SMD-FPTP electoral system naturally favors the dominant party of the moment.

Table 5.6: Results of 2002 Kenyan Parliamentary Elections

Party	Votes	% of Total	Seats	% of Total	Disprop. Index
NARC	2,697,450	45.82%	125	59.5%	14
KANU	1,652,767	28.07%	64	30.4%	2
FORD-P	492,350	8.36%	14	6.6%	-2
Safina	209,151	3.55%	2	1.0%	-2
FORD-A	82,505	1.40%	2	1.0%	0
Sisi Kwa Sisi	35,826	0.61%	2	1.0%	0
Shirikisho	14,114	0.23%	1	0.5%	0
Others (25)	702,883	11.96%	0	0.0%	-12
Total	5,887,046	100%	210	100%	—

Source: Tabulated from Electoral Commission of Kenya Figures

NARC's electoral victory over KANU in 2002 heralded much rejoicing and expectations of a new mode of politics. Indeed, one of NARC's principal campaign pledges was a new constitutional dispensation for the country within the first one hundred days of its presidency, granted that the constitutional review process was already at the advanced drafting stage. On assumption of power in January 2003 however, the target date for a new constitution was pushed forward by six months. Ten months down the road, the constitutional review process was adjourned to January 2004! In January 2004, President Kibaki promised that all efforts would be made to have a new constitution by June 30, 2004. This date also passed with the promise unmet and with Kibaki and his cronies now evasive about setting a deadline. The stalling of the process is a function of disagreement over power sharing between the presidency and a proposed premiership. Those who had advocated for this arrangement during the Moi incumbency such as President Mwai Kibaki, Minister Kiraitu Murungi, parliamentarian Koigi wa Wamwere, and clergymen Peter Njenga and Timothy Njoya among others, became its chief opponents. Concentration of power in the presidency was bad under Moi; it became okay once they assumed power—a classical failure of the shoe-on-the-other-foot test (see Nasong'o, forthcoming).

The foregoing vindicates Harbeson's (1999: 51) assertion that Kenya " . . . provides one of the clearest examples in Africa of the precariousness of undertaking multiparty elections as the first step toward democracy before inter-party agreement has been forged and the fundamental rules of the game reformed." He rightly concludes that donor pressure upon the Kenyan government to permit multiparty elections should, in retrospect, have extended to fashioning a broader multiparty agreement on reforming the rules of the game, and perhaps to electing a constituent assembly to draft a new constitution. However, though external actors should take some of the blame, the greater blame lies squarely with opposition politicians in Kenya. They seem not to be committed democrats but strategically sing the democratic song as a way of facilitating their own stab at power. Once in power, they revert to their true colors. It may thus be argued that the social struggles for democracy across time and place are fundamentally aimed at serving sectional interests though they may at times, through the stroke of luck, serve the interests of the larger society in general (see Hamalengwa, 1992).

This eventuality is a function of the paradox of political liberalization without fundamental restructuring of political processes and institutions to positively reshape the strategic context of political competition and the management of public affairs. John Harbeson argues that the push for democratization in the early 1990s suffered from a disproport᠂ ᠃ate emphasis on the conduct of initial, national-level multiparty elections. This temporally constrained, election-centric conception of transition phases according to Harbeson (1999: 42–43), lies in the implicit excessive expectations of this period. The expectations included the presumptions that: (1) Democratic transitions will necessarily produce regime change from an incumbent authoritarian to a new democratically inclined regime. (2) Initial multiparty elections and/or regime change will ipso facto generate the momentum necessary to produce subsequent, broader patterns of democratization. (3) This momentum will be sufficient to generate the means for the fulfillment of the broader array of democratization tasks in the consolidation phase. (4) The initial multiparty elections taking place at the national level will lead to democratization at the subnational levels. (5) The polity itself will remain sufficiently stable to sustain transition and subsequent consolidation phases of democratization.

Obviously, these assumptions were mistaken. Accordingly, as Reynolds and Sisk (1998: 11) argue, there is a growing sense both in academic and policy circles that the promotion of rapid democratization in Africa at the beginning of the 1990s, with its emphasis on multiparty elections without much attention to electoral systems design, was misguided at best, a fundamental mistake at worst. However, this may be so in countries such as Kenya and Zambia, where opposition forces squandered the chances for forcing incumbents into renegotiating new rules of the game. In others such as Benin, Malawi, Mali, Mozambique, and South Africa among others, having started off with constitutional reengineering, they have bright prospects for democratic consolidation.

CONCLUSION

This chapter has focused on the role of electoral system design in the new multiparty elections in Africa with specific reference to the cases of Kenya and Zambia. It has noted that electoral systems are designed to perform three key functions. First, they serve to translate the votes cast into seats in a legislative chamber, and into the selection of executives. Second, electoral systems serve as channels for holding representatives and executives accountable to the electorate. In essence, they bestow the electorate with the right to renew or revoke the mandate of their governors at regular intervals. Third, electoral systems perform the normative function of structuring the boundaries of acceptable political discourse by providing incentives to competitors for power, especially political parties, to couch their appeal to the electorate in distinct ways thus providing them with clearly delineated alternative political agendas. The chapter has noted that the two electoral dimensions that have significant implications for electoral outcomes and the quality of representation are electoral formula and constituency size.

In respect to constituency size, it was noted that the incumbent KANU regime in Kenya used electoral constituency malapportionment to create more constituencies in areas that were overwhelmingly pro-KANU. This strategy assured KANU of more seats in parliament following the 1992 and 1997 elections even with fewer overall votes, but was a gross violation of the cardinal democratic principle of fair representation and equality of the vote. With regard to electoral formula, on the other hand, it was observed that both Kenya and Zambia use SMD-FPTP systems, which require a mere plurality of the votes cast for one to win the presidency. As a result, the incumbent in Kenya won the first and second multiparty elections in 1992 and 1997 with only 37 and 41 percent of the votes cast respectively against the combined opposition's 63 and 59 percent respectively. It was argued that had the electoral formula required an absolute majority for one to win, a run-off between the incumbent and his closest rival could easily have resulted in the defeat of the incumbent as happened in the first multiparty elections in Benin in 1991, Mali in 1992, and Madagascar in 1993. The Zambian opposition was lucky in this regard in the sense that they managed to unite into one party and thus forced a majoritarian political outcome by default in the country's first multiparty elections in 1991. However, the inequity of the Zambian electoral system was illustrated in the third multiparty elections in 2001 when the eventual winner, Levy Mwanawasa, garnered a mere 28 percent of the votes cast, with 72 percent split out amongst ten opposition candidates, with the closest competitor to the eventual winner garnering 27 percent of the vote.

In the final analysis, it may be concluded from the foregoing analysis that electoral system design is of crucial importance to the cause of promoting and consolidating democracy. As the evidence examined in this chapter amply demonstrate, the type of electoral system under which elections are held has far-reaching implications for the competitiveness of the political game, as well as for the quality and fairness of representation. It thus is no wonder that African countries that reverted to multiparty politics following a comprehensive review of their constitutions enhanced electoral competitiveness providing, in the process, circumstances under which incumbent authoritarian regimes could be defeated. In the quest for redesigning the strategic environment of political engagement in democratizing countries, therefore, no exercise is as important as designing an electoral system that not only enhances fair competition and ensures just representation, but one that also enhances political cooperation across social groups and thus serves the function of conflict mitigation in multiethnic societies. In any event, the electoral system is the sole institution that helps to determine what parties look like, who is represented in parliament, and ultimately, who governs.

Chapter Six
Rational Politics and Democratization

According to George Tsebelis (1990: 40), the rational choice approach assumes that individual action is an optimal adaptation to an institutional environment while interaction between individuals is assumed to be an optimal response to each other. Hence the prevailing institutions, or the rules of the game, determine the behavior of actors, which in turn produces political or social outcomes. The assumption is that whatever rational actors do, be they individuals, political parties, interest groups, or governments, they consider net payoffs, which may be material or psychological, egoistic or altruistic. Nonetheless, as Margaret Levi (1999: 20) points out, although the choice of each actor may be intentional and individually rational, the results may seem unintentional and socially irrational to many. It is in regard to this that Tsebelis argues that seeming suboptimal choices by actors indicate the presence of "nested games" wherein events or strategies in one arena influence the way the game is played in another arena. Based on the assumption of rationality, therefore, this study has so far delineated the nature of the strategic interaction among the key political actors in Zambia and Kenya; the forms of constraint appertaining thereto; the search for equilibrium between the political forces at play, and how these processes impacted upon electoral outcomes in the two countries between 1991 and 2002.

Chapter One focused on the emergence of authoritarianism in Africa as embodied in the rise of the single-party state system soon after political independence. It argued that virtually all African countries emerged into independence under nascent multiparty political systems but political consolidation by the dominant political elite saw the outlawing of opposition political parties. The parties of independence in Kenya and Zambia, as elsewhere in Africa, were not all-encompassing nationalist movements. Their capacity for mobilization and control was increasingly circumscribed once independence was attained. The new political elite faced spirited opposition and challenge from both ethnoregional and ideological groups, which undermined their power positions. To maximize their power and insure themselves against competition, therefore, the dominant elite rationalistically opted for single-party authoritarianism, which they justified as a logical response to the politics of fragmentation and a basis for the onerous task of nation building. For all practical purposes, Chapter One contended that the actualization of the authoritarian paradigm in Africa was a deliberate rational choice on the part of the dominant political elite to maximize and monopolize power and thus reign supreme. This eventuality was a result of the strategic interaction between the incumbent political elite and the nascent opposition parties within the rubric of weak political institutions and fragile constitutional frameworks.

The cases of Kenya and Zambia, especially the latter, amply illustrate how the single-party state rationally emerged out of a bitter and prolonged political conflict, which had demonstrated the difficulties the leadership faced in asserting control. In Kenya, the groups that faced each other in KANU in the mid-1960s were ideologically oriented, with leftists who espoused radical agrarian reforms, Africanization of the economy, and land redistribution, pitted against the conservatives who ruled out nationalization of the economy and wished to maintain the pre-independence status quo for their own self-aggrandizement. Within UNIP in Zambia at the same time, the political groups that competed for the control of the party and government policies were generally ethnoregional groups, which responded to their constituents in the provinces, regions, and localities. In both countries, this party factionalism and sectionalism became apparent in 1966. In Zambia it climaxed in the formation of the UP by dissidents from UNIP led by Nalumino Mundia. The UP was a result of growing disenchantment and relative deprivation felt by many political leaders of Lozi origin within UNIP over what they regarded as the neglect of Barotseland (now Western Province) in terms of system distributive outputs. It was also in view of what they regarded as Bemba domination of the party. In Kenya, on the other hand, party factionalism culminated in the resignation of Vice President Oginga Odinga and his formation of the KPU following an orchestrated move to marginalize him and his fellow progressives from the center of power.

Once the single-party system was established in both Kenya and Zambia, as elsewhere in Africa, provision was made for the supremacy of the party organs over state organs and the notion of single-party rule was objectified and elevated to the level of a hegemonic ideology. This was done by attributing political independence to the dominant party; objectifying the party as the embodiment of nationalism; projecting it as a moral community; equating the party with the state and presenting it as the agent of development; and positing the single-party system as a reflection of traditional African democracy. By using the ideology of the one-party state, African leaders sought to transform their regimes towards actualization of political unanimity. They went about this through various ways. These included co-optation, intimidation, exile, or deportation of political opponents. Other mechanisms included modification of the electoral system to make competition impossible; transformation of the inherited constitution to centralize wide discretionary power into the executive and to restrict the role of representative institutions such as parliament. This authoritarian paradigm of governance also saw the increasing use of a criterion of political loyalty to select key administrators; administrative control over local government; reduction of the independence of the judiciary; as well as governmental control over the mass media, both print and electronic. Furthermore, it witnessed the erosion of consultation within the party and of accountability of the leadership to the members, even as the language of collective leadership was invoked. In other words, it was the antithesis of the democratic mode of governance.

The fact that in their quest to maximize their self-interest, rational actors face both institutional and environmental constraints is illustrated by the analysis of the push for democratization in Chapter Two. Whereas incumbent regimes both in Kenya and Zambia, and Africa generally would have preferred to maintain a monopoly over political power within the purview of single-party states, they were forced by environmental circumstances to open up political space to competition. Churches, university student organizations, NGOs, as well as professional organizations such as the Law Society of Kenya constituted the main institutional opponents of the single party system in Kenya. Intellectuals and university students in Zambia also constituted significant opposition to the single-party state, but of critical importance was the role of the labor movement as well as the business community. These internal political forces were augmented by a number of key factors in the international environment to constrain the viability of single-party systems in Africa. The first external factor was the collapse of the totalitarian communist regimes of Eastern Europe, an eventuality that served to energize the pro-democracy forces in Africa and to legitimize demands for political change. The second key factor was the economics of SAPs. This had its greatest impact in Zambia where implementation of IMF/World Bank austerity measures led to riots in major cities that essentially marked the beginning of the end of the Kaunda regime. Third was the aid crunch especially against Kenya by both the country's bilateral and multilateral lenders, all of whom predicated further lending on political liberalization.

In the face of the above forces, the incumbent regimes in Kenya and Zambia faced narrowed choices. In Zambia, President Kaunda opted for a referendum to decide on whether to adopt multiparty politics. He then postponed it, but ultimately opted for multipartyism without the referendum. In so doing, Kaunda sought to steal the initiative for political change from the MMD, which, gauging from the popular turnouts at its political rallies, was sure to win the referendum. In addition, by acceding to multi-partyism much earlier than the referendum would have allowed, Kaunda acted in his own self-interest. He thereby afforded himself a whole year to repackage his party and political agenda in readiness for the electoral showdown in October 1991. Kenya's President Moi faced similar options. First, he constituted a committee to collect views from Kenyans on the future of the party system. Whereas the committee, in spite of overwhelming evidence to the contrary, reported that majority Kenyans were for the continuity of the single-party system; and a KANU National Delegates Conference gathered in 1991 at Kasarani, Nairobi was ready to rubber-stamp the committee's "findings," Moi announced, to the surprise of the delegates, that it was time for political pluralism. In so doing he, like Kaunda, sought to stem the tide of agitation for political change and to placate external aid donors, as well as to control the momentum for political change to his own advantage.

At the end of the day, Kaunda was overwhelmingly vanquished in the first multiparty elections of October 1991. Indeed, the tide against Kaunda was such that Zambians averred that, "[i]f a frog stands against Kaunda, we will elect the frog!" For his part, Moi emerged victorious in the 1992 elections in spite of the popular slogan "Moi must go!" and even went on to win again with an improved tally of votes in 1997. Whereas there are a number of factors that account for this eventuality, this study hypothesized three principal explanatory variables. First, it was hypothesized that the nature and structure of the politically active civil society organizations is an important factor in determining the success of the new democratic paradigm over the old authoritarian forces. Secondly, the study hypothesized that the instrumentalist mobilization of politicized ethnicity and its deployment in the service of ethnic bossmen is an important explanatory variable in the electoral victory or defeat of incumbent authoritarian regimes. Finally, it was hypothesized that the third key determinant of the electoral victory or defeat of the incumbent authoritarian regimes in their first contest with opposition political parties was electoral system design.

With regard to the first hypothesis, the analysis in Chapter Three demonstrated that the nature, organization, and resource base of the politically active civil society organizations is an essential variable in explaining incumbent regime change and/or continuity in the face of democratization. With regard to Zambia, The key political actor within civil society ranks was the labor movement led by the Zambia Congress of Trade Unions— ZCTU. The autonomous ZCTU provided channels through which economic grievances were expressed and organized into an electoral bid for state power. ZCTU's organizational structures served an imperative role of mobilizing support for MMD, with trade union offices all over the country serving as recruiting centers for the new party. The ZCTU had a relatively sound resource base based on membership dues; hence members had a stake in transition politics and remained politically mobilized. In Kenya on the other hand, the equivalent of ZCTU, the Central Organization of Trade Unions—COTU, had been affiliated to the ruling party, KANU by 1991, and its leaders co-opted for their own self-aggrandizement and to the political advantage of the ruling elite. Consequently, the labor movement in Kenya remained politically obtuse. The key political player on the part of civil society organizations was the NGO movement. The limitation of this eventuality is that NGOs are non-membership organizations that are largely urban-based, whose activities remain sporadic, disconnected, and largely suspended from the mass publics. Furthermore, NGOs are highly donor dependent, are accountable to their benefactors, and lack collaborative synergy even among themselves, hence unlike the labor movement in Zambia, they failed to marshal the support necessary to effect political change in Kenya.

The second hypothesis relating to the role of ethnicity in electoral politics of transition was analyzed in Chapter Four with particular reference to the cases of Kenya and Zambia. It was noted that ethnicity is both functional and dysfunctional relative to the purposes for which it is mobilized. On the positive side, ethnicity provided a basis for organization of resistance against colonialism and for mobilization of nationalist movements in the fight for independence in Africa. Secondly, it provided the basis for adaptation to the uncertainty and insecurity caused by the rapid changes introduced by colonialism. Thirdly, ethnicity provides a sense of belonging as part of an interdependent layer of social relations between the individual and the state. It thus cushions the individual from the negative effects of alienation inherent in a modern complex society. Fourthly, ethnic movements raise issues concerning discrimination and oppression and thus contribute to democratic practice by demanding equity and justice in the distribution of public goods and services. Finally, mobilization of various ethnic populations behind various factions of a nation's elite contributes to decentralization of power, which is healthy for the institutionalization of democratic freedoms.

It was observed, however, that ethnicized politics is anathema to democratic transition in Africa. Chapter Four demonstrated that compared to Zambia, Kenya has a very high rate of ethnic politics that manifests itself in ethnic bloc-voting and ethnically exclusive political parties. This ethnicization of the political arena in Kenya has served to accentuate suspicion and rivalry and thus heightened the perception of political engagement as a zero-sum game. Overall, the high rate of politicized ethnicity in Kenya is caused by the unwillingness of elite actors to collaborate across ethnic divides. Yet it is incumbent upon the elite to establish credible multiethnic parties to facilitate mass support for such parties. Whereas cross-ethnic parties engendered a maximum coalition on the part of the Zambian opposition forces leading to their electoral victory in 1991, lack of elite collaboration is the principal explanation for the ethnic fragmentation of the Kenyan party system that was a major causal variable for the electoral defeat of the opposition in Kenya in 1992 and 1997. Indeed, when the political elite in Kenya learnt from their 1992 and 1997 electoral experience and decided to come together in a grand alliance in 2002, they trounced the incumbent KANU regime.

Finally, in respect to the role of the electoral system design, it was noted in Chapter Five that the type of electoral system, especially the system's electoral formula and constituency size had serious implications for electoral outcomes in the first multiparty elections in Africa, as well as for the quality and fairness of representation. For instance, the incumbent KANU regime in Kenya used electoral constituency malapportionment to create more constituencies in areas that were overwhelmingly pro-KANU. This strategy assured KANU of more seats in parliament even with fewer overall votes, but was a gross violation of the cardinal democratic principle of fair representation and equality of the vote. With regard to electoral formula, on the other hand, it was observed that both Kenya and Zambia use SMD-FPTP systems, which require a mere plurality of the votes cast for one to win a political seat, including the presidency. As a result, the incumbent in Kenya won the first multiparty elections in 1992 and 1997 with only 37 and 41 percent of the votes cast respectively against the combined opposition's 63 and 59 percent respectively. It was argued that had the electoral formula required an absolute majority for one to win, a run-off between the incumbent and his closest rival could easily have resulted in the defeat of the incumbent as happened in the first multiparty elections in Benin in 1991, Mali in 1992, and Madagascar in 1993. The Zambian opposition was lucky in this regard in the sense that they managed to unite into one party and thus forced a majoritarian political outcome by default in the country's first multiparty elections in 1991. However, the inequity of the Zambian electoral system was illustrated in the third multiparty elections in 2001 when the eventual winner garnered a mere 28 percent of the votes cast against his closest competitor's 27 percent. 72 percent of the vote was split out amongst ten opposition candidates. Electoral system design thus has a significant impact on electoral outcomes, with regime change in the first multiparty elections occurring mainly in countries where the electoral systems were redesigned to facilitate fair competition such as requirement for an absolute majority to win the presidency. Examples here include Benin, Central African Republic, Congo-Brazzaville, Madagascar, Mali, and Sierra Leone.

THE QUESTION OF RATIONALITY

The rationality undergirding the emergence of single-party authoritarianism in Africa as well as the environmental constraints on the continued viability of the single-party system has been elaborated above. Nonetheless, a major question remains to be addressed: what was rational about the role of civil society organizations, ethnicity, and electoral system design as discussed in Chapters Three, Four, and Five? The significance of this question warrants separate analysis of each of the three variables.

Civil Society and Rational Politics

The centrality of the labor movement as a component of civil society in the victory of the opposition MMD over the incumbent UNIP in Zambia in 1991 has been underscored. The structure of the labor movement was invaluable in mobilizing support for the new party. In addition, the apparent honesty and sincerity of Chiluba, the opposition presidential candidate, who was fresh from the ranks of civil society and represented long-standing opposition to the Kaunda regime, put the opposition on a moral high ground. It is noteworthy, however, that the MMD was not, in fact, formed by Chiluba, nor by those who had stood firm against single-party authoritarianism over time. The party was formed in May 1990 first as a movement by two prominent ex-UNIP politicians, former finance minister Arthur Wina as its leader, and former foreign affairs minister, Vernon Mwanga as his deputy. Prominent UNIP politicians joined MMD, including Humphrey Mulemba, a UNIP MP and ex-UNIP secretary general; Ludwig Sondashi, a UNIP MP and former member of UNIP Central Committee; former solicitor general Levy Mwanawasa (who succeeded Chiluba as president in 2001); former Speaker of the National Assembly, Robinson Nabulyato; and former minister for mines, Andrew Kashita (Ihonvbere, 1996a: 149; Donge, 1995: 199).

These prominent former UNIP politicians had fallen out of favor with President Kaunda. For them therefore, the legitimization of the forces of political change simply provided them with a chance to get back at their former boss and secure their lost sinecure positions. As Chabal and Daloz (1999) argue, the MMD unity was a clear division between two kinds of MMD supporters. First was the group of "big men" who were rationalistically ready to play the record of renewal, safe in the knowledge that their financial support for the opposition would give them the pride of place in the new government. The second group of MMD supporters was a variety of young hopefuls often politically sophisticated and well informed about the world beyond Africa but largely bereft of the resources necessary to acquire political prominence. Since the first group did not include any obvious candidates for leadership, they readily threw their support behind Frederick Chiluba—the living star from the second group—with a reputation for having hitherto steadfastly refused co-optation into ruling circles (Chabal & Daloz, 1999: 34).

Once he assumed power, therefore, Chiluba remained torn between the demands of his powerful backers, who expected rapid payoffs, and the expectations of the population at large. He thus faced contradictions between his original promise to reform and the distributive imperatives on which his shot-term legitimacy rested, at least in the eyes of those who sponsored him. In the final analysis, the new president resorted to old-style practices of governance and, despite his pronouncements, effectively renounced any attempt at a radical reform of the political system. Against this background, corruption became rampant and endemic in the new government. As Julius Ihonvbere (1996: 185) notes, "[t]he corruption within the MMD is adjudged to be more pervasive, more sophisticated, and more damaging than what had obtained under Kaunda." In any event, after assuming power, the MMD did not attempt to restructure or reconstitute the Zambian state to reflect an emergent democratic political dispensation. Instead, as Julius Nyang'oro (1997) notes, it retained in large measure the ministers, institutions, and policies of the Kaunda regime and succumbed to the same authoritarian tendencies that characterized UNIP during its hey-day. This, in the words of Mphaisha (1996) amounted to a "retreat from democracy."

Indeed, as Bornwell Chikulo (2000) writes, contrary to general expectations that political and economic liberalization would reduce the level of corruption, under the Chiluba regime corruption became a very serious problem. It not only became widespread but endemic and systemic, especially among cabinet ministers and other officials. Such corruption included abuse of office and graft; theft and financial mismanagement; drug trafficking; and looting of commercial banks (see Nasong'o, 2003; Chikulo, 2000: 164–171). President Chiluba went so far as to use the powers vested in him by the Corrupt Practices Act of 1980 to shield senior cabinet ministers from prosecution as recommended by the Anti-Corrup-tion Commission. This led Dean Mungomba, Zambia Democratic Con-gress (ZDC) leader to argue thus:

> . . . [i]t is evident, therefore, that the Chiluba regime has reached the pathological condition of systemic corruption. . . . nothing much has been done to curb the spread of corruption owing to the fact that Presi-dent Chiluba, Defense Minister Ben Mwila, and Finance Minister Ronald Penza are the most corrupt individuals in the country. . . . Between Mwila, Chiluba and Penza they have turned this country and its economy into three competing enterprises. (Chikulo, 2000: 176–177)

Yet in spite of overwhelming evidence of corruption against the top echelon of the MMD leadership, Chiluba refused to acknowledge that corruption was indeed a problem. He parried charges against senior government offi-cials and challenged the public and Western donors to produce evidence of corruption. Consequently, none of Chiluba's corrupt ministers was prose-cuted and only a few token dismissals were made to placate international donors.

President Chiluba's reluctance to act against corruption was initially explained by apologists of his regime, who gave him the benefit of doubt, as a problem of weak leadership, with Chiluba being portrayed as a weak leader, unable to control his colleagues, and indecisive on disciplinary mat-ters. The second explanation is, however, more plausible. This explains Chiluba's condoning of corruption in terms of the fact that it was pay-back time for him with regard to the network of political predators and oppor-tunists who had joined and financed the MMD during its formative years of the early 1990s. "These political predators were subsequently rewarded with appointments to top positions in the MMD government and are now sharing the spoils of power, while the 'reformists' have left, citing corruption and failure to implement policy and electoral promises as the rationale for their exit" (Chikulo, 2000: 177). Against this background, Bornwell Chikulo notes that a general perception emerged viewing Chiluba's reluctance to act against corruption as emanating from the fact that corruption was personally beneficial to him and his collaborators.

It may be posited, further, that Chiluba's motive for failing to act firmly against corruption may not merely have been due to personal gain but may also be interpreted as a rational quest for political survival by an embattled president. As Mphaisha (1996: 81) states:

> Leaders like Chiluba use political patronage to co-opt their critics because they know that those affected either want material gain or want to protect their business interests through the possession of politi-. cal power. It is mainly this realization that explains the Chiluba government's emphasis on economic reforms, which have been intended to benefit MMD leaders through the purchase of parastatal organizations and winning of government contracts.

It thus is no wonder that authoritarianism and its associated malaise of corruption became even more endemic in Chiluba's Zambia in spite of the change of regime and the democratic credentials with which the new president rode to power.

With regard to Kenya, civil society organizations (CSOs) contributed immensely to the process of pushing for the opening up of political space, and have continued to articulate the interests of the common people vis-à-vis the state. Although much of the criticism of CSOs in Kenya has been on the fact that they are largely urban based and disconnected from the masses they purport to represent, Stephen Orvis (2003) shows in his empirical study of four NGOs in Kenya,[1] that these organizations have shifted their attention to focus on the rural areas. In so doing, Orvis posits, they have begun to have a measurable impact on citizen understanding of politics. Nonetheless, the same rationalistic tendency toward self-interest within the ranks of Kenyan CSOs can be deduced. As noted in Chapter Three, these social formations were thrust onto the political stage as political norm setters and agents of political change by the policy shift on the part of international development financiers in the late 1980s. Donors shifted away from channeling development resources via state apparatuses to channeling the same through civil organizations. This policy shift was a function of the perception of the African State as too corrupt, opaque, and overly bureaucratic. For their part, NGOs as representatives of civil society were envisioned as bastions of liberty, transparency, and accountability; and thus they were regarded as the natural allies of the poor. Yet most of these organizations, just like the single-party state institutional legacy they seek to deconstruct, operate under highly personalized leaderships, which, though largely benevolent, as Ndegwa (1996) holds, are nevertheless unaccountable.

It is significant to note, further, that the unbridled enthusiasm with the political role of civil society in the early 1990s eschewed discussion of the requisite conditions for the social differentiation between civil society, political society, economic society, and parochial society. As a result, hastily constituted NGOs were funded to undertake political projects in the name of civic education, political mobilization, and shielding individuals from oppressive states. In addition, the democratic nature and orientation of CSOs in Africa was taken for granted, an assumption that was inherently without merit since the CSOs leadership is self-appointed and largely wanting in democratic credentials and orientation. It would seem that by the turn of the 1990s, authoritarianism was so entrenched in most African States that anyone purporting to be anti-establishment was regarded as a democrat. Arguably, most leaders of CSOs in Africa rationalistically seized the opportunity spawned by the evangelism for democracy and joined the democracy bandwagon not necessarily to serve the purpose of democratization, but their own selfish primitive accumulation interests. Given the worsening economic circumstances in Africa by the turn of the 1980s, a situation that was compounded by the implementation of SAPs, and the predication of aid to economic and political conditionality, the arena of privilege for ambitious and calculating individuals shifted from the state to the NGO world. As Wafula Buke (2004) rightly observes, the expansion of the NGO sector weakened the near monopoly of the state as an employer:

> The NGO sector provided an alternative and a lucrative one too . . .
> ·Through their funds, donor agencies inherited all the key personnel in
> the previously illegal organizations [fighting against authoritarianism
> as a patriotic duty], gave them bigger salaries, myriad benefits and priv-
> ileges but armed them with their own agenda . . . for the first time in
> the history of our country, it became paying to participate in the strug-
> gle against an incumbent government.

Clearly, therefore, some of the CSOs, especially as manifested in NGOs, share the alignment and project of the state-based elite in the form of self-advancement and personal accumulation. The emergence of what have come to be termed "MONGOs" (my own NGO) or "briefcase NGOs" in Kenyan political parlance, that are run as personal or family outfits points to this eventuality. Against this background, it is the chief executives of the NGOs who, in the process, get "empowered" partly vis-à-vis the state but mainly vis-à-vis rank and file members of civil society. As argued elsewhere, the speed with which some NGO executives transform themselves from modest living standards to bourgeois lifestyles complete with state-of-the-art limousines and palace-like residences is a glaring pointer to the fact that some of these outfits are largely avenues for accumulation within civil society much as the state has remained an arena for self-aggrandizement with regard to the political class. In essence, they are sources of "primitive accumulation" within a political game of democratization (see Nasong'o, 2002a, 2002b: 11–12; Gibson, 1994: 24). For example, in 2001, the executive director and trustees of SAREAT (Series on Alternative Research in East Africa Trust—an NGO established to promote good governance through research and publication) were taken to court by the FORD Foundation for misappropriating millions of dollars in grants to the NGO. The NGO has since closed down and its former executive director now works for another NGO!

Two other examples include the Institute for Civic Education in Africa (ICEDA) and the Civic Resources and Information Centre (CRIC). Both of these received the bulk of their funding from the United States Agency for International Development (USAID) and the Swedish International Development Agency (SIDA), the two leading providers of political aid to Kenyan CSOs. The two NGOs wound up when financial and programmatic audits could no longer justify their continued existence. With regard to ICEDA, its leader, a well-respected cleric and crusader for political pluralism, could not account for funds his organization received for a number of projects. Similarly, CRIC received funding for eight projects between 1995 and 1998, which was diverted and squandered. Ironically, as Owiti (2000) notes, though financial malfeasance was suspected early in both cases, funding continued and, in the interregnum, the chief executive of the CRIC, an esteemed democracy crusader within donor circles, received the prestigious Martin Luther King Jr. award for exemplary young leaders!

A fourth most bizarre case of the opportunism replete within CSO ranks involves a leading light in the civil society realm in Kenya. In this case, the CSO operative feigned injury on the budget day fracas of 1997,[2] got himself admitted into a Nairobi hospital and called the boss of a donor agency from his hospital bed to brief him on his "ordeal" that day. The donor, who had been procrastinating in approving a proposal by the "injured" civil society luminary promptly approved the proposal, had funding for the proposed project processed, and visited the guy in hospital, check in hand! (see Nasong'o, forthcoming; Owiti, 2000: 17). It is in view of this that Peter Wanbali (2001) contends that civic education is "puerile nonsense" that opportunist traders masquerading as principled civil society activists have used to cheat millions of dollars out of the gullible wallets of well-funded groups in Western countries.

The rational self-interest of CSOs is further manifested in the fact that most of them start off as specialists in particular social domains but over time, branch off into other areas with a view to attracting funding from as many sources as possible, and also in response to changing donor priorities. The reliance of these organizations on external sources of financial support forces them to strive to win the approval of Western donors, lenders, nations, and international monitors, rather than the loyalty and support of domestic constituencies, turning them into programmatic appendices of international funding agencies. Given this reality, most of these organizations are unable to effectively counter accusations that they are in the service of foreign rather than local interests. As noted in Chapter Three, the organizations' external linkages directly impinge upon their agendas and performance. Under such circumstances, their contribution to democratic transition remains only incidental rather than fundamental.

Finally, a close observation of the Kenyan politics of transition reveals that some of the civil society operatives strategically use their political activism for change to build their own individual political profiles with an eye on parleying into electoral politics. They later use their "democratic credentials" to launch political careers and to negotiate for prime positions at the national table of "eating chiefs" (see Amutabi, forthcoming). Notables among this group in Kenya include the likes of Kivutha Kibwana of the NCEC fame, former LSK chairman, Paul Muite, and human rights crusaders and prodemocracy activist lawyers Kiraitu Murungi and Mirugi Kariuki, among others. All these personalities used their prominent roles in the prodemocracy movement within the realm of civil society to launch successful political careers. In the NARC government that assumed power after the December 2002 electoral ouster of the KANU regime, Kibwana was appointed assistant minister of state in the president's office, Murungi became minister for justice and constitutional affairs, while Muite assumed the chairmanship of the Parliamentary Select Committee on constitutional reform. All of them transformed from the prodemocracy and human rights firebrands of the Moi era to anti-constitutional review, hawkish defenders of the same authoritarian institutional legacy that NARC inherited from KANU and which they had built their democratic credentials fighting against. The sense of betrayal on the part of Kenyans in view of these developments is well captured by Rana Warah (2004: 14), who laments:

> [t]hen [under Moi], we knew we had a dictator as president and found ways to survive in a hostile, autocratic environment; today, our so-called liberators have proved to be no better than wolves in sheep's clothing. Our sense of betrayal today is far greater than it was even three years ago, because everyone we thought was on our side, was actually only looking out for himself and herself.

Mahmood Mamdani (1995) couldn't have been more right in his perspective of civil society as a realm of contradictory possibilities in which demands of social movements, like those for democracy and human rights, ought not to be viewed as general demands of civil society against the state. Indeed, reaching beyond these assumptions fathoms and clarifies the fact that for the Kibwanas, Muites, Kariukis, and Murungis of Kenya, they were anti-authoritarianism under KANU not because they were prodemocracy but simply because they were left out of the gravy train. For them, democracy simply meant creating the requisite conditions for them to replace the previous KANU regime so that they could also enjoy the same enormous powers that the authoritarian institutions afforded the previous regime. For instance, in justifying opposition to the creation of the position of prime minister, NARC minister for transport and communications, John Michuki, argued that establishing such a position to reduce the powers of the presidency was only necessary when Moi was in power " . . . because we wanted one of our own to share power with him." For him, President Kibaki is "a good man" and there thus is no longer need to care about the enormous powers of the presidency! (Kendo, 2003).

Rationality and Ethnic Politics

On the face of it, it is apparent that the maximum coalition that involved a cross-section of ethnic and interest groups within the MMD would be the most rational strategy for the opposition to adopt in order to oust an incumbent regime. In this case, all the forces ranged against President Kaunda collaborated and mobilized across ethnic divides for purposes of effecting regime change in October 1991. They even went so far to pick an individual from within the ranks of civil society, untarnished by involvement in the power politics of the one party state, and presented him to the electorate as the alternative to the discredited Kaunda, and the symbol of a new dawn. On the other hand, the extent of ethnic politics in Kenya, the ethnic fragmentation, and the tendency for each major political elite to go it alone appears so irrational. In fact, as demonstrated in Chapter Four, it was this reality of ethnic politics that fragmented opposition votes in Kenya both in 1992 and 1997, leading to the incumbent regime to retain power on both occasions. What was rational about this ethnic fragmentation that was so detrimental to the interests of the opposition?

As noted in Chapter Four, the emergence of the original FORD in Kenya was reminiscent of the MMD in Zambia and for some time, the popularity of FORD, gauged from the crowds it attracted at its political rallies, was a waking nightmare for the incumbent KANU. The tide of opposition and public opinion against KANU was so intense that it was assumed the opposition would triumph in the first multiparty elections. It was on the basis of this assumption that politicians in the opposition began to position themselves as advantageously as possible for purposes of securing key positions in the new political dispensation that was expected to be ushered in by the elections. Accordingly, as Walter Oyugi (1998: 302) observes, the jostling for power increasingly " . . . assumed ethnic character with Kikuyu delegations made of prominent personalities in FORD reportedly visiting Matiba regularly in London to impress on him that a leadership vacuum existed in the party." This was presumably on account of the advanced age of the de facto FORD leader, Oginga Odinga. The rivalry for FORD's presidential ticket between Matiba and Odinga intensified on the former's return from London where he had spent close to a year recuperating from a stroke he suffered while in detention for his presumed role in instigating the 1997 *Saba Saba* riots. Within this context, Masinde Muliro, a Luhyia, made a bid for the same ticket with a view to emerging as a compromise candidate between Odinga and Matiba. Unfortunately, Muliro, arguably Kenya's most principled politician of rare political sobriety, passed away under mysterious circumstances on August 14, 1992.[3]

The rivalry over the FORD leadership and presidential ticket culminated in the party's split into FORD-A, led by Kenneth Matiba, a Kikuyu, and FORD-K, led by Oginga Odinga, a Luo, with the situation in the opposition compounded by the formation of the DP, led by Mwai Kibaki, another Kikuyu. The DP was formed in December 1991 by a section of wealthy Kikuyu associated with the former GEMA on realization that the GEMA community lacked credible representation in the then interim FORD leadership. As noted in Chapter Four, a prominent DP supporter told his listeners while on a recruitment mission in a social club in Nairobi: "Who is Gachoka to represent Kikuyu interest? Does he measure up to Odinga, Muliro and Shikuku?" (Oyugi 1998: 303). When it appeared during the May-November 1992 period that Matiba might not be a serious candidate on account of the state of his health and wrangling within FORD-A, where Martin Shikuku, the secretary general, also made a bid for the party's ticket for the presidency, it was to the DP that most of the Kikuyu defecting from KANU turned following the dissolution of parliament. It was against this background that the opposition vote in 1992 was divided between Matiba, Kibaki, and Odinga, allowing the incumbent President Moi to sail through. Indeed, it is arguable that had there been only one Kikuyu opposition candidate in 1992, it is likely that he would have won. This is borne out by the fact that the combined vote for the two Kikuyu candidates, Mwai Kibaki and Kenneth Matiba, who drew their main support from the same constituency, was 45.78 percent of the total votes cast, compared to the eventual winner's (President Moi's) 36.91 percent.[4]

It is apparent therefore, that the choices, decisions, and actions of opposition politicians in Kenya were rational and strategic at the individual level. However, cumulatively, they seem to have been so erratic and irrational. This reality of the Kenyan politics dovetails with Margaret Levi's (1999: 20) observation in regard to the rational choice approach that although the choice of each actor may be intentional and individually rational, the results may seem unintentional and socially irrational to many. It is in regard to this that George Tsebelis argues that seeming suboptimal choices by actors indicate the presence of "nested games" wherein events or strategies in one arena influence the way the game is played in another arena. In respect to the Kenyan situation, the opposition politicians were not only playing the game at the national level where unity was needed to supplant the incumbent regime, but they were also playing to their ethnic constituencies in order to advance their political currency at the national level as explained below. The game of national transitional politics was thus nested within the game of advancing sectional and ethnic interests.

Nevertheless, if the three opposition politicians in 1992 were convinced that the end of the KANU regime was assured in the 1992 polls hence their selfish individual desire to replace Moi, what was rational about four more opposition candidates contesting against Moi in the 1997 polls? Was it a case of failure to learn from the 1992 opposition experience? This time round, opposition presidential candidates chose to strategically take advantage of their ethnically exclusive parties to force a run-off between Moi and his closest opponent. As elaborated in the section below, a rule was passed prior to the 1992 multiparty elections requiring a presidential winner to garner, in addition to a plurality of the national votes, at least 25 percent of the votes cast in at least five of the country's eight administrative provinces. These provinces in fact coincide with ethnic regions. With

FORD-K's Michael Wamalwa of Western Province, NDP's Raila Odinga of Nyanza, DP's Mwai Kibaki of Central, and SDP's Charity Ngilu of Eastern Province, it was calculated that these opposition candidates would lock out Moi from their ethnoregions of Luhyia, Luo, Kikuyu, and Kamba respectively, given their ethnically cohesive party support. They thus envisaged a presidential run-off by default in which one of them would trounce Moi. Once again, this was a miscalculation. Given KANU's multiethnic character (see Chapter Four), it managed to muster enough votes in Western, Nyanza, and Eastern Provinces to fulfill the 25 percent rule. It was only in Central Province among the Kikuyu that KANU was completely shut out.

Finally, the ethnic division in Kenya can also be explained in terms of the nature of the Kenyan politics right from independence compared to that of Zambia. In Zambia, Kenneth Kaunda pursued the politics of inclusion wherein the idea of maximum coalition was fostered, with key positions in government shared out on a balancing basis among the major ethnic groups in Zambia. This eventuality was a function of the fact that Kaunda himself was not a Zambian by birth. He was born in Malawi but moved and settled in Eastern Zambia with his missionary father as a young boy. To ensure support for himself and his UNIP government, therefore, Kaunda resorted to the politics of inclusion. On the other hand, Kenyan politics from the very beginning tended to be exclusive. For one to acquire political currency at the national level, one had to demonstrate that he had the following and loyalty of his own ethnic group. By sticking it out and contesting for the presidency on the basis of their ethnically exclusive parties in 1992 and 1997 therefore, Kenyan opposition politicians were simply boosting their bargaining power at the national level. It was within this context that when Michael Wamalwa, Charity Ngilu, and Raila Odinga "gave up" their presidential ambitions to support Mwai Kibaki in 2002, they were handsomely rewarded in proportion to the size of the ethnic constituency they brought to the table.

Indeed, the sharing of the key posts reflected a strategic calculation on the basis of the size of support each key politician brought to the coalition. Kibaki, from the most populous Kikuyu community was the sole opposition presidential candidate; Michael Wamalwa, from the second most populous Luhyia community was the running mate and vice president designate; Raila Odinga, from the Luo, the third most populous community was offered premiership; while Charity Ngilu and Kipruto Kirwa, from the Kamba and Kalenjin, two less populous communities were offered deputy premierships in the memorandum of understanding that sealed opposition unity against KANU in the December 2002 elections.[5]

Electoral System Design and Rational Choice

As shown in Chapter Five, the first multiparty elections in Zambia and Kenya in 1991 and 1992 respectively were held without a comprehensive restructuring of the electoral systems, and the rules of the game generally, of the two countries. The only thing that was done to the electoral rules of Zambia and Kenya was a single amendment to sections 2(A) and 4 of the Kenyan and Zambian constitutions respectively to legalize multiparty politics. The rest of the electoral system design including the first-past-the-post, winner take all mechanism, single-member constituency electoral districts, as well as electoral commissions constituted solely by the incumbents in the two systems without any form of vetting remained in place. The electoral rules were thus stacked against the opposition in the two countries in a big way. Indeed, it as in recognition of this reality that a group calling itself the Middle Ground Group (MGG) emerged in the case of Kenya with the sole purpose of persuading the three leading opposition presidential candidates—Oginga Odinga, Kenneth Matiba, and Mwai Kibaki—to agree on supporting just one of them in order to boost the chances of defeating the incumbent President Moi. However, the efforts of the MGG, led by Wangari Maathai among others, did not succeed. The key question then, is: why did the opposition in the two countries choose to go to the polls knowing that the electoral system was not in their favor? What was rational about this option?

The answer to the above question is provided by Josep Colomer (2000) according to whom such multiparty elections within a context of non-democratic rules of the game constitute strategic transitions and are, therefore, rational. Colomer, drawing from his analysis of transition politics in the former communist countries of Eastern Europe, contends that in the quest for democratic transition, authoritarian incumbents and their democratic oppositions always arrive at an intermediate formula between dictatorship and democracy:

> In order to be agreeable, a provisional compromise must include the calling of a multiparty election not securing an absolute winner. On the one hand, the rulers can rely upon their advantage as incumbents to turn the compromise into a lasting 'semidemocratic' regime, which would allow them not to be expelled from power or even to recover some of their previously challenged positions. On the other side, the democratic opposition can envisage the agreement as a mere transitory stage, giving it some chance of gaining power and introducing further reforms, which can lead to the eventual establishment of a democratic regime. (Colomer, 2000: 1–2)

Colomer argues that the uncertainty of further developments, which greatly depend on undetermined electoral results, makes the agreement rational for actors with different expectations. Indeed, this situation obtained both in Kenya and Zambia. Once multipartyism was legalized and the October 1991 elections called in Zambia, one of the key promises of the MMD during the campaign was that it would rewrite the constitution to strengthen the protection of civil liberties and to ensure the de-linkage of party and government. It however took two years after the elections before the Mwanakatwe Constitutional Commission (MCC) was appointed for this purpose in November 1993. After the MCC submitted its proposals to the MMD government in June 1995, the government resisted strong domestic and donor pressure to publish the MCC's draft document for public debate prior to editing by the MMD government. The MMD government further insisted that the document be ratified only by the Zambian parliament in which the MMD enjoyed an 83.33 percent majority. The MMD government thus went ahead to revise the draft constitution without the requisite public debate, a move that was essentially self-serving and not in the interests of advancing the cause of democracy.

As noted in Chapter Five, in one of its most serious departures from democratic practice, the MMD revised the draft constitution to restrict eligibility to run for president to third generation Zambians, a stricture that explicitly curtailed Kaunda's rematch with Chiluba in the 1996 elections. The amendments also required traditional chiefs to abdicate their chieftaincy before becoming eligible for elected office, a provision that also targeted Kaunda's vice presidential running mate, Senior Chief Inyambo Yata who was sure to draw wide support for Kaunda from the Lozi of Western Province. In effect, the MMD government disregarded the recommendations by the MCC, Western donors, and civil society that any new constitution should be ratified by a national referendum or a constituent assembly rather than by parliament. Now that they were in power, it was no longer in their interest to allow for a democratic constitutional review process that would have had the effect of diluting their power. Instead, the new political elite used their positions to consolidate their power and maximize their chances for reelection in 1996. Having been so blatantly targeted by the constitutional amendments, UNIP, the biggest opposition party at the time, boycotted the 1996 elections, leaving the MMD to have a field day. It is for this reason that John Harbeson (1999) rightly notes that far from strengthening and creating momentum for democracy, the 1996 Zambian elections had the opposite effect.

Furthermore, as Jan Van Donge (1995) notes, Chiluba maintained the presidential system yet he campaigned on the issue of returning Zambia to the parliamentary Westminster model that would have given the people's representatives greater power over policy making and the running of public affairs. He appointed and fired at will heads of parastatals and surrounded himself more and more with advisors. Chiluba maintained Kaunda's security apparatus and even resorted to declaring a state of emergency for some time, an act he considered an inexcusable arrogation of power by Kaunda when the situation was reversed. Donge explains this continuity in political strategy and modus operandi as crafty moves by political actors. It is based on rational calculations for power maximization and maintenance.

The same case applied to Kenya, where no pact preceded the first multiparty elections in 1992. Although there was no redesigning of the electoral rules, the tide against the incumbent KANU regime of President Moi was so much so that opposition politicians believed Moi would be routed. Each of the key opposition politicians thus jostled to be the one to succeed the incumbent. Failure on the part of the three opposition presidential contenders to unite, however, cost them victory. Following their electoral defeat, they joined forces to agitate for a change of electoral rules to level the playing field. Political activism in this regard was led by the National Convention Executive Council (NCEC) as elaborated in Chapter Five. The efforts culminated in the IPPG compromise of 1997 that was supposed to have been minimal reforms on the electoral system to pave way for the 1997 elections after which an elaborate process to review the constitution was to be put in place. The main amendment that the opposition sought to exploit by going to the polls in 1997 was one enacted in April 1992 that provided that a presidential victory required not only a simple majority of the votes cast, but also at least 25 percent of the votes cast in at least five of the country's eight provinces.[6]

In the 1997 elections, the opposition had four main presidential contenders, Michael Wamalwa of Western Province; Charity Ngilu of Eastern Province; Raila Odinga of Nyanza Province; and Mwai Kibaki of Central Province. This time round, this was a strategic move on the part of the opposition. The calculation was that given the overwhelming vote for the opposition in the 1992 elections, President Moi would be locked out of the four provinces from which the opposition candidates hailed, to force a runoff between him and the leading opposition contender. Once again, the opposition miscalculated, using the advantages of incumbency, the KANU candidate prevailed once again, having been shut out only in Central Province. Moi's lowest vote share, amounting to two percent of the votes cast, was in the Kikuyu dominated Central Province. His largest shares were in Northeastern Province, 78 percent, and in Rift Valley Province, 66 percent (Haugerud, 1995: 25). Against this background, John Harbeson (1999: 51) argues that:

> Kenya thus provides one of the clearest examples in Africa of the precariousness of undertaking multiparty elections as the first step toward democracy before inter-party agreement has been forged and the fundamental rules of the game reformed. Lacking such an agreement, opposition parties and civil society have remained futilely dependent upon a manifestly unsympathetic government to initiate further democratization.

The greatest exemplification of rational calculation on the part of politicians in Kenya came in the run-up and aftermath of the December 2002 elections. Having been beaten twice before, the opposition now found common ground and united under a grand alliance called National Alliance Rainbow Coalition (NARC) to which the existing opposition political parties became corporate members. Under the arrangement, Mwai Kibaki was made the sole opposition presidential candidate with Michael Wamalwa as his running mate and vice president designate. Raila Odinga was to become prime minister, and Charity Ngilu his deputy, positions that did not exist, but that NARC undertook to create under a new constitution that they promised to put in place[7] within one hundred days of their administration. Completing the constitutional review process and promulgating a new constitution within the first one hundred days was one of the key campaign planks for NARC. However, after winning and assuming office on December 30, 2002, the new NARC government now pushed the date for a new constitution to June 2003. Come June, the deadline was pushed to end of 2003. In October 2003, the proceedings of the National Constitutional Conference under the direction of the Constitution of Kenya Review Commission (CKRC) at Bomas of Kenya, Nairobi, were adjourned to January 12, 2004, with President Kibaki and the justice and constitutional affairs minister, Kiraitu Murungi promising a new constitution by June 2004![8] This date also came and passed with the powers-that-be now evasive about setting a deadline within which a new constitution would be in place.

Obviously, it was no longer in the self-interest of the new power holders to speed up the constitutional review process. In fact, the idea of creating the position of prime minister, a promise that convinced Raila Odinga to support Mwai Kibaki for president and to rally his supporters behind the opposition coalition, became a major sticking point. Key supporters of the new president argued that such an eventuality would create two centers of power, which would be a recipe for instability. However, as already pointed out above, it was the minister for transport and communications, John Michuki who let the cat out of the bag on this issue. He asserted that they had agitated for the creation of the position during their opposition days simply to facilitate "one of our own to share power with Moi." Now that Moi was no more, he asserted, there was no need for the position of prime minister because Kibaki, unlike Moi, was "a good president"! (see Kendo, 2003). In this self-interested scheme of things, power concentration in the presidency was bad when Moi was in power; it was okay for the Michukis, Murungis, and Mirugis among others, now that they were in power. The mood of despair in view of this is captured by V. G. Simiyu, who observes:

> . . . what has annoyed people is that this [NARC] leadership, elected on a democratic platform, the leaders themselves were perceived as the torchbearers of democracy, then they have just sunk to the same disease of ethnicity, of personality cult, and hardened drunkenness with power. It is fantastic how people can turn around. I know power has no logic, power has no emotions, but it is baffling that people all of a sudden we now see them in their true colors that even the democratic agenda was only a bogey to get to political power. It is really unfortunate.[9]

Against this background, it is no wonder that the constitutional review process in Kenya that was set in motion in 2000 has become a game of musical chairs. This reality lends credence to Munyonzwe Hamalengwa's (1992) argument to the effect that the struggles for democracy are not, in actuality, a disinterested pursuit for societal good. All these struggles, he argues, be they in Africa, Asia, Latin America, or Eastern Europe among other areas, have been organized and vented by particular interests. They are fundamentally aimed at serving the interests of particular segments of the populace, though they may at times serve the interests of the larger society in general. In view of the foregoing, John Harbeson (1999) rightly observes that without agreement among the parties on the basic rules of the game prior to the initial multiparty elections, no semblance of democratically legitimated constraints existed that could restrain the abuses of democratic practice by the victors.

Arguably, therefore, domestic and external donor pressure upon the Moi and Kaunda regimes in Kenya and Zambia to permit multiparty elections should, in retrospect, have included the crafting of a broader multiparty agreement on restructuring the rules of the game. In addition, and perhaps most importantly, it should have included a provision for electing a constituent assembly to draft a new constitution prior to the first multi-party elections in the two countries as happened in the cases of Benin, Mali, Malawi, Mozambique, and South Africa among other African countries.

CONCLUSION

This chapter has analyzed the role of civil society organizations, ethnicity, and electoral system design in the democratization process in Africa from the standpoint of the rational choice perspective. It has demonstrated that the push for democratization and the stonewalling of the process are a function of the selfish strategic considerations of the dominant political elite at particular historical moments. In the case of Zambia in 1991, the MMD campaigned on the promise to rewrite the constitution to advance democracy once in power. Subsequently, after assuming power, the new MMD government restricted the debate on the new constitution to parliament in which it had an absolute majority. At the end of the day, the new constitution that emerged constricted political space in Zambia to the extent that it disqualified former President Kaunda from running in the 1996 elections on the grounds that he was not third generation Zambian. Similarly, in Kenya, the NARC leaders were the foremost proponents of constitutional review for purposes of devolving the overwhelming presidential powers that made the position an imperial presidency. Once they assumed power in 2002, however, they changed tune and constitutional review ceased to be the urgent priority it had been. In both cases, therefore, the democrats of yesteryears turned reactionaries once in power because of selfish rational calculations.

What this chapter illustrates is that individual political action is a self-interested optimal adaptation to an institutional environment while interaction between political actors is an optimal response to each other. In other words, prevailing rules of the game determine the behavior of actors, which cumulatively generate political outputs. To ensure that political action and the strategic interaction of key political actors as they maneuver to maximize their interests are mediated in ways that ensure the greatest good to the greatest number, it is imperative to redesign the rules of engagement. However, as the cases of Benin, Malawi, Mali, and South Africa illustrate, this must be accomplished at critical junctures that engender uncertainty, which ensures that the strategic considerations of the dominant political actors are not brought to bear upon the process. Quite paradoxically, the opportunity for such constitutional engineering existed in both Kenya and Zambia but was squandered by opposition politicians who were more interested in merely replacing the incumbents. In Kenya, this moment of political opportunity obtained during the conjuncture in which the original FORD managed to push for the return to multiparty politics. At this juncture, the incumbent KANU regime was very vulnerable and could easily have been pushed to acquiesce to re-writing the constitution before the first multiparty elections. A similar opportunity obtained in Zambia the moment Kaunda agreed to a referendum to decide on whether to reintroduce multipartyism or not, then recapitulated on the referendum. This was the moment he could have been pushed to allow the restructuring of the political system. Opposition forces in both countries failed to seize upon these windows of political opportunity as they selfishly jostled amongst themselves to replace the incumbents.

Chapter Seven
Prospects for Democratic Consolidation

The process of democratization in Africa has produced mixed results. As the analysis in the foregoing chapters demonstrates, the contention between the established authoritarian paradigm and its resurgent democratic counterpart continues. Consequently, a number of African and Africanist scholars who have analyzed the transition politics in Africa paint two contradictory scenarios about the possibilities for democratic consolidation on the continent. One is overly pessimistic about the prospects of democracy on the continent. I call this group the "demo-pessimists." The other is largely optimistic about the eventuality of democratic consolidation in Africa, I call this group the "demoptimists."

THE PESSIMISTIC PROGNOSIS

A number of scholars have taken a critical analysis of the politics of transition in Africa and concluded that the prospects for consolidating democracy in Africa are dismal at best, non-existent at worst. The African and Africanist scholars who fall within this pessimistic prognosis category—the demo-pessimists—can be grouped into five analytical schools: the rational instrumentalists, the political economy theorists, those who take the social capital perspective, the "Leninist approach" analysts, as well as some who take the institutionalist perspective. Though they take divergent approaches in their analyses, these scholars arrive at more or less the same pessimistic conclusions in regard to the prospects for democracy in Africa.

The Rational Instrumentalists

Among the rational instrumentalists, perhaps none provides a more sting-
ing indictment of the political process of change in Africa than Patrick Chabal and Jean-Pascal Daloz (1999). The two scholars argue that there
prevails in Africa a system of policies that are inimical to socio-economic
development, as it is usually understood in the West. Taking a rational
instrumentalist view of politics in Africa, they contend that political disorder has been instrumentalized in virtually all African states in ways that
have made it a major resource for political actors. As a result, they contend,
there is no incentive to work for a more institutionalized ordering of society. On the contrary, there is an in-built bias in favor of greater disorder
and against the formation of the Western-style legal, administrative, and
institutional foundations required for socio-economic development.
According to Chabal and Daloz, therefore, the prospects for political institutionalization in Africa are limited. They conclude that it is unlikely that
the democratic experiments in Africa will lead to the establishment of the
constitutional, legal, and bureaucratic political order required for fundamental reform:

> Such change will have to be driven by popular will. Only when ordi-
> nary African men and women have cause to reject the logic of personal-
> ized politics, seriously to question the legitimacy of the present political
> instrumentalization of disorder and struggle for new forms of political
> accountability, will meaningful change occur. Tempting as it is to think
> that political liberalization, the so-called democratization of Africa,
> will facilitate such change, there is in the foreseeable future little likeli-
> hood that it will. (Chabal & Daloz, 1999: 162–163)

Taking the same line of argument, Richard Joseph (1998) asserts that
the democratization process in Africa has only resulted in what he calls
semi-authoritarian regimes that are fashioned in direct response to external
forces. In order to obtain international attention, approval, and respectabil-
ity and therefore ensure continued flow of foreign aid, Africa's reluctant
converts to democracy " . . . conduct a balancing act in which they impose
enough repression to keep their opponents weak and maintain their own
power while adhering to enough democratic formalities that they might just
pass themselves off as democrats" (Joseph, 1998: 14). It is on this basis that
Joseph points out that in this age of symbols and images, the phenomenon
of democracy-as-presentability has now emerged. In this emergent scenario,
elections, which are seen as symbols of democracy, are easy to capture on
film thereby making democracy part of the fashionable attire of modernity

notwithstanding the nature of the body donning the said attire. In essence, the label is more important than the labeled.

The strategic maneuvers of the dominant political elite in pursuit of their own self-interests are evident in efforts at political reform both in Kenya and Zambia. In the case of Zambia, Chiluba campaigned in 1991 on the promise that as president, he would enact a new constitution to advance the cause of democracy. Once in power, however, he restricted discussions on the new constitution to parliament in which his MMD party had absolute control. As a consequence a constitutional provision was made restricting presidential candidacy to third generation Zambians thereby disqualifying former President Kaunda, Chiluba's only viable opponent, from running in 1996. At the end of the day, the transition from Kaunda's UNIP to Chiluba's MMD regime in Zambia was essentially a transition from a de jure one-party state to a dominant-party state (see Burnell, 2001; Mphaisha, 2000; Phiri, 1999; Donge, 1995). Very little changed by way of the mode of governance and the management of public affairs. It is for this reason that Mphaisha (1996) contends that Chiluba's second tenure as president (1996–2001) marked a "retreat from democracy."

The same strategic maneuvers on the part of the political elite have remained characteristic of the political reform process in Kenya. Support for the constitutional review process in the country has remained dependent on the strategic considerations of the key political actors. During the Moi regime as elaborated in Chapter Five, the opposition politicians were the key proponents of a people-driven constitutional reform process and agitated for the devolution of the overwhelming powers of the presidency. Once they assumed power under the NARC coalition in December 2002, however, the same politicians now argued the case for a small group of "experts" to write the constitution and marshaled forces to stonewall and torpedo the review process. As Adams Oloo (2004) rightly observes, the opposition political elite's support for and interest in the review process under Moi was not driven by a commitment to genuine reform, but rather by the strategic need to facilitate the evolution of a coalition that could be used to defeat KANU. This same view is held by Wambui Kiai who, convinced that the new government lacks a common ideology and has fractured into self-interested factionalism, asserts: "I think so much of what they were doing was just to remove Moi, I don't know if they have properly conceptualized what is democratization, or about what is the Kenya we want . . ."[1] Like Chabal and Daloz, therefore, Oloo contends that underlying the elite's lack of support for political reform is its fear of institutionalization of politics and the likely emergent social order:

Institutionalization comes with the need for evolution of an inclusive process and a mechanism for bringing in the excluded. Indeed, it is for this reason that devolution is one of the most contentious issues in the review process. Devolution in its pure sense threatens the hegemonic exercise of political power by the elite who do not want to cede even the smallest amount of power to a perceived or real alternative "center of power." (Oloo, 2004: 15–16)

In spite of having promised a new constitution within one hundred days of its assumption of power, therefore, more than two years into its tenure, the NARC government is nowhere near to delivering on this promise. The constitutional review process has remained the game of musical chairs it was under the former KANU regime.

The Political Economy Theorists

The second group of demo-pessimists is comprised of the political economy theorists, who find a strong correlation between economic development and the nurturing and consolidation of democracy. Theorists in this category argue that democracy requires certain minimum levels of economic development without which it is futile to expect democracy to take root. The foremost proponent of this view is Samuel Huntington (1997, 1991). Huntington (1997: 5) observes, for instance, that " . . . all the wealthiest countries in the world, except Singapore, are democratic, and almost all the poorest countries in the world, with the notable exception of India and perhaps one or two others, are not democratic." Quoting Seymour Martin Lipset, Huntington advances several reasons why economic development has a strong positive effect on democratization. First, he points out that economic development involves higher levels of urbanization, literacy, and education, and involves a shift in occupational structure with a decline in the size and importance of the peasantry, and the development of a middle class and an urban working class. The latter groups increasingly want a voice in and influence over policies that affect them; and with higher levels of education, they are able to organize trade unions, political parties, and civic associations to promote their interests.

Additionally, it is observed that economic development produces more resources, public and private, for distribution among groups in society. Politics becomes less and less of a zero-sum game and hence compromise and consensus are engendered. Thirdly, economic growth produces a more complex economy that becomes increasingly difficult for the state to control. The inevitable easing of state control of the economy that follows facilitates the creation and growth of independent centers of power based on private control of capital, technology, and communications. The bourgeoisie who own these assets demand a political system in which they are able to exercise influence, one that is not dominated by a military junta, a politburo, or a dictator and his sycophants. Finally, it is posited that while in the short term rapid economic growth often exacerbates income inequalities, in the longer term, it produces greater equality in income distribution; " . . . it is incompatible with gross inequalities in wealth and income. Economic growth eventually reduces these inequalities and hence facilitates the emergence of democracy" (Huntington, 1997: 5).

The above arguments dovetail with the postulations of Marxist theorists of history according to whom when human dexterity or the means of production change, they change the social division of wealth and labor which, in the final analysis, compels changes in the structure and exercise of public authority. The logic of this paradigm, argues Andrew Janos (1997: 122), is that when politics is changing, the logical sources of change are in the domains of economics and what he calls "techne." It is against this economic interpretation of political development that Africanist scholars like Robert Bates (1999) and David Simon (2002) are skeptical about the possibilities of consolidating democracy in Africa amidst poverty. Bates in particular argues that historically, democracy accompanies economic prosperity; it is the result of growth and rising per capita incomes. But, he asserts, democratic reform in Africa has occurred at the nadir of Africa's postindependence economic history. He thus concludes that the widespread political reform in Africa is shallow, its breadth notwithstanding. Without socio-economic transformation, the logic of the political economy argument goes, democracy will remain an illusion in Africa. Authoritarianism will persist based on the politics of prebendalism in which state offices " . . . are regarded as prebends that can be appropriated by office holders who use them to generate material benefits for themselves and their constituents and kin groups" (Dommen, 1997: 488).

The Social Capital Proponents

The third category of demo-pessimists includes those who take the social capital approach. Concurring with the political economy theorists on the economic basis of democracy, theorists taking this perspective argue that the lack of the requisite economic conditions for democracy in Africa results from the lack of social capital among African societies (see Schedler, 1998; Simone & Santi, 1998; Chege, 1997; Esman & Uphoff, 1984). According to A. M. Simone and K. P. Santi (1998), social capital are those features of social organization such as reciprocity networks, norms and trust relations that make people collectively productive and which facilitate mutually beneficial cooperation. "They are resources that are neither traditional capital nor human capital but a system of human relationships that we engage in to solve every day problems" (Simone & Santi, 1998: 18).

This perspective blames the lack of indigenous commercial progress in Africa on lack of social capital and the prevalence instead of " . . . force of custom, rigidity of status, collectivism of the extended family, the clan, the village, or tribe . . ." (Chege, 1997: 214). Banfield (1958) refers to this phenomenon as "amoral familism" which he describes as " . . . the inability of the villagers to act together for their common good or, indeed, for any common end transcending the immediate material interest of the nuclear family" (see Putnam et al, 1988: 224). This lack of the spirit of associationism across the parochial identities of family and ethnicity, it is argued, has over time hindered the development of a corporatist culture, which is the fount of the capitalist ethic of liberalism and, according to social capital theorists, the engine of democratic advancement.

Putnam et al (1988: 226), among the chief proponents of the social capital approach to economic and political development, posit that associationism, the essence of social capital, has positive effects both "internally" on individual members of communities and "externally" on the wider polity. Internally, as Putnam et al (1988: 227) argue, members of associations display higher political sophistication, social trust, political participation, and what they call "subjective civic competence." Externally, it is posited that interest articulation and interest aggregation are enhanced by a dense network of secondary associations. In view of this, one would expect that the emergence and proliferation of NGOs among other civil society organizations committed to myriad socio-economic and political agendas in Africa fulfill these conditions. Exponents of the social capital thesis, however, argue that most of these organizations are largely elitist, urban-based, external dependent, and thus detached from the communities they seek to transform. Milton Esman and Norman Uphoff (1984), for instance, contend that from the point of view of social engineering, organizations implanted from the outside, or imposed from above, as are most NGOs, are incapable of generating social capital among communities. "The most successful local organizations are those that represent indigenous, participatory initiatives in relatively cohesive communities" (Esman & Uphoff, 1988: 40).

Indeed, while acknowledging that democracy NGOs have begun to have some measurable impact on citizen understanding of politics in Kenya with their increasingly noticeable rural presence, Stephen Orvis (2003: 247) nevertheless argues that they have " . . . done so by relying on ethnic, clan, partisan, and other 'non-civil' networks to build supporters." Accordingly, to Korwa Adar (1998), "ethnicity and ethnic kings" constitute the "enduring dual constraints" to Africa's democratic electoral experiments. Overall, therefore, social capital theorists take the view that democracy cannot be realized in African states given their social and economic precariousness. They contend that successful strategies of democratization must shift from the political approach, especially by external forces seeking to force a redistribution of political power in Africa through political pressure. Attention should be refocused instead on channeling more resources to the creation and nurturing of social capital, which is the key to effective economic development and political transformation.

The "Leninist Approach" Analysts

In the fourth category of demo-pessimists are the "Leninist approach" analysts who argue that the possibilities of democratic consolidation in Africa are bleak because of the "Leninist option" adopted in the push for African democratization (see Nasong'o, 1998; Ottaway, 1997). According to this school of thought, faced with the reality of lack of the requisite conditions for the emergence and practice of Western-style liberal democracy, democratic evangelists opted for the Leninist approach towards democratizing Africa. Long before Lenin appeared on the Russian political scene, Karl Marx had hypothesized that a socialist revolution could only take place in an industrialized society with a large proletariat. These social conditions, according to Marx, could be achieved naturally through the forces of dialectical materialism that have characterized the history of human development since antiquity (see Marx & Engels, 1992 [1888]). According to this Marxist interpretation, the principle of dialectical materialism is that the driving force of human life is the quest for economic welfare. The essential purpose of all ideas and institutions be they economic, political, religious, or whatever, is to safeguard economic interests. At any given stage of economic development, there is a ruling class, which, by monopolizing the ownership of land, factories, technology, or other sources of wealth, is in a position to dominate the entire society. Great as its power may be however, such a ruling class is basically unstable. In the course of time, new sources of wealth are discovered and lead to new forms of economic organization. New classes emerge to exploit these opportunities thus challenging the monopoly of the older ruling class. Dialectically speaking, the established order is a thesis that inevitably produces its own antithesis in the form of a new revolutionary class. The result, according to

Karl Marx, is a revolutionary crisis or synthesis in which the new class, having gradually grown stronger than the old, overthrows its former rulers and completely refashions society in accordance with its own interests (see Leonard, 1974; Marx & Engels, 1992 [1888]).

Vladmir Lenin, however, was impatient with Marx's dialectical prescriptions. Faced with the reality that Russia was nowhere near to satisfying the prerequisites to a successful socialist revolution and unwilling to let history take its full course, Lenin chose to design a shortcut through political organization, the formation of a strong vanguard party, and the education of the masses to convert them into new socialist beings. In this way, he sought to socially engineer the socio-economic conditions deemed indispensable to the maintenance of a socialist system (Ottaway, 1997: 10).

In similar manner, though even the most optimistic crusaders of democratization implicitly recognized that conditions in Africa were not favorable to liberal democracy, they devised a shortcut. This comprised economic sanctions, civic education, and sheer political pressure in the belief that external pressure, support for democratization, and expertise could make elections happen, strengthen parties, and create institutions. On the overall, the onus for pushing forward the democratic wheel was placed on "civil society" however conceptualized. Under the Russian revolution, the Soviet socialist person was to be created by Lenin through the political process of forced collectivization, centralized economic planning, and nationalized ownership of the means of production and distribution. In similar manner, the new African democratic citizen was to be created through deliberate civic education by so-called grassroots NGOs in order to provide and strengthen the social underpinnings of the new democratic structures.

At the end, Leninism failed to realize increased popular welfare and international competitiveness. It gave rise instead to a military-industrial complex based on the technologies of destruction and premised on the philosophy of "the state for the state" (Janos, 1996: 130). It eventually collapsed under the weight of its own efforts to keep up with the Western world. In the same vein, so the argument goes, the "Leninist approach" to democratization in Africa has at best only led to minimalist forms of democracy, or "democracy with adjectives" (Collier & Levitsky, 1997). The result is what some analysts call "feckless democracy" (Carothers, 2002), "choiceless democracy" (Mkandawire, 1999), "illiberal democracy" (Zakaria, 1997), "electoral democracy" (Diamond, 1996: 20), or "delegative democracy" (O'Donnell, 1994). In this regard, "genuine democracy" remains as elusive as ever. In the face of this, some scholars conclude that with regard to Africa, the "third wave" (of democratization) is over (Diamond, 1996). Similarly, in his analysis of the "third wave of democratization" in Africa, Crawford Young (1994, 1999) sees only "ambiguities and contradictions of a political imperative." In the same vein, Julius Ihonvbere (1996b) takes a critical look at what he calls "Africa's non-transition to democracy" and rhetorically asks: "where is the third wave?" Following in Ihonvbere's intellectual footsteps, Godwin Murunga casts "a critical look at Kenya's non-transition to democracy" and concludes that the decade of multiparty politics in Kenya has been a wasted period: " . . . the often eulogized transition to democracy actually never occurred" (Murunga, 2002:90). Accordingly, the Leninist approach, Ottaway (1997) contends, is incapable of producing tenable and enduring results.

The Institutionalists

Fifth and finally is the demo-pessimist group of scholars that take an institutionalist approach to political analysis. This school of thought argues that the personalized nature of the democratic crusade in Africa[2] and transition to multiparty politics without restructuring the strategic environment of political engagement is a pointer to the shallow nature of the African political transition (see Nasong'o, 2003a; Harbeson, 1999; Bratton & Posner, 1999; Bates, 1999; Ihonvbere, 1997; Mbaku, 1997). As Mukum Mbaku (1997) posits, to make certain that the present transitions lead to the establishment of viable political and economic systems, African countries must begin with proper constitution making, including provision of appropriate facilities for all relevant population groups to effectively participate in constitutional discourse. "Unless effective and self-enforcing social contracts which must flow from the political cultures of these polities are produced, the continent is unlikely to see any significant improvement in human development" (Mbaku, 1997: 49).

With specific reference to the 1992 and 1997 elections in Kenya, for instance, Robert Bates (1999) asserts that Kenya is an exemplar of most African states where rival political parties enter elections without posing a serious threat to autocratic incumbents. For his part, Rok Ajulu (2000) asserts that despite the introduction of "democracy" and multiparty politics in Kenya, nothing much seems to have changed. If democratization is understood broadly to include ingredients such as periodic elections, a free press, respect for human rights, an independent judiciary, rule of law, and a greater role for civil society, Ajulu posits, then clearly, Kenya's multiparty process does not seem to be headed in that direction. In Ajulu's opinion, political processes since the opening up of democratic space in 1990 have not been about deliberate construction of democratic institutions. Rather, over the last decade, Kenya has witnessed consistent attempts by the ruling elite to close the democratic space altogether. Ajulu thus concludes that democracy, either in its minimalist form, that is, the procedural form of democracy, or its substantive form, that is, regular electoral contestation combined with the strengthening of independent institutions within the state and civil society, has failed to take root in the country.

This institutionalist view is further reiterated by George Ayittey (2002: 9) who asserts that faced with pressure to democratize their "abominable systems," African authoritarian leaders simply pack the electoral commissions with their cronies, manipulate the electoral rules, and hold what he calls "kokonut elections" to return themselves to power. In essence, the process of democratization in Africa has led to what Thandika Mkandawire (1999) terms as "choiceless democracy." Accordingly, Richard Joseph (1998) concludes that within the decade of the 1990s, Africa moved from *abertura* (political opening) to closure. As such, Claude Ake (1996) summarizes the pessimistic prognosis, the continent remains caught between a discredited authoritarian past and a democratic future that refuses to arrive.

THE OPTIMISTIC PERSPECTIVE

The above conclusions by the demo-pessimists are not without merit. Indeed, it is noteworthy that the process of democratization goes through three major phases. The first is political opening, marked by democratic ferment and political liberalization that culminates in the appearance of cracks in an incumbent authoritarian regime. This gives way to the second phase of breakthrough when an incumbent authoritarian regime collapses leading to the emergence of a new democratic regime. This is then followed by the third and final phase of democratic consolidation. The last phase is a slow but purposeful process in which democratic forms are transformed into democratic substance, with the political elite getting habituated to the new rules of political engagement (see Nasong'o, forthcoming; Carothers, 2002; Manning, 2002).

From the analysis in the foregoing chapters, it is evident that with regard to most African countries, including Kenya and Zambia, the process of democratization has gone through the first two stages and the countries are now in the murky waters of the third phase. To argue, therefore, that the transition to democracy never took place (Murunga, 2002), or that the democratization process in Africa has resulted in a non-transition to democracy (Ihonvbere, 1996b), and that thus the third wave in Africa is over (Diamond, 1996) is to miss the point. It is to erroneously assume that transition to democracy is an event that takes place once and for all. Yet it is an arduous process replete with advances and retreats as the key political actors jostle and strategize to advance, protect, and maximize their positions. It is at this point, therefore, that the demoptimists differ with the demo-pessimists (see Murunga & Nasong'o, forthcoming; Manning, 2002; Chweya, 2002; Owuoche & Jonyo, 2002; Goldsmith, 2001; Ruto & Njoroge, 2001; Chweya & Nasong'o, 1996). As Carrie Manning argues:

> . . . by framing the problem in this way [democratization in Africa as having only led to virtual or illiberal democracy], we may be missing important opportunities to inform our theoretical and conceptual understanding of democratization and state building in contexts in which democracy emerges not as the natural or logical culmination of a long-term process of social, economic, or political development, but as an artificially imposed solution to economic, political, and social ills. (Manning, 2002: 6–7)

The merit of the pessimistic prognosis notwithstanding, therefore, a more careful and nuanced analysis of the concrete dimension of democracy, of the balance sheet of the immeasurable sacrifices of sweat, tears, and blood that have been shed at the altar of democracy in Africa reveals plenty of evidence indicating that the process of democratization in Africa has yielded concrete positive results. Evidence in this regard can be grouped into three broad analytical categories. First is a juxtaposition of the political realities obtaining now with the political situation prior to the onset of the politics of transition in the early 1990s to gauge what has been achieved along the democratization trajectory. Second is recourse to the perspectives of those who have lived the experience of authoritarianism and the politics of transition. What do they say about the impact of the democratization process? Third, and derived from the foregoing two categories, is an analysis of the available evidence of democratic consolidation as advanced by some of the leading demoptimists among African and Africanist scholars.

The Balance Sheet: Then and Now

One of the key elements of a democratic system is the existence of contending political forces in the name of political parties vying for the prime spot on the political stage. Prior to the onset of the wave of democratization in Africa in the early 1990s, as elaborated in Chapter One, opposition forces were criminalized, illegitimated, and forced to operate underground in places where they had the audacity to exist. The first major impact of the forces of democratization has been the legitimization of the voices of political dissent internal to the African states that had for long operated mainly underground in opposition to the authoritarian incumbents. Prior to the transition to multiparty politics, such political dissenters in countries like Kenya and Zambia were dismissed as communist agitators and disgruntled elements that could not be allowed to operate freely. These alternative political forces were criminalized, and so intensely cracked down upon that they were forced to operate underground. With the advent of democratization, however, they found leeway to operate covertly and canvass for support as legitimate opponents of the incumbent regimes. Most of these political dissenting groups reconstituted themselves into potent prodemocracy movements, such as Movement for Freedom and Justice (MFJ) in Ghana, FORD in Kenya, Campaign for Democracy and National Democratic Coalition (NADECO) in Nigeria, AFORD in Malawi and Caucus for National Unity (CNU) and MMD in Zambia, among others. Some of these movements later transformed themselves into opposition political parties, emerging as effective representatives of alternative political views in legislatures across Africa. In this way, parliaments in most of the African states are undergoing transformation from being mere rubber stamps of the capricious whims of the executive to being important forums for policy debate and legislative action.

The second major impact has been the elevation of the role of civil society in the political process as elaborated in Chapter Three. According to advocates of the centrality of civil society to democratic politics, civil society was the hitherto missing key to sustained political reform, legitimate states and governments, improved governance, viable state-society and state-economy relationships, and prevention of political decay. This emphasis led to what Naomi Chazan (1994) has described as an explosion of associational life in Africa with important political dimensions. Accordingly, in countries as diverse politically as Gabon, Kenya, Nigeria, Tanzania, Zaire, and Zambia, civil liberties unions, human rights organizations, political debating forums, countrywide welfare and service organizations were formed. These institutions have not only contributed to what is described as a veritable explosion of associational life in Africa but also injected an explicitly political dimension into the associational arena, pressing for guarantees for basic human rights and advocating democratic reforms. The vibrancy of this civil society phenomenon in the political process has led Perlas to contend that the end of the Cold War did not mark "the end of history" as Francis Fukuyama (1989) enthusiastically declared. Instead, it heralded the beginning of history, as " . . . an empowered civil society will begin to write the script for the new history" (Perlas, 1999: 137). In spite of the contested nature of the civil society conceptualization, and the limitations of its promise as midwife of regime change and agent of political transformation, therefore, the rise and centrality of CSOs in Africa's transition politics is a conjuncture that has spawned a new kind of political economy in which the role of the state is increasingly being challenged.[3]

The third major characteristic feature of democratic politics is the institution of a limited mandate for political leaders. Prior to the democratization process of the 1990s, the idea of a limited mandate in Africa only applied to parliamentarians, and even so, only to a limited extent. The chief executives, on the other hand, had open-ended mandates. This is what explains the fact that leaders like Mobutu Seseko of the former Zaire ruled for thirty-two years, from 1965 to 1997; Hastings Kamuzu Banda of Malawi even declared himself Life President and reigned for thirty years, from 1964 to 1994. Similarly, Kenneth Kaunda in Zambia ruled for 27 years (1964–1991), while Daniel arap Moi was in power for 24 years (1978–2002). In countries where there were changes in political leaderships, this was effected either by death of the incumbent, or by way of military coups rather than via the civility of limited mandates. Emblematic of the coup as the mode of change of political leadership is Nigeria with two coups in 1966, followed by coups in 1975, 1976, 1983, and 1985 (see Nasong'o, 2003b). Hence the established governance paradigm was either single-party authoritarianism or military dictatorship.

However, the politics of transition has essentially spelled the beginning of the end of authoritarianism as an established mode of political leadership in Africa. In the new politics of democratization, emphasis has been placed on circumscription of presidential tenure to two terms, invariably of five years each, and to political pluralism, which has resulted in political competition, and a limited mandate for leaders. In this event, hitherto authoritarian leaders find themselves increasingly incapable of reproducing themselves in power. Indeed, some of them, like the self-styled Malawian life president, Hastings Kamuzu Banda, Zambia's long serving President Kenneth Kaunda, and Benin's perennial President Mathieu Kérékou found themselves casualties of the new competitive politics. Other countries that witnessed change in government through elections in the 1990s include Cape Verde, Mali, Madagascar, Namibia, and South Africa (Ellis, 2000: 43). In the final analysis, it is the circumscription of presidential tenure to two terms that facilitated Kenya's President Moi's retirement and the assumption of power by a coalition of opposition political parties, whose presidential candidate, Mwai Kibaki, walloped Moi's chosen successor, Uhuru Kenyatta, in the December 2002 elections by garnering almost two thirds of the votes cast.

Indeed, the departure of Jerry Rawlings from power in Ghana after serving two elective terms in January 2001 and the assumption of power by an opposition party following the December 2000 elections, as well as the two-term tradition established in Tanzania since 1985 and that is taking root in South Africa, constitute a clear manifestation of the fact that this new kind of politics is taking root in Africa. The fact that the limited mandate tradition has been locked in place in Tanzania was confirmed by a top CCM official in response to a query by a journalist. Asked what would happen if word went round in Tanzania to the effect that President Benjamin Mkapa wanted to stay in power after his constitutionally allowed two terms that end in October 2005, the official chuckled bemusedly before saying: "Although we would have a hearty laugh about the joke, his family would get worried about his mental health" (Buwembo, 2004).

The fourth significant impact of the politics of transition is the sense of empowerment that opposition political forces now enjoy and the effect of this on the politics of change. Whereas in the single-party era, the "maximum leader" was viewed as infallible and those around him kow-towed to his whimsical and capricious wishes without question, the new politics of multiparty democracy has emboldened alternative political views not only in the opposition but, even more significantly, within incumbent parties. For instance, Kaunda's successor in Zambia, Frederick Chiluba, found stiff opposition even from within his own party, MMD, in early 2001 when he sought to have the constitution changed to allow him run for a third term. Kamuzu Banda's successor in Malawi, Bakili Muluzi faced similar opposition in 2004 when he also tried to engineer a constitutional amendment to allow him run for a third term. Both cases constitute a significant pointer to the institutionalization of a limited mandate for African leaders, which is a major characteristic of democratic politics. In this event, African leaders will no longer find it easy to perpetuate themselves in power as they were wont to do during the "party-state" era.

Fifth, and equally important, is the effect of the liberalization of the channels of political communication in the unfolding political developments in Africa. At the height of the era of authoritarianism, the flow of information was tightly controlled by the state regimes, which controlled the main channels of political communication including the print and electronic media. Under these circumstances the incumbent political elite essentially engaged in a propagandist top-down flow of information intended to secure public cooperation and support (see Wanyande, 2002; Chweya & Nasong'o, 1996). African publics were thus denied access to alternative political views, as holders of these views were unable to address themselves to the people. Concomitant with the process of democratization has come the opening up of the channels of political communication with the result that a number of alternative channels that are independent of the state have sprung up in Kenya, Malawi, Tanzania, Zambia, and elsewhere on the continent. Accessibility to alternative political information has in turn functioned to enable African publics to begin to understand the actions of their political leaders and the nexus between those actions and popular goals. Consequently, meaningful articulation of interests and exercise of political influence over leaders on the part of the people has emerged and, as such, activism for good governance is no longer the proverbial cry in the wilderness that it used to be.

Overall, Zambia, the first case of a political transition to multipartyism that resulted in the defeat of an incumbent in October 1991, is emblematic of the foregoing political developments. Although Chiluba's performance as president fell way below expectations and seriously undermined his democratic credentials, Jan Kees van Donge (1995) argues that there were distinct differences between the Kaunda and Chiluba periods. Zambia under Chiluba became a much more open society where criticism was much more tolerated. Kaunda was always wont to present himself as above party politics and did not deign to debate with those who criticized him. At best he answered his critics. But Chiluba had to face his critical challengers in press conferences and on television. Donge observes that these changes may be seen as embedded in the emergence of new professional groups in Zambia, which define themselves much more independently of the state and politics. Politicians in Kenya and Zambia as elsewhere in democratizing Africa, can now proliferate much more easily outside the party structure dominated by the president. In fact, all political parties have to cope with intense internal competition for leadership. This development is partly a result of the political transition to multipartyism, and partly a manifestation of a struggle between generations. "Old names which have been around in . . . politics since independence continue to remain important in all parties, and political strife in all parties is regularly expressed in terms of a generational struggle" (Donge, 1995: 194).

Similarly, the Kenyan press has emerged as a critical guardian of the national interest in terms of keeping the new NARC government on its toes. In the previous oppressive KANU era, acts of corruption were perpetrated without much coming to the public light. In the new expanded political space, however, acts of malfeasance are promptly reported by the empowered media. It was within this context, for instance, that the twin Anglo Leasing & Finance Ltd. scams that would have cost the Kenyan government nearly Sh7 billion was reported by a vigilant media, with the effect of nipping the would-have-been mega-billion scam in the bud. The scams involved the controversial Sh4 billion deal for the construction of a CID Forensic Laboratory for which the government paid KSh241 million (US$ 3.21 million) without any work having been done. This was compounded by the decision by government officials to expand an KSh800 million passport issuing equipment contract to one costing Sh2.7 billion and then issued it to the shadowy Anglo Leasing and Finance Ltd. without competitive bidding, and paid KSh.900 million (US$ 12 million) as commitment fee (see Irungu, 2004). Following reportage of the scandals, the popular outcry that followed resulted in the monies paid out being wired back to treasury and the projects cancelled. In addition to the role of the media, this eventuality was also a function of an increasingly alert and critical public fed on high expectations of leadership probity, which has made it impossible to conjure up and execute mind-boggling acts of corruption that were the order of the day during the single-party authoritarianism.

Perspectives from Lived Experience

The positive impact of the process of democratization in Africa is best illustrated by views from African citizens who have lived the experience of authoritarianism and the transition political conjuncture. The views of a cross-section of respondents, collected via a field survey in the spring of 2002 and summer of 2003 largely tally with the above "balance sheet." First, the respondents were asked to state what they considered to be the main achievements of the democratization process in response to which the following was stated.

The first was stated as the regaining of confidence among African citizens as a result of the reassertion of their freedom of expression and conscience. Recognizing that prior to1990 there was a lot of fear among the people, fear that was justified by the system of terror unleashed by the single-party system in which no mortal felt safe, respondents asserted that in the new politics of democratization, citizens no longer whisper their political opinions, but state them openly. As Peter Wanyande noted: "I think citizens have . . . become much more freer, much more willing and able to talk about government, to talk about public affairs, and indeed to express their political views fairly openly, which is something that was not done in the pre-1990 years. That is important."[4] This new found openness, as Winnie Mitullah noted, "enabled people to start talking; people began engaging with the state, raising questions."[5] The second major achievement was stated as the increasing political awareness among citizens, which is a form of political empowerment. According to Joseph Khaemba, this awareness was lacking in the single-party era because people's minds were skewed towards just one particular line of thought. It was one party, and that was it. But with the advent of multiparty politics in this country (Kenya), he noted,

> . . . you find that people are now able to start to realize, to start to view things differently, and to start appreciating that at least there must be some change of thought. And the mere fact that a person is in a position of leadership does not mean that he is always right. You can still be challenged, people are aware of what is happening, and people are coming up and querying so many decisions that were being made by the executive. And I think that is a major, major achievement because prior to that in the [19]80s you couldn't query what a local administrator said or did, you couldn't query what a district officer did, you couldn't query the provincial administration, the presidency, the ministers, and name it.[6]

Third, respondents also identified as a major impact of the democratization process, the opening up of the hitherto circumscribed political space. The manifestation of this, they noted, is the proliferation of political parties to compete for power with incumbent parties. For instance, when UNIP's Kaunda was disqualified from running for the presidency in Zambia in 1996, four other parties emerged to compete for power with the incumbent MMD, with more others being formed in the run-up to the 2001 elections.[7] A further manifestation of the opened up political space was viewed as the emergence of a number of civil society organizations to occupy a space that had been hitherto completely closed to them. On the other hand, it was noted, the existing ones, those that were there by the time the political space was opened up have become much more vibrant, much more active.

The fourth major impact of the democratization process identified by respondents was the defeat of the incumbent regimes in Kenya and Zambia, especially the defeat of incumbent parties that had been in power in both countries since independence. As Peter Wanyande (personal interview, 2003) argued, "one measure of democracy is the ability of opposition parties to take over power and to do so peacefully, and that has been done in the year 2002 when we had NARC take over power from KANU." Mbosonge Mwenechana (personal interview, 2002) noted the same in regard to the shift of power from UNIP to MMD in Zambia in 1991. Omo Omoruyi[8] observed that for long, African politicians went into elections with a single-minded idea of winning. They did not believe in losing as they believed that a winner is for all time and a loser is also for all time. However, the changed fortunes in regard to regime change in Zambia, in Omoruyi's (personal interview, 2002) view, had the effect of instilling in African political leaders the sense that democracy is a behavioral thing based on continuous contestation, that today's loser will be tomorrow's winner. It is in view of these developments that David Makali noted:

> I think first of all, change has come, change of whatever nature from one regime to another for us has been a welcome thing because we had been under oppression for a long time. We are hoping that we are in less oppressive time with a government that is more sensitive hopefully, to human rights, more responsive to people's needs and more accountable and transparent in terms of governance as it were so that transition is clear that we are in new times.[9]

Finally, respondents were asked to comment on the prospects for democratic consolidation and once again, they were very positive about this eventuality. The first to be pointed out were statements from government officials, particularly ministers that pointed to some commitment not to return to the dark days of one party dictatorship. Second, respondents pointed to the determination of citizens and the kind of enlightenment that they demonstrate as a positive development that is likely to be carried through the consolidation phase of democratization. Joseph Khaemba (personal interview, 2003) put it most strongly:

> I am optimistic about the prospects of democratic consolidation. There is no changing, no reverse, no going back. If the current government makes the mistake of repeating the things that the KANU government did, I tell you the resistance that is going to be in this country, the alternative forces that are going to come up in this country would be too strong for anybody to withstand it. And I saw it during the campaign, because I was one of the aspirants . . . So I am optimistic that things are going to be better than they have been in the past.

The greatest vindication of Khaemba's observation is symbolized by the successful resistance that Zambia's Fredrick Chiluba and Malawi's Bakili Muluzi faced when they attempted to cling to power after their second tenure by orchestrating constitutional amendments to enable them run for a third term in 2001 and 2004 respectively.

Similarly, David Makali (personal interview, 2003) also noted that the prospects are very bright, that Kenya is going to be a democratic country because of the lessening of ethnicity. The older generation is, according to Makali, being replaced with "a new generation of our age taking over, moving up and taking over a significant position in society and that is not prejudiced like our predecessors who were really raised on ethnic consideration. Ours is cross cutting and there is a lot of intermarriage." In this way, Makali noted, Kenya is becoming really cosmopolitan, a development that offers good prospects for political campaigns from non-ethnic perspectives and viewpoints.

Another characteristic pointer to the prospects for democracy is a host of attempts being made in both Kenya and Zambia to reinvigorate public institutions and therefore, to move away from a system of personal rule to a system in which the government relies on institutions to govern. Such institutionalization, as Neo Simutanyi pointed out, is key to consolidating democracy and, if followed through, would lead to complete supplanting of personal rule in the democratizing countries of Africa.[10] Concomitant with this is the sense of hope and renewal generated by the transition from one regime to another via the ballot box. This view was captured by Wambui Kiai (personal interview, 2003) who observed that in 2001, Kenyans were a beaten people who were demoralized and wondering what to do: "I know quite a number of scholars had begun searching outside because they said if KANU was going to come [win the 2002 elections], out we go."

Nonetheless, whereas the overwhelming majority of those interviewed[11] were enthusiastically optimistic about democratic consolidation in Kenya and Zambia, and indeed in the rest of the democratizing countries of Africa, there were two of them that were largely pessimistic about this eventuality, one Kenyan and one Zambian. The Zambian, Dr. Neo Richard Simutanyi (informal conversation, 1998) was simply not impressed by Chiluba's poor academic credentials, terming him an illiterate incapable of comprehending the institutional basis of governance. Chiluba, in Simutanyi's view, was overly diminutive, not just in physical status, but also in intellectual abilities. Not much could therefore be expected of him in terms of shifting the governance paradigm in Zambia. The pessimistic Kenyan, Dr. Vincent G. Simiyu, was particularly disappointed and frustrated by the self-interested power struggles within the emergent factions in the new ruling NARC coalition, on account of which he was pessimistic about the prospects of political and socio-economic renewal in Kenya. He asserted:

> I am pessimistic because by December [2002 when NARC took over]
> we were talking all over, and I talked so many times all over, that at
> least now we have an opportunity to lay the groundwork for the indus-
> trialization of this country. That is the only way we can create wealth.
> You cannot industrialize when you have all these petty squabbles and
> lack of self confidence, lack of transparency among the leaders them-
> selves, you know, behaving like capitalists and communists embracing
> each other and stabbing each other at the back, I mean you can't, you
> can't.[12]

This pessimism notwithstanding, however, empirical evidence does suggest
that the positive impact of the democratization process in Africa is irreversible. It may be a slow, arduous, and messy process, but there is concrete
evidence, as espoused by demoptimists, that it is undergoing consolidation.

Evidence of Democratic Consolidation

Unlike in the pre-1990 period, political competition has become the key
characteristic feature of the political terrain across Africa in the period following the 1990s wave of democratization on the continent. Robert Bates
(1999: 91) notes that as of 1995, 60.4 percent (29) of sub-Saharan Africa's
48 executives were elected in elections in which they faced rivals backed by
an opposition party. This was a remarkable improvement from two
decades earlier in 1975 when only 3 (6.3 percent) had been so chosen. Similarly, in 1995, 72.9 percent (35 of 48) of Africa's states had legislatures
chosen in competitive elections in which candidates faced rivals sponsored
by an opposition party. Again, this was a remarkable achievement over the
1975 state of continental political affairs when 24 of Africa's 48 states (50
percent) lacked any form of legislature. It is noteworthy that these changes
are not only remarkable, but also largely irreversible as illustrated by available evidence indicative of democratic consolidation in Africa.

If, as noted above, Chabal and Daloz (1999) are the chief proponents
of the pessimistic prognosis, Arthur Goldsmith is the foremost exponent of
the optimist perspective in regard to the prospects of democratic consolidation in Africa. Based on his empirical study of *Donors, Dictators and
Democrats in Africa,* Arthur Goldsmith (2001) observes that the continent
is definitely on the road to democratic consolidation since the 1990s. He
identifies four types of evidence that demonstrate the fact that democracy is
consolidating in Africa. The first set of evidence is that across the continent,
more liberal rules of political engagement are being adopted. For instance,
in 1980, only 25 of the 48 sub-Saharan African states (52%) had a fixed
term of office for the chief executive; in 1995, the number had grown to 33

(68.7%). Similarly, in 1980, only 24 of the 48 sub-Saharan African countries (50%) allowed multiple parties to contest legislative elections; by 1999, all 48 sub-Saharan African countries except 5—Democratic Republic of Congo, Eritrea, Rwanda, Somalia, and Swaziland—(89.5%) had conducted multiparty elections. Goldsmith argues that one of the essential conditions for a democratic system is that there is inclusive electoral participation; and asserts that many recent African contests meet this test as supported by voter turnout figures. While voter participation is under 30 percent of the eligible population in several countries, the average for the continent was nearly 60 percent during the 1990s. The lowest turnouts are often in countries where the contests are the least competitive, including Burkina Faso and Zimbabwe. Given the logistical difficulties of voting in many parts of Africa, the average rate of voter participation is respectable according to Goldsmith. For comparison, he notes, Africa's average voter turnout in recent leadership elections is only about 10 to 15 percentage points below the rate in many European countries, and is about 10 percentage points higher than the rate in recent United States presidential contests (Goldsmith, 2001: 423).

The second type of evidence is the growing number of competitive elections in Africa in recent years. It is noteworthy that meaningful elections were largely unknown during most of the post-colonial era. Following an initial contest before independence, autocratic civilian and military governments took control in the majority of the countries. The entire sub-Saharan region (48 countries) held only 126 elections for the top national office in the thirty years between 1960 and 1989 as indicated in Table 7.1 below. Most of these elections were non-competitive, with an average winner's share of close to 90 percent of the votes cast. The 1990s, as Goldsmith (2001) shows, broke form. During the decade, African countries held 78 top leadership elections, more than half as many as in the previous three decades. All but five countries in the region were involved. The elections became tighter and competitive, with the average winner's share dropping more than 20 percentage points, to around two thirds of the votes cast, from an average total for all the countries of 87.9 percent between 1960 through 1989, to an average total of 66.5 percent between 1990 through 2000 (Goldsmith, 2001: 421; see also Bates 1999: 91). For instance, whereas Chiluba won the presidency in Zambia with over 75 percent of the votes cast in 1991, his victory declined to 72 per cent in 1996 and, in 2001, his designated successor, Levy Mwanawasa, faced so tough a competition that he won with a mere 28 per cent to his closest rival, Anderson Mazoka's 27 percent of the total valid votes cast (see Nasong'o, 2004a).

According to Goldsmith, African heads of state are having more diffi-culty resisting their challengers under the new rules of political engagement. As Table 7.1 below illustrates, no incumbent leader ever lost an election in Africa until 1982, when Sir Seewoosagur Ramgoolam's parliamentary gov-ernment was handed electoral defeat in Mauritius. Thereafter, between 1990 and 2000, opposition candidates defeated incumbents or their designated replacements on twenty-one more occasions. Goldsmith argues that the threat of losing an election may account for the increasing rate of leaders' retirements—nine in the 1990s versus only eight in the previous three decades: "Rather than risk humiliation at the polling booth, many leaders may choose to give up public office" (Goldsmith, 2001: 422). Arguably, however, a further explanation lies in the institution of a limited mandate on executive leadership, which is a key characteristic of democracy. This is what explains the departure from power of the likes of Bakili Muluzi of Malawi (2004), Daniel arap Moi of Kenya (2002), Fredrick Chiluba of Zambia (2001) Jerry Rawlings of Ghana (2000), and Hassan Mwinyi of Tanzania (1995), among others. Without the limited mandate introduced by the new democratic politics, these leaders would almost certainly still be in power, or at least, would not have relinquished power at the time they did.

The third type of evidence is reflected in the declining number of coups d'etat as elections become more spirited in Africa. Goldsmith notes that counting the number of successful coups shows this, including victories

Table 7.1: Number of Leadership Transitions in Sub-Saharan Africa (48 Countries), 1960–1999

Mode of change	1960–69	1970–79	1980–89	1990–99	Total
Overthrown in coup, war, or killed	28	30	23	25	106
Died of natural or accidental causes	02	03	04	03	12
Retired	01	02	05	09	17
Lost election	00	00	01	21	22
Other: interim or caretaker regime	06	08	04	14	32
All leadership transitions	37	43	37	72	189

Source: adapted from Goldsmith, 2001: 422

in civil war and foreign invasion in each of the last four decades, while at the same time adjusting for the number of years of national independence. He writes: "The rate of military take-overs has dropped almost by half, falling from 0.087 per country year in the 1960s, to 0.046 per country year in the 1990s" (Goldsmith, 2001: 424). Even where coups have taken place, Goldsmith argues that new political attitudes among elites plus new expectations among citizens and international donors appear to be altering the outcomes of such coups that still occur. It is becoming the norm for coup leaders to step aside quickly, after organizing internationally acceptable elections. He gives the examples of Niger and Guinea-Bissau, both of which had coups in 1999, and both held elections for civilian governments before the year ended. In both cases international observers certified that the electoral process was reasonably free of fraud and intimidation. Similarly, the 1991 coup in Mali can be said to have been a coup for democracy. It deposed a dictator, Moussa Traoré, keen on forcefully subverting the democratic movement, and brought to power Amadou Toumani Touré, who organized successful elections within a year and led the military back to the barracks (see Vengroff & Kone, 1995). When post-coup elections are run unfairly, angry citizens may take to the streets and force those responsible to flee, as happened to Côte d'Ivoire's General Robert Gueï in October 2000.

According to Julius Nyang'oro (1997), military coups have become so unpopular in Africa that coup attempts are scoffed at by civilians and foreign governments. Such was the case in São Tome and Principe in July 1995 and in Comoro Islands in September/October 1995. In the case of São Tome and Principe, two days after the takeover, civilian control was reestablished after the military quickly realized that it could not make a credible argument to the population to support the intervention. "Only a few years ago, such intervention would have been accepted without fanfare" (Nyang'oro, 1997: 112). In the case of the Comoros, the old mercenary, Colonel Bob Denard found out that the old practice of mercenary armies coming in and taking over African governments—sometimes with the acquiescence of foreign powers—was no longer acceptable behavior internationally. France, the old colonial power, was forced to denounce Bob Denard and actually sent a military force to the Comoros to put a stop to Denard's antics.

The fourth and final evidence of democratic consolidation in Africa is the fact that overall indices of political freedom, which capture the above three types of evidence have been on the rise since the 1990s as indicated in Table 7.2 below. The first set of data is Raymond Gastil's index of political freedom, currently updated annually by Freedom House. The starting point for Gastil's index is a pair of checklists, one for political rights to participate

Table 7.2: Comparative Democracy Indices in Africa, 1989 and 1999

	Political Freedom Index 1= Least Free 7= most Free		Democracy Index 0=Least Open 10= Most Open	
Year	1989	1999	1989	1999
Mean Score	2.4	3.6*	0.8	3.0*
No. of States	47	48	41	41

Source: Goldsmith, 2001: 425
* Significantly different from the 1989 score at 99 percent confidence level

freely in the political system and one for political liberties to develop views and institutions separate from the state. Each country is ranked on a seven-point scale from "not free" to "free." These are combined into the seven-point political freedom score, recorded so that higher scores represent greater freedom, i.e., high degree of free and competitive elections, competitive autonomous parties, and provisions for political opposition. Between 1989 and 1999, the average African country improved its rating from a mean score of 2.4 to 3.6, a change that Goldsmith (2001) finds to be statistically significant at 99 percent confidence level.

The second overall indicator of democratization in Africa shown in Table 7.2 above is the democracy index started by Ted Robert Gurr and now updated by the University of Maryland's Polity98 Project. This dataset focuses on eight indicators of political authority and regime type for 177 countries. Gurr's democracy index attempts to measure the general openness of the political structure, scored on a zero-to-ten scale, and based on characteristics of a country's party system, electoral process, and executive. Again, the improvement from a mean score of 0.8 in 1989 to a mean score of 3.0 in 1999 is found to be statistically significant at 99 percent confidence level. This reality leads Goldsmith to conclude that generally, the evidence supports a mildly buoyant view of African democratization since the end of the Cold War. The level of democracy may be low compared to the old democracies of the Global North, and the new systems are not yet consolidated in most African countries. Nonetheless, in spite of the false starts and reversals, political trends in Africa are slowly but surely moving toward democracy (Goldsmith, 2002: 418–419). Indeed, despite the contradictions and ambiguities in Africa's democratic transition (see Young 1999; 1994), the continent has covered quite some distance from the single-party political authoritarianism of the period preceding the 1990s.

CONCLUSION

That the democratic transition in Africa since the 1990s has spawned a political conjuncture in which competition for political power among political parties is now the norm rather than the exception cannot be belabored. The fact that twenty-one incumbents, or their designated successors, were defeated in elections in Africa in the 1990–99 decade, compared to only one in the previous three decades, is ample testimony to the new political dispensation on the continent. This is buttressed by the new sense of empowerment on the part of the African citizen resulting from the liberalization of the channels of political communication, the enhanced freedom of expression and association, the increasing centrality of civic organizations in political processes, and the institution of limited mandate for executive leadership. However, this eventuality should warrant neither celebration nor complacency for, the shift to effective democratic institutionalization is yet to be accomplished.

In the first place, although there were 78 top leadership elections in Africa in the 1990s, more than half the number in the previous three decades, only 21 of them (26.9%) led to power transition from an incumbent party to an opposition one. Second, of the 21 democratic power transitions in the period 1990–99, four occurred in two countries—twice in both Benin and Mauritius. Hence, only 19 of 48 sub-Saharan African countries (39.5%) experienced a shift of power from one party to another during the period. Third, though the average winner's share of votes cast in the 1990s went down to 66.5 percent from 87.9 percent in the previous three decades, compared to more established democracies, this margin of victory is still lopsided. For instance, available evidence shows that in the history of the U.S., no president has ever won two thirds of the popular vote. The mean score for presidential victories is 51 percent. Similarly, no British party has won even half of the votes cast in the ten general elections between 1964 and 1997. Even in established democracies where rules demand a runoff for two top candidates where none secures an absolute majority in the first round, as is the case in France, the pattern is the same. Jacques Chirac was elected in the second round with only 52.6 percent of the vote in 1995. His predecessor François Mitterrand, having lost one earlier contest with 49.2 per cent, won his two consecutive seven-year terms by 54 per cent and 51.8 percent (see Goldsmith, 2001).

The lopsided nature of presidential victories in Africa and the dominance of incumbent victory are indicative of the still uncompetitive nature of the electoral process. As Van de Walle (2003) notes, the nature of the emergent party system in Africa is such that with very few exceptions such as Kenya and Ghana, the parties that won the first multiparty elections have almost invariably remained in power. On the positive side, therefore, political liberalization led to the emergence of multiparty political systems across the continent. However, the downside is that in most countries, this was not coupled with a transformation of political institutions to reflect the new political reality and enhance the possibilities for fair competition. Most opposition political parties in Africa thus face significant institutional constraints that curtail their ability to effectively organize and sell their political agendas to the electorate. The challenge to democratic consolidation in Africa thus lies in redesigning the strategic environment of political competition by way of constitutional engineering to provide for new rules of the political game that ensure fair competition and accountable governance. Without this, the transition to political pluralism may easily remain stuck at the breakthrough stage with the consolidation stage proving intractable to navigate.

In this regard, it is somewhat disappointing that for most of the African states, political transition was narrowly interpreted in terms of minimalist democratic tenets whereby multiparty politics is legalized and new leaders are elected. Whereas this has led to the supplanting of long-serving regimes in a significant number of cases as pointed out above, it is paradoxical that the forces of democratization have not, for the most part, even deigned to question the nature and structure of the African colonial state together with its boundaries. The colonial state was constructed to serve external interests. As such, its political and administrative structures were over-centralized. To facilitate broad-based democracy and political participation, therefore, this colonial state needs to be deconstructed with a view to devolving power to the localities through mechanisms that are broadly agreed upon. As Marina Ottaway (1999: 309) notes, perhaps it is only Ethiopia that has gone this far in terms of state reconstruction. The country's transformation followed the 1991 military defeat of Mengistu Haile Mariam's regime. But the victors did not simply set up a new government. First, the two movements that defeated Mengistu, the Eritrean People's Liberation Front (EPLF) and the Ethiopian People's Revolutionary Democratic Front (EPRDF), agreed to partition the country to create Eritrea in 1993 via a referendum in Eritrea. Second, the EPRDF transformed the new Ethiopia from a unitary state to a federation of ethnic regions. Ironically, unlike the rest of the African countries, Ethiopia is the only one that escaped the depredations of colonialism save for a four-year period of Italian occupation between 1936 and 1941.[13]

In the final analysis, democracy has to be understood as existing at the abstract, practical, and concrete levels. At the abstract level, democracy is an intellectual creation, a mentally visualized reality postulated as a model of the possible and desirable in matters of social co-existence and the government of citizens in a society. In its practical form, democracy consists of the ways and means of translating the democratic ideal into a concrete reality. This is what the democratization process in Africa has been all about. The concrete dimension of democracy comprises the balance sheet of the past and present efforts to install a democratic order (see Nasong'o, 2001a; Gitonga, 1987). As evidenced from the analysis of African and Africanist demo-pessimists and demoptimists above, Africa has covered much distance from the days of single-party monolithism, yet a lot more remains to be covered before African countries reach the democratic promised land. Towards this end, there is imperative need for restructuring the colonial state and redesigning the strategic environment of political engagement on the part of all African states for purposes of enhancing the consolidation of the democratic gains so far achieved. Otherwise the contention between democracy and authoritarianism will continue for the foreseeable future, with democratic elections yielding authoritarian regimes because of over-centralized and undemocratic institutions of governance.

Notes

NOTES TO CHAPTER ONE

1. Neopatrimonialism is a system in which the chief executive maintains authority through personal patronage rather than ideology or law. Herein, patron-client relationships that generate loyalty and dependence pervade the formal political and administrative systems as leaders occupy bureaucratic offices less to perform public service than to acquire personal wealth and status. They maintain their positions by doling out personal favors both within the state and society (see Bratton & van de Walle, 1994).

2. For a critique of the rational choice theory, see D. P. Green & I. Shapiro, *Pathologies of Rational Choice Theory: A Critique of Applications in Political Science* (New Haven: Yale University Press, 1994).

3. Towards this end, the country was divided into seven Regions and one Area, Nairobi, the seat of the central government. The Regions were Western, Nyanza, Rift Valley, Central, Eastern, Coast, and Northeastern. These reverted to their current status as administrative provinces when *Majimboism* was officially abolished in 1966.

4. Personal interview with Dr. V. G. Simiyu, Professor of History, University of Nairobi, Kenya, August 15, 2003.

5. Bildad Kaggia was one of the six freedom fighters convicted at the sham trial at Kapenguria in northern Kenya for "masterminding" the Mau Mau war of independence. The others were Jomo Kenyatta, Kung'u Karumba, Achieng' Oneko, Paul Ngei, and Fred Kubai.

6. The independence constitution in Kenya provided for the special election of twelve parliamentarians whereby once elected by universal adult suffrage, the Lower House of Parliament constituted itself into an electoral college for this purpose. The provision was later amended to provide for the direct nomination of the twelve by the president.

7. The Gikuyu, Embu, and Meru are closely related ethnic groups of Central and Eastern Kenya. Through GEMA, the elite of these communities came to dominate the country's political economy under the Kenyatta regime.

8. Ten of the 75 seats at Zambia's independence were reserved for the minority Whites. These seats were subsequently abolished in 1968.

9. It does seem that Kaunda's resignation was a rational strategic maneuver aimed at making himself indispensable and strengthening his hand in an effort to deal decisively with the crisis of factionalism in the party.

10. The Tanzanian one-party experiment has been hailed as a model example of a deliberate effort to strike a balance between popular participation and central control, both key ingredients of national development. Indeed, the greatest achievement of the experiment was the integration of Tanzanian society and promotion of a sense of nationhood that remains unparalleled elsewhere in Africa.

11. The recommendation in this regard was for an incumbent to be eligible for reelection only once; but this was ultimately rejected and the incumbent given a free hand to contest for the presidency as many times as he wished.

12. TANU merged with Zanzibar's Afro-Shirazi Party in 1977 to become Chama Cha Mapinduzi (CCM)—Revolutionary Party.

13. To Nyerere, such difference is a difference over fundamentals, which inevitably involves disunity and potential revolution.

NOTES TO CHAPTER TWO

1. J. M. Kariuki's body was found by a Maasai herdsman in the Ngong forest on the outskirts of Nairobi after having gone missing for a couple of days during which time the government claimed he was on a trip to Zambia. A parliamentary select committee chaired by Elijah Wasike Mwangale investigated the murder and found the government culpable.

2. See Ngugi wa Thiong'o's novel, *Petals of Blood,* which depicted the sense of disillusionment with independence on the part of the masses in Kenya— the flowers of independence had turned out to be petals of blood!

3. This list of students is only illustrative; it is by no means exhaustive. For a detailed account of student activism and the consequences for the students involved, see Klopp & Orina (2002); and Amutabi (2002).

4. For a detailed account and assessment of NGOs and other civil society organizations in the democratization process in Kenya, see Chapter Three.

5. In early 1980, the Zambian government uncovered "a serious coup plot" in which locals had allegedly recruited "Kantangese mercenaries" to help them overthrow the Kaunda government. Later, in October 1980, eight people were arrested and charged with treason, among them three prominent businessmen, Valentino Musakanya, Edward Shamwana, and Yoram Mumba. Others were military officers, Brig. Gen. Godfrey Miyanda, Gen. Christopher Kabwe, Mjr. Anderson Mporokoso, and Mjr. McPherson Mbulo. Pierce Annfield, a European also allegedly involved in the plot was tried in absentia as he had fled the country by the time of the arrests.

6. The Zambian High Court, which, unlike the case in Kenya, remained independent under Kaunda, released the detainees following their application of the writ of harbeas corpus, an action that embarrassed the UNIP government.

7. This statement on the part of labor leaders was an insurance against state harassment since anyone perceived to be disloyal within the rubric of the

one-party state risked detention without trial, as indeed, Chiluba, the ZCTU president, was at some point.

8. The economic crisis was a consequence of plummeting copper prices at the international market on which the Zambian economy heavily relied as a source of public revenue.

9. Indeed, prior to the KANU delegates meeting of 1991, a committee under the chairmanship of Vice President George Saitoti, had toured the country to collect views on the future of the political system. Despite popular views to the contrary, the committee emerged with a report to the effect that Kenyans were supportive of the continuity of the one-party state.

10. *Kwacha* is the name of the Zambian currency.

NOTES TO CHAPTER THREE

1. Personal interviews with Mbosonge Mwenechana and Omo Omoruyi, spring 2002; Peter Wanyande, Vincent Simiyu, Wambui Kiai, Mwenda Mbatiah, Kakai Wanyonyi, David Makali, Joseph Khaemba, and Winnie Mitullah, summer, 2003.

2. As a consequence, it is assumed that civil society organizations are in constant confrontation with the state. Indeed, some scholars argue that a civil society exists only in so far as it is self-consciously autonomous and in opposition to the state. See for instance, Pietrowski (1994); and Callaghy (1994).

3. The assumption here is that the state is inherently opaque, corrupt, repressive, and exploitative, while civil society organizations are regarded as bastions of transparency, accountability, and hence the natural allies of the people in their daily struggles for survival.

4. A number of parties were formed along a colorful spectrum such as the Theoretical Spiritual Political Party (TSPP); Christian Alliance for the Kingdom of Africa (CHAKA); National Alliance for Democracy (NADA); and Movement for Democratic Process (MDP), none of which managed to garner enough support to field candidates.

5. *Mwakenya* is a Swahili acronym standing for Muungano wa Wazalendo wa Kuikomboa Kenya—Patriotic Union for the Liberation of Kenya.

6. Forum for Restoration of Democracy-Asili (FORD-A) was the Kikuyu faction led by Kenneth Matiba with the support of Martin Shikuku, a Luhyia; while Forum for Restoration of Democracy-Kenya (FORD-K) remained dominated by the Luo with the support of Michael Wamalwa and the Bukusu sub-group of the larger Luhyia ethnic group. Nonetheless, it was FORD-K that managed to win at least a parliamentary seat in all of the country's eight provinces in 1992, a feat that eluded even the incumbent KANU as it was completely locked out of Central Province.

7. An example is the Series on Alternative Research in East Africa Trust (SAREAT), a local NGO in Nairobi, committed to promoting an alternative political view in East Africa that was taken to court by the Ford Foundation in 2001 for colluding with one of the Foundation's Nairobi Program officers to misappropriate the Foundation's grants to the NGO.

The NGO has since closed down and its former chief executive now works for another NGO.

NOTES TO CHAPTER FOUR

1. For instance, faced with riots and political strife following the assassination of Tom Mboya, a Luo, in 1969, the Kenyatta regime in Kenya resorted to oathing in Kenyatta's ethnoregion of Kiambu by which the Kikuyu vowed on pain of death to support Kenyatta and ensure that the presidency remained in the "House of Mumbi" (among the Kikuyu) and that in any event, it did not cross River Chania, i.e., go beyond Kenyatta's Kiambu district.
2. At this particular moment in time, the Kikuyu accounted for only 17 percent of the Kenyan population. Their 30 percent share of the cabinet positions was, therefore, way out of proportion relative to the ratio of their population to the rest of Kenyans.
3. When Odinga fell out with Kenyatta in 1966 and set up the KPU, Kenyatta used his control of the legitimate means of coercion to curtail the new party's national ascendancy and thus successfully projected it as an ethnic Luo party, portraying its key Kikuyu supporters like Bildad Kaggia as Kikuyu sellouts. Ultimately, Kaggia succumbed to ethnic pressure and resigned from his KPU vice presidency.
4. This does not necessarily denote the practice of voting for a candidate from one's ethnic group.
5. For details on the third multiparty elections in Zambia in 2001 and Kenya in 2002, see Chapter Five.
6. These figures do not include those of fringe presidential candidates whose total votes were of little consequence to the electoral outcome one way or the other.
7. Tony Gachoka, a political nonentity whose only claim to prominence was his editorship of the fiercely anti-Moi weekly *Finance* magazine, was the only Kikuyu holding a position in the interim FORD leadership that was dominated by political heavyweights and veterans like Masinde Muliro, Oginga Odinga, and Martin Shikuku.
8. Kenneth Matiba suffered a stroke while in detention for his perceived role in instigating the 1991 *Saba Saba* (July 7) riots. Despite close to one year's hospitalization in London, he never fully recovered from the effects of the stroke.

NOTES TO CHAPTER FIVE

1. Prior to this, the Institutional Revolutionary Party (*Partido Revucianario Institucional*—PRI) ruled uninterrupted for 71 years beginning 1929 in spite of the fact that elections were regularly held in Mexico during the period.
2. As one of the poorest countries in the world, with the lowest levels of GNP per capita, among the lowest Human Development Index, with a history of

political intolerance, social strife, regional socio-economic imbalance, and possessing few natural resources to attract international interest, Mozambique lacked in all socio-economic and political factors held as conducive to democracy.

3. Zambia had operated without the position of vice president since the inception of de jure single-party rule in 1972 when the position was abolished and one of non-executive prime minister (appointed by the president) created.

4. Mauritius was the first country in Africa to go through such an electoral transfer of power when the incumbent regime of Sir Seewoosagur Ramgoolam was handed electoral defeat by the opposition in 1982.

5. Anderson Mazoka maintained a lead over Levy Mwanawasa from the time the vote counting began through the results from 130 of Zambia's 150 constituencies. It was only with the returns from the 20 final constituencies that Mwanawasa opened a 16,298 votes lead with 456,308 votes against Mazoka's 440,010 votes.

6. The additional five seats for the Rift Valley shown in Table 5.4 were created in the run-up to the 1997 general elections.

7. In this event, membership to the ECK was expanded from 5 to 21 members with additional commissioners nominated by parliamentary parties in proportion to their parliamentary strength.

NOTES TO CHAPTER SIX

1. Orvis's study is an in-depth analysis of the civic education and paralegal work of the Catholic Justice and Peace Commission (CJPC), the Greenbelt Movement, International Commission of Jurists-Kenya Chapter, and the Education Centre for Women in Democracy (ECWD).

2. The fracas was a result of demonstrations at Parliament Building mobilized by CSOs to interrupt the reading and passage of the budget on June 19, 1997 in protest against the failure of government to institute a constitutional review process. The government unleashed its paramilitary police on the protesters resulting in skirmishes in which several people were seriously injured.

3. Masinde Muliro passed away suddenly on August 14, 1992 at Jomo Kenyatta International Airport, Nairobi on arrival from the UK where he had gone to seek support for his presidential bid. Suspicion about Muliro's death heightened after the government hastily convened a press conference at the airport to which Muliro's personal physician, Dr. Arthur Obel, was ferried to declare, without the benefit of an autopsy, that cardiac arrest was the cause of the veteran politician's death. Justice Bena Lutta was to later describe Muliro in a eulogy as "the best president Kenya never had."

4. It should be noted, however, that the rivalry between Matiba and Kibaki reflected the sectional interests among the Kikuyu. During the Kenyatta presidency, the Kikuyu of Kiambu had vowed to ensure that the presidency remained within Kiambu. It was now time for disproving these Kiambu Mafia, hence the rivalry between Matiba from Murang'a, and Kibaki from Nyeri.

5. It is noteworthy that the positions of prime minister and two deputies did not exist, but the opposition coalition undertook to finalize the constitutional review process within one hundred days of their assumption of power, which would create the new positions. Needless to say, this never came to pass. This eventuality generated bad blood within the ruling coalition between President Kibaki and his close ethnoregional backers who felt secure in the constitutional status quo and Raila Odinga and his close associates who felt betrayed by the disregard of the memorandum of understanding once victory was achieved.

6. This amendment was enacted by the KANU regime prior to the 1992 elections as a way of tripping up the opposition. The assumption was that only KANU could afford to meet the requirement because of the advantages of incumbency, while even if an opposition presidential candidate won an overall majority, they were unlikely to meet the requirement given their ethnically exclusive party support (see Chapter Four).

7. The constitutional review process had been underway since 2000, and by this point in time, it had come up with a draft document that was the subject of deliberations by a National Constitutional Conference at the Bomas of Kenya, Nairobi.

8. The review process was adjourned ostensibly to allow parliamentarians, who constituted one third of the delegates reviewing the draft constitution, to attend to urgent parliamentary business. Kiraitu Murungi's assurance of a new constitution by June 2004 was a mere tactical response to Kenya's donors who, in a meeting in Nairobi in November 2003 voiced their misgivings about the new government's commitment to the review process, which appeared suspect.

9. Personal interview with Dr. V. G. Simiyu, Professor of History, University of Nairobi, Kenya, August 15, 2003.

NOTES TO CHAPTER SEVEN

1. Personal interview with Ms. Wambui Kiai, Acting Director, School of Journalism, University of Nairobi, Kenya, July 8, 2003.

2. Emblematic of the personalized nature of the democratic crusade were the slogans "Moi Must Go!" in Kenya and "Kaunda Walala (No More)!" in Zambia. It is as if getting rid of Moi and Kaunda would, in and of itself, rid Kenya and Zambia of their socio-economic malaise. Yet Moi and Kaunda represented an institutionalized mode of politics that needed to be deconstructed if a new mode of governance was to be realized (see Nasong'o, 2003a, Ihonvbere, 1997).

3. As noted earlier, this eventuality has been helped by the policy shift on the part of aid donors away from development funding through states to channeling these resources via civil society organizations. The downside to this reality is that the CSOs are unable to effectively counter accusations that they are in the service of foreign rather than local interests, as they have no effective control over agenda-setting and defer to the dictates of their benefactors.

4. Personal interview with Dr. Peter Wanyande, Associate Professor of Political Science, University of Nairobi, Kenya, August 15, 2003.
5. Personal interview with Dr. Winnie Mitullah, Senior Research Fellow, Institute for Development studies, University of Nairobi, August 13, 2003.
6. Personal interview with Mr. Joseph Khaemba, an aspirant for the Kimilili parliamentary seat, Bungoma District, in the 2002 elections in Kenya, Nairobi, August 15, 2003.
7. Personal interview with Mr. Mbosonge Mwenechana, a Zambian graduate student of economics, Boston, June 22, 2002.
8. Personal interview with Dr. Omo Omoruyi, former Director of the Nigerian Center for Democratic Studies, who observed both the Zambian and Kenyan first multiparty elections, Boston, May 23, 2002.
9. Personal interview with Mr. David Makali, Director, Media Institute, Nairobi, July 23, 2003.
10. Informal discussion with Dr. Neo Richard Simutanyi, Lecturer in Political Science, University of Zambia, Chicago, July 1998.
11. The interviewees included David Makali, Johnstone Ojwang, Joseph Khaemba, Kakai Wanyonyi, Mbosonge Mwenechana, Mwenda Mbatiah, Neo Richard Simutanyi, Omo Omoruyi, Peter Wanyande, Vincent G. Simiyu, and Winnie Mitullah.
12. Personal interview with Dr. V. G. Simiyu, Professor of History, University of Nairobi, Kenya, August 15, 2003.
13. Ethiopia's Emperor Menelik II successfully warded off colonial designs over his empire when he decisively defeated the Italians in the battle of Adowa in 1860, thereby asserting his country's independence. Indeed, when the League of Nations was formed in 1919, Ethiopia was one of its founding members. Mussolini's invasion of Ethiopia in 1936 was an act of revenge against Italy's humiliating defeat at the hands of Ethiopia more than seven decades earlier.

Bibliography

Abbink, J. and Hesseling, G. eds. 2000. *Election Observation and Democratization in Africa*. London: Macmillan Press.

Adar, K. G. 2000a. "Assessing Democratization Trends in Kenya: A Post-mortem of the Moi Regime," *Commonwealth and Comparative Politics*, 38, 3, 103–130.

———. 2000b. "The Internal and External Contexts of Human Rights Practice in Kenya: Daniel arap Moi's Operational Code," *African Sociological Review*, 4, 1, 74–96.

———. 2000c. "The Interface between Political Conditionality and Democratization: The Case of Kenya," *Scandinavian Journal of Development Alternatives and Area Studies*, 19, 2–3, 71–104.

———. 1999. "The Interface between Elections and Democracy: Kenya's Search for a Sustainable Democratic System, 1960s–1990s," in J. Hyslop, ed. *African Democracy in the Era of Globalisation*. Johannesburg: Witwatersrand University Press, 340–360.

———. 1998. "Ethnicity and Ethnic Kings: The Enduring Dual Constraint in Kenya's Multiethnic Democratic Electoral Experiment," *The Journal of Third World Spectrum*, 5, 2, 71–96.

———. 1995. "Kenya-U.S. Relations: A Recapitulation of the Patterns of Paradigmatic Conceptualization, 1960s–1990s," in G. M. Munene et. al, eds. *The United States and Africa: From Independence to the End of the Cold War*. Nairobi: East African Educational Publishers, 89–104.

Adhiambo-Oduol, J. 2002. *Leadership, Civil Society and Democratization in Kenya*. Addis Ababa: ECA.

Ajulu, R. 2002. "Politicised Ethnicity, Competitive Politics and Conflict in Kenya: A Historical Perspective," *African Studies*, 61, 2, 251–268.

———. 2000. "Thinking Through the Crisis of Democratization in Kenya: A Response to Adar and Murunga," *African Studies Review*, 4, 2, 133–157.

———. 1995. "The Left and the Question of Democratic Transition in Kenya: A Reply to Mwakenya," *Review of African Political Economy*, 22, 64, 229–235.

Ake, C. 2000. *The Feasibility of Democracy in Africa*. Dakar: CODESRIA.

———. 1996. *Democracy and Development in Africa*. Washington, DC: Brookings Institution.

———. 1991. "Rethinking African Democracy," *Journal of Democracy*, 2, 1, 32–44.

Alexander, D. 1993. *The Development of Workers' Education and Political Change in Zambia.* Edinburgh: Edinburgh University Press.

Amutabi, M. N. Forthcoming. "Ethnicity and Political Transition in Kenya," in G. R. Murunga and S. W. Nasong'o, eds. *Struggles for Democracy in Kenya: Gains, Limitations, and Prospects.* Dakar: CODESRIA.

———. 2002. "Crisis and Student Protest in Universities in Kenya: Examining the Role of Students in National Leadership and the Democratization Process," *African Studies Review,* 45, 2, 157–178.

Anderson, B. 1983. *Imagined Communities: Reflections on the Origins and Spread of Nationalism.* London: Verso.

Arrow, K. J. 1951. *Social Choice and Individual Values.* New Haven: Yale University Press.

Assensoh, A. 1998. *African Political Leadership: Jomo Kenyatta, Kwame Nkrumah and Julius Nyerere.* Malabar, Florida: Krieger Publishing Company.

Atieno-Odhiambo, E. S. 2002. "Hegemonic Enterprises and Instrumentalities of Survival: Ethnicity and Democracy in Kenya," *African Studies,* 61, 2, 223–249.

Ayittey, G. B. N. 2002. "Biting their own Tails: African Leaders and the Internalist Intricacies of the Rape of a Continent," Keynote Address to SORAC Conference on Internalist vs. Externalist Interpretations of African History and Culture, Montclair State University, New Jersey, November 7–9.

Azarya, V. 1994. "Civil Society and Disengagement in Africa," in J. W. Harbeson et. al, eds. *Civil Society and the State in Africa.* Boulder: Lynne Rienner, 83–100.

Banfield, E. 1958. *The Moral Basis of a Backward Society.* Chicago: The Free Press.

Barkan, J. D. 1994. "Elements and Institutions of Good Governance and Accountability," in O. Owiti and K. Kibwana, eds. *Good Governance and Accountability in Kenya: The Next Step Forward.* Nairobi: Claripress, 27–31.

———. 1993. "Kenya: Lessons from a Flawed Election," *Journal of Democracy,* 4, 3, 85–99.

———. 1987. "The Electoral Process and Peasant-State Relations in Kenya," in F. M. Hayward, ed. *Elections in Independent Africa.* Boulder: Westview Press, 213–237.

———., P. Densham, and G. Rushton. 2001. "Designing Better Electoral Systems for Emerging Democracies." www.uiowa.edu/~electdis/

———., and N. Ng'ethe. 1998. "Kenya Tries Again," *Journal of Democracy,* 9, 2, 32–48.

Barreto, A. A. 2001. *The Politics of Language in Puerto Rico.* Gainesville: University Press of Florida.

Barth, F., ed. 1969. *Ethnic Groups and Boundaries: The Social Organization of Culture Difference.* Boston: Little, Brown, & Co.

Bates, R. H. 1999. "The Economic Bases of Democratization," in R. Joseph, ed. *State, Conflict, and Democracy in Africa.* Boulder: Lynne Rienner, 83–94.

Bayart, J. F. et. al. 1999. "From Kleptocracy to the Felonious State?" in Bayart, J. P. et. al., *The Criminalization of the State in Africa.* Oxford: James Currey & Bloomington, IN.: Indiana University Press, 1–31.

Baylies, C. and M. Szeftel. "The Fall and Rise of Multiparty Politics in Zambia," *Review of African Political Economy,* No. 54, 75–91.

——., and M. Szeftel. 1982. "The Rise of a Zambian Capitalist Class in the 1970s," *The Journal of Southern African Studies,* 9, 3, 201–209.

Beckman, B. 1998. "The Liberation of Civil Society: Neo-Liberal Ideology and Political Theory in an African Context," in M. Mohanty, et. al., eds. *People's Rights: Social Movements and the State in the Third World.* London: Sage, 45–62.

Bediako, K. 1995. *Christianity in Africa: The Renewal of non-Western Religion.* Edinburgh: Edinburgh University Press.

Bentham, J. 1988 [1781]. *The Principles of Morals and Legislation.* Amherst, New York: Prometheus Books.

Bratton, M. 1998. "Second Elections in Africa," *Journal of Democracy,* 9, 3, 51–66.

——. 1994. "Economic Crisis and Political Realignment in Zambia," in J. A. Widner, ed. *Economic Change and Political Liberalization in sub-Saharan Africa.* Baltimore: Johns Hopkins University Press, 101–128.

——. 1994. "Civil Society and Political Transitions in Africa," in J. W. Harbeson, et. al., eds. *Civil Society and the State in Africa.* Boulder: Lynne Rienner, 51–81.

——., and D. N. Posner. 1999. "A First Look at Second Elections in Africa, with Illustrations from Zambia," in R. Joseph, ed. *State, Conflict, and Democracy in Africa.* Boulder: Lynne Rienner, 377–407.

——., and N. van de Walle. 1997. *Democratic Experiments in Africa: Regime Transitions in Comparative Perspective.* Cambridge, UK: Cambridge University Press.

——., and N. van de Walle. 1994. "Neopatrimonial Regimes and Political Transitions in Africa," *World Politics,* 46, 4, 453–489.

——., and D. Rothchild. 1992. "The Institutional Bases of Governance in Africa," in G. Hyden and M. Bratton, eds. *Governance and Politics in Africa.* Boulder: Lynne Rienner, 263–284.

Brown, S. 2002. "Quiet Diplomacy and Recurring 'Ethnic Clashes' in Kenya," in American Political Science Association Annual Meeting, Boston, USA, August 29-September 1.

——. 2001. "Authoritarian Leaders and Multiparty Elections in Africa: How Foreign Donors Help to Keep Kenya's Daniel arap Moi in Power," *Third World Quarterly.* 22, 5, 725–739.

Buke, W. 2004. "We can Do without NGOs," *East African Standard,* Nairobi, June 4.

Burnell, P. 2001. "The Party System and Party Politics in Zambia: Continuities, Past, Present and Future," *African Affairs,* 100, 399, 239–263.

——. 1995. "The Politics of Poverty and the Poverty of Politics in Zambia's Third Republic," *Third World Quarterly,* 16, 4. 675–690.

Buwembo, J. 2004. "Why Do African Presidents want to Serve Life Sentences in State House?" *The East African,* November 29.

Callaghy, T. M. 1994. "Civil Society, Democracy, and Economic change in Africa: A Dissenting Opinion about Resurgent Societies," in J. W. Harbeson, et. al., eds. *Civil Society and the State in Africa.* Boulder: Lynne Rienner, 231–253.

Caporaso, J. A. 1978. "Dependence, Dependency, and Power in the Global System," *International Organization,* 32, winter.

Carothers, T. 2002. "The end of the Transition Paradigm," *Journal of Democracy*, 13, 1, 5–21.

CDCM [Center for International Development and Conflict Management]. 1999. Polity98 Project http://www.bsos.umd.edu/cidcm/polity/

Chabal, P. and J. P. Daloz. 1999. *Africa Works: Disorder as Political Instrument*. Oxford: James Currey & Bloomington: Indiana University Press.

Chan, S. 2000. *Zambia and the Decline of Kaunda, 1984–1998*. New York: The Edwin Mellen Press.

Chazan, N. 1994. "Engaging the State: Associational Space in Sub-Saharan Africa," in J. S. Migdal, et. al. *State Power and Social Forces: Domination and Transformation in the Third World*. Cambridge: Cambridge University Press, 255–289.

Chege, M. 1997. "Introducing Race as a Variable into the Political Economy Debate of Kenya: An Incendiary Idea," *African Affairs* 97, 387, 209–230.

——. 1996. "Africa's Murderous Professors," *The National Interest*, 9, 46.

——. 1993. "The Kenya December 1992 General Elections," *CODESRIA Bulletin*, 1.

Chikulo, B. C. 2000. "Corruption and Accumulation in Zambia," in K. R. Hope and B. C. Chikulo, eds. *Corruption and Development in Africa: Lessons from Country Case-Studies*. London: Macmillan, 161–182.

——. 1980. "The 1978 Zambian Elections," in *Evolving Structure of Zambian Society*. Proceedings of a seminar held at the Centre of African Studies, University of Edinburgh, May 30–31.

Chweya, L. ed. 2002. *Electoral Politics in Kenya*. Nairobi: Claripress.

——., and S. W. Nasong'o, 1996. "Political Communication: Its Role in State-Civil Society Contest in Kenya," in 10th Biennial Conference of the African Council for Communication Education, Cape Town, South Africa, November 15–19.

Clapham, C. and J. A. Wiseman. 1995. "Assessing the Prospects for the Consolidation of Democracy in Africa," in J. A. Wiseman, ed. *Democracy and Political Change in Sub-Saharan Africa*. London: Routledge, 220–232.

Colburn, F. D. 1994. *The Vogue of Revolution in Poor Countries*. Princeton: Princeton University Press.

Collier, D. and S. Levitsky, 1997. "Democracy with Adjectives: Conceptual Innovation in Comparative Research," *World Politics*, 49, April, 430–451.

Colomer, J. M. 2000. *Strategic Transitions: Game Theory and Democratization*. Baltimore: Johns Hopkins University Press.

Connor, W. 1994. *Ethnonationalism: The Quest for Understanding*. Princeton, NJ: Princeton University Press.

Coolidge, J., and S. R. Ackerman. 2000. "Kleptocracy and Reform in African Regimes: Theory and Examples," in K. R. Hope, and B. C. Chikulo, eds. *Op. Cit*, 57–86.

Cornell, S. 1996. "The Variable Ties that Bind: Content and Circumstances," *Ethnic and Racial Studies*, 9, 2.

Cruz, C. 2000. "Identity and Persuasion: How Nations Remember their Pasts and Make their Futures," *World Politics*, 52, 3, 275–312.

Dahl, R. 1982. *Dilemmas of Pluralist Democracy*. New Haven: Yale University Press.

Danziger, J. N. 2005. *Understanding the Political World*. New York: Pearsons Education.

Davidson, B. 1992. *The Black Man's Burden: Africa and the Curse of the Nation-State*. New York: Random House.

Diamond, L. 1999. *Developing Democracy toward Consolidation*. Baltimore: Johns Hopkins University Press.

———. 1996. "Is the Third Wave Over?" *Journal of Democracy*, 7, 3, 20–37.

Diang'a, J. W. 2002. *Kenya 1982: The Attempted Coup*. London: PenPress.

Dommen, D. 1997. "Paradigms of Governance and Exclusion," *Journal of Modern African Studies*, 35, 3, 483–494.

Donge, J. K. 1995. "Kaunda and Chiluba: Enduring Patterns of Political Culture," in J. Wiseman, ed. *Democracy and Political Change in Sub-Saharan Africa*. London: Routledge, 193–219.

Downs, A. 1957. *An Economic Theory of Democracy*. New York: Harper and Row.

Easterly, W. and R. Levine. 1997. "Africa's Growth Tragedy: Policies and Ethnic Divisions," *Quarterly Journal of Economics*, 112, 4.

Ellis, S. 2000. "Elections in Africa in Historical Context," in J. Abbink, and G. Hesseling, eds., *Op. Cit.*, 37–49.

Eriksen, T. H. 1993. "Ethnic Classification: Us and Them," *Ethnicity and Nationalism: Anthropological Perspectives*. London: Pluto Press, 18–35.

Fatton, R. Jr. 1995. "Africa in the Age of Democratization: The Civic Limitations of Civil Society," *African Studies Review*, 38, 2, 67–99.

Foeken, D. and T. Dietz. 2000. "Of Ethnicity, Manipulation and Observation: The 1992 and 1997 Elections in Kenya," in J. Abbink, and G. Hesseling, eds., *Op. Cit.*, 122–149.

Frank, A. G. 1970. "The Development of Underdevelopment," in R. Rhodes, ed. *Imperialism and Underdevelopment: A Reader*. New York: Monthly Review Press.

Freedom House, 1999. Annual Survey of Freedom Country Scores. http://www. freedom house.org.rankings.pdf/

Fukuyama, F. 1989. "The End of History?" *The National Interest*, 16, 3–18.

Galtung, J. 1971. "A Structural Theory of Imperialism," *Journal of Peace Research*, 8, 2, 81–117.

———. 1967. *Capitalism and Underdevelopment in Latin America*. New York: Monthly Review Press.

Gertzel, C. ed. 1984. *The Dynamics of the One-Party State in Zambia*. Manchester: Manchester University Press.

———. et. al. 1984. "Introduction: The Making of the One-Party State," in C. Gertzel, ed. *Ibid.*, 1–28.

Gibson, N. 1994. "Fanon's Humanism and the Second Independence in Africa," in McCarthy-Arnolds, et. al., eds. *Africa, Human Rights, and the Global System: The Political Economy of Human Rights in a Changing World*. Westport: Greenwood, 23–34.

Gibson, S. 1999. "Aid and Politics in Malawi and Kenya: Political Conditionality and Donor Support to the 'Human Rights, Democracy and Governance' Sector," in L. Wohlgemuth, et. al., eds. *Common Security and Civil Society in Africa*. Uppsala: Scandinavian Institute of African Affairs.

Gimode, E. Forthcoming. "The Role of the Police in Kenya's Democratisation Process," in G. R. Murunga and S. W. Nasong'o, eds. *Op. Cit.*

Glickman, H. 1998. "Ethnicity, Elections, and Constitutional Democracy in Africa," in T. C. Sisk, and A. Reynolds. *Elections and Conflict Management in Africa.* Washington, DC: United States Institute of Peace, 37–54.

Goldsmith, A. A. 2001. "Donors, Dictators, and Democrats in Africa," *Journal of Modern African Studies,* 39, 3, 411–436.

Green, D. P. and I. Shapiro. 1994. *Pathologies of Rational Choice Theory: A Critique of Applications in Political Science.* New Haven: Yale University Press.

Gulhati, R. 1989. *Impasse in Zambia: The Economics and Politics of Reform.* Washington, DC: The World Bank.

Gupta, A. 1974. Trade Unionism and Politics on the Copperbelt," in W. Tordoff, ed. *Politics in Zambia.* Berkeley: University of California Press, 288–319.

Hamalengwa, M. 1992. *Class Struggles in Zambia and the fall of Kenneth Kaunda.* Lanham, MD: University Press of America.

Harbeson, J. W. 1999. "Rethinking Democratic Transitions: Lessons from Eastern and Southern Africa," in R. Joseph, ed. *State, Conflict, and Democracy in Africa.* Boulder: Lynne Rienner, 39–55.

——. 1994. "Civil Society and Political Renaissance in Africa," in J. W. Harbeson, et. al., eds. *Civil Society and the State in Africa.* Boulder: Lynne Rienner, 1–34.

Hartman, D. 1999. "Kenya," in D. Nohlen, et. al., *Elections in Africa: A Data Handbook.* Oxford: Oxford University Press, 475–494.

Haugerud, A. 1995. *The Culture of Politics in Modern Kenya.* Cambridge, UK: Cambridge University Press.

Himbara, D. 1994. *Kenyan Capitalists, the State and Development.* Nairobi: East African Educational Publishers.

Hobsbawm, E. 1993. "Introduction: Inventing Traditions," in E. Hobsbawm and T. Ranger, eds. *The Invention of Tradition.* Cambridge, UK: Cambridge University Press, 1–14.

Hope, K. R. 1997. *African Political Economy: Contemporary Issues in Development.* Armonk, NY: Sharpe.

——., and B. C. Chikulo, eds. 2000. *Corruption and Development in Africa: Lessons from Country-Case Studies.* London: Macmillan.

Horowitz, D. L. 2000. *Ethnic Groups in Conflict.* Berkeley: University of California Press.

Hulterström, K. 2004. *In Pursuit of Ethnic Politics: Voters, Parties, and Policies in Kenya and Zambia.* Uppsala: Uppsala University Press.

——. 2002. "A Conceptualization of Ethnic Politics: Bloc Voting and Party Support in Kenya and Zambia," in Conference on Consolidation in New Democracies, Uppsala University, June 8–9.

Human Rights Watch. 1993. *Divide and Rule: State-Sponsored Ethnic Violence in Kenya.* New York: Human Rights Watch.

Huntington, S. M. 1997. "After Twenty Years: The Future of the Third Wave," *Journal of Democracy,* 8, 4, 3–12.

——. 1991. *The Third Wave: Democratization in the Late Twentieth Century.* Norman: University of Oklahoma Press.

Hyden, G. and M. Bratton. 1992. *Governance and Politics in Africa*. Boulder: Lynne Rienner.

Ihonvbere, J. O. 2000. *Africa and the New World Order*. New York: Peter Lang Publishing.

——. 1997. "On the Threshold of another False Start? A Critical Evaluation of Prodemocracy Movements in Africa," in E. I. Udogu, ed. *Democracy and Democratization in Africa*. Leiden: Brill, 125–142.

——. 1996a. *Economic Crisis, Civil Society, and Democratization: The Case of Zambia*. Trenton, NJ and Asmara: Africa World Press.

——. 1996b. "Where is the Third Wave? A Critical Evaluation of Africa's Non-Transition to Democracy," *Africa Today*, 43, 4, 343–368.

——. 1996c. "The Crisis of Democratic Consolidation in Zambia," *Civilisations*, 43, 2, 83–109.

Irungu, G. 2003. "Donors Alarm as Graft Smears Kibaki's Team," *Daily Nation*, Nairobi, Thursday November 27.

Jackson, R. and C. Rosberg. 1982. *Personal Rule in Black Africa*. Berkeley: University of California Press.

Janos, A. C. 1997. "Paradigms Revisited: Productionism, Globality, and Postmodernity in Comparative Politics," *World Politics*, 50, 1, 118–149.

Jonyo, F. 2002. "Ethnicity in Multiparty Electoral Politics," in L. Chweya, ed. *Op. Cit.* 86–107.

Joseph, R. ed. 1999. *State, Conflict, and Democracy in Africa*. Boulder: Lynne Rienner.

——. 1998. "Africa, 1990–1997: From Abertura to Closure," *Journal of Democracy*, 9, 2, 3–17.

Kamwambe, N. 1991. *Frederick Chiluba: Is He Riding A Tide of Fortune?* Lusaka: Shelley's Printers.

Katumanga, M. 2002. "Internationalisation of Democracy: External Actors in Kenya Elections," in L. Chweya, ed. *Op. Cit.* 173–196.

——. 2000. "Civil Society and the Politics of Constitutional Reform in Kenya: A Case Study of the National Convention Executive Council (NCEC)," Research Report. Institute of Development Studies, UK.

Kaunda, K. 1973. *The Leadership Code and Responsibilities of the Leadership in the Creation of a New Social Order*. Lusaka: Government Printer.

Kendo, O. 2003. "It is Ufungamano Group that Employed 'Wanjiku,'" *East African Standard*, Nairobi, September 18.

Kibwana, K. et. al. 1996. *The Anatomy of Corruption in Kenya: Legal, Political, and Socio-Economic Perspectives*. Nairobi: Clarion.

Klopp, J. M. 2002. "Can Moral Ethnicity Trump Political Tribalism? The Struggle for Land and Nation in Kenya," *African Studies*, 61, 2, 269–294.

——. 2001. "Pilfering the Public: The Problem of Land Grabbing in Contemporary Kenya," *Africa Today*, 47, 1, 5–26.

——., and J. R. Orina, 2002. "University Crisis, Student Activism, and the Contemporary Struggle for Democracy in Kenya," *African Studies Review*, 45, 1, 43–76.

Lambert, Y. 1993. *Ghana: In Search of Stability, 1957–1992*. Westport: Praeger.

Lange, M. -F. 2000. "Elections in Mali (1992–7): Civil Society Confronted with the Rule of Democracy," in J. Abbink and G. Hesseling, eds., *Op. Cit.*, 228–254.

Leonard, W. 1974. *The Three Faces of Marxism.* New York: Holt, Rinehart & Winston.

Levi, M. 1999. "A Model, a Method, and a Map: Rational Choice in Comparative and Historical Analysis," in M. I. Lichbach, and S. Zuckerman, eds. *Comparative Politics: Rationality, Culture, and Structure.* New York: Cambridge University Press, 19–41.

Leys, C. 1975. *Underdevelopment in Kenya: The Political Economy of Neo-Colonialism, 1964–1971.* London: Heinemann.

Lijphart, A. 1998. *Electoral Systems and Party Systems: A Study of Twenty-Seven Democracies, 1945–1990.* New York: Oxford University Press.

Lonsdale, J. 1994. "Moral Ethnicity and Political Tribalism," in P. Kaarsholm and J. Hultin, eds. *Inventions and Boundaries: Historical and Anthropological Approaches to the Study of Ethnicity and Nationalism.* Roskilde University.

Lopes, C. 1996. "The Africanisation of Democracy," *African Journal of Political Science*, 1, 2, 139–153.

Magnusson, B. A. 1999. "Testing Democracy in Benin: Experiments in Institutional Reform," in R. Joseph, ed., *Op. Cit.*, 217–237.

Maipose, G. S. 1996. "Central Government Administration: Problems and Prospects in Load and Capacity," in O. Sichone and B. Chikulo, eds. *Democracy in Zambia: Challenges for the Third Republic.* Harare: SAPES Books.

Makinda, S. K. 1992. "Kenya: Out of the Straitjacket, Slowly," *The World Today*, 48, 10, 188–192.

Mamdani, M. 1995. "A Critique of the State and Civil Society Paradigm in Africanist Studies," in M. Mamdani and E. Wamba-dia-Wamba, eds. *African Studies in Social Movements and Democracy.* Dakar: CODESRIA, 602–616.

Manning, C. L. 2002. *The Politics of Peace in Mozambique: Post-Conflict Democratization, 1992–2000.* Westport: Praeger.

Marx, K. and F. Engels. 1992 [1888]. *The Communist Manifesto.* New York: Bantam Books.

Matanga, F. K. 2000. "Civil Society and the Politics of Democratization in Africa," in P. G. Okoth and B. A. Ogot, eds. *Conflict in Contemporary Africa.* Nairobi: Jomo Kenyatta Foundation, 56–63.

Mazrui, A. A. 1972. *Cultural Engineering and Nation-Building in East Africa.* Evanston, IL: Northwestern University Press.

Mbaku, J. M. 2000a. *Bureaucratic and Political Corruption in Africa: The Public Choice Perspective.* Malabar, FL: Krieger Publishing Company.

——. 2000b. "Controlling Corruption in Africa: A Public Choice Perspective," in K. R. Hope and B. C. Chikulo, eds., *Op. Cit.*, 119–136.

——. 1997. "Effective Constitutional Discourse as an Important First Step to Democratization in Africa," in E. I. Udogu, ed. *Democracy and Democratization in Africa.* Leiden: Brill, 39–51.

Mbikusita-Lewanika, A. 1990. *Milk in a Basket! The Political-Economic Malaise in Zambia.* Lusaka: Zambia Research Foundation.

Meyns, P. 1992. "Civil Society and Democratic Change in Africa: The Cases of Cape Verde and Zambia," in *African Development Perspectives Yearbook,* Vol. 3, 582–599.

Migdal, J. S. 1988. *Strong Societies and Weak States: State-Society Relations and State Capacity in the Third World*. Princeton: Princeton University Press.

Miguel, E. 2004. "Tribe or Nation? Nation Building and Public Goods in Kenya versus Tanzania," *World Politics*, 56, 3, 327–362.

Mkandawire, T. 1999. "Crisis Management and the Making of Choiceless Democracies," in R. Joseph, ed., *Op. Cit.*, 119–136.

Mogire, E. O. 2000. "The State and Internal Political Conflicts in Africa: The Case of Kenya," in P. G. Okoth and B. A. Ogot, eds. *Conflict in Contemporary Africa*. Nairobi: Jomo Kenyatta Foundation, 128–140.

Molteno, R. 1974. "Cleavage and Conflict in Zambian Politics: A Study in Sectionalism," in W. Tordoff, ed. *Politics in Zambia*. Berkeley: University of California Press, 62–106.

Momba, J. C. 2000. "Political Culture and the Limits of Institutional Reforms: Implications for the Future of the Democratisation Process in Zambia," in K. K. Prah, and A. G. M. Ahmed, eds. *Africa in Transformation: Political and Economic Transformations and Socio-economic Development Responses in Africa*. Addis Ababa: OSSREA, 207–231.

——. 1993. "Uneven Ribs in Zambia's March to Democracy," in P. A. Nyong'o, ed. *Arms and Daggers in the Heart of Africa: Studies in Internal Conflict*. Nairobi: Academy Science Publishers, 181–208.

Mphaisha, C. J. J. 2000. "The State of Democratization in Zambia," *Commonwealth and Comparative Politics*, 38, 3, 131–146.

——. 1996. "Retreat from Democracy in Post One-Party State in Zambia," *Commonwealth and Comparative Politics*, 2, 34, 65–84.

Mueller, S. 1984. "Government and Opposition in Kenya," *Journal of Modern African Studies*, 22, 3, 399–427.

Mufune, P. 1988. "The Formation of Dominant Classes in Zambia: Critical Notes," *Africa Today*, 35, 2, 5–20.

Mugambi, J. N. K. ed. 1997. *Democracy and Development in Africa: The Role of Churches*. Nairobi: All Africa Conference of Churches.

Muigai, G. 1995. "Ethnicity and the Renewal of Competitive Politics in Kenya," in H. Glickman, ed. *Ethnic Conflict and Democratization in Africa*, Atlanta: The Africa Association Studies Press, 161–196.

Munene, M. 2001. *The Politics of Transition in Kenya*. Nairobi: Friends-of-the-Book Foundation/Quest & Insight Publishers.

——. 2000. "Crisis and the State in Kenya, 1995–1997: An Appraisal," in P. G. Okoth and B. A. Ogot, eds. *Conflict in Contemporary Africa*. Nairobi: Jomo Kenyatta Foundation, 152–176.

——. 1993. "The Diplomatic Collision Course: The U.S. and Kenya in the Post-Cold War Period," in P. G. Okoth and P. K. Kakwenzire, eds. *The Americas Before and After Columbus*. Kampala: United States Information Service, 80–98.

Mungai, K. 2005. "More Legislators?" *The Standard Online*, Nairobi, February 6.

——. 2002. "Distribution of Parliamentary Seats Unfair," *East African Standard*, December 25.

Murunga, G. R. 2004. "The State, its Reform and the Question of Legitimacy in Kenya," *Identity, Culture, and Politics*, 5, 1, 228–263, Dakar: CODESRIA, ICES.

——. 2002. "A Critical Look at Kenya's Non-Transition to Democracy," *Journal of Third World Studies,* XIX, 2, 89–111.

——. 2000. "Civil Society and the Democratic Experience in Kenya: Review Essay," *African Sociological Review,* 4, 1, 97–118.

——. 1999. "Urban Violence in Kenya's Transition to Pluralist Politics, 1982–1992," *Africa Development,* XXIII, 1 & 2.

——., and S. W. Nasong'o. eds. Forthcoming. *Struggles for Democracy in Kenya: Gains, Limitations, and Prospects.* Dakar: CODESRIA.

Mutoro, H., L. Chweya, and W. Nasong'o. 1999. "Political Leadership and the Crisis of Development in Africa: Lessons from Kenya," in R. Gosh, et. al., eds. *Good Governance and Sustainable Development: The Indian Ocean Region.* New Delhi: Atlantic Publishers, 67–82.

Mwagiru, M. 2002. "Elections and the Constitutional and Legal Regime in Kenya," in L. Chweya, ed. *Op. Cit.* 28–51.

Mwakikagile, G. 2001. *Ethnic Politics in Kenya and Nigeria.* Huntington, NY: Nova Science Publishers.

Mwanakatwe, J. M. 1994. *End of Kaunda Era.* Lusaka: Multimedia Publications.

Nasong'o, S. W. Forthcoming. "Negotiating New Rules of the Game: Civil Society and the Kenyan Transition," in G. R. Murunga and S. W. Nasong'o, eds., *Op. Cit.*

——. 2004a. "Democracy and Political Competitiveness in Africa: The Primacy of Electoral System Design," in 47th/37th Annual Meeting of the African Studies Association/Canadian Association of African Studies, New Orleans, November 11–14.

——. 2004b. "La Sociedad Civil y la Democratización Africanas: La Dinámica de las Fuerzas Externas," *Estuios de Asia y Africa,* XXXIX, 1, 75–94.

——. 2003a. "The Paucity of Personalized Democratic Crusades: Kenya and Zambia from an Institutional Perspective," in 46th Annual Conference of the African Studies Association, Boston Sheraton, October 6–8.

——. 2003b. "Ethnonationalism and State Integrity in Africa: Cultural Objectification and the Rwandan Genocide," *Canadian Review of Studies in Nationalism,* XXX, 1–2, 53–63.

——. 2002a. "Kenya's Multiparty Elections in a Comparative East African Perspective," in L. Chweya, ed. *Op. Cit.,* 197–225.

——. 2002b. "Civil Society and African Democratisation: The Flip Side of the Coin," *Studies in Democratisation,* e-Journal of the Center for the Study of Democracy, Northeastern University, Boston, Fall 2002: http://www.csd.neu.edu

——. 2001a. "The Illusion of Democratic Governance in Kenya," in R. Dibie, ed. *The Politics and Policies of Sub-Saharan Africa.* Lanham, MD: University Press of America, 117–133.

——. 2001b. "Civil Society and African Democratization: The Dynamics of External Forces," in Canadian Association of African Studies Annual Conference on 'Africa: Between the Demons of the Past and the Promise of the Future.' Quebec: Université Laval, May 27–30.

——. 2000. "Resource Allocation and The Crisis of Political Conflicts in Africa: Beyond the Inter-Ethnic Hatred Thesis," in P. G. Okoth and B. A. Ogot, eds.

Conflict in Contemporary Africa. Nairobi: Jomo Kenyatta Foundation, 44–55.

——. 1998. "From Christian Evangelism to Democratic Evangelism: The Paucity of the Leninist Approach," in 11th Biennial Conference of the African Council For Communication Education, on 'Communication and Good Governance,' Kenya College Of Communications Technology, Nairobi, Kenya, 9th-15th October.

——. 1997. "Democratization and Human Rights Issues in Kenya: The Role of American Ambassadors William Attwood and Smith Hempstone," in Sixth Regional Colloquium on American Studies in East Africa, Egerton University, Njoro, Kenya, August 7–12.

National Democratic Institute and Carter Center, 1992. *The October 31, 1991 National Elections in Zambia.* Washington, DC: National Democratic Institute for International Affairs.

Ndegwa, S. N. ed. 2001. *A Decade of Democracy in Africa.* Leiden: Brill.

——. 1996. *The Two Faces of Civil Society: NGOs and Politics in Africa.* West Hartford: Kumarian.

Neocosmos, M. 1993. *The Agrarian Question in South Africa and 'Accumulation from Below.'* Uppsala: Scandinavian Institute of African Studies.

Neumann, J. Von and O. Morgenstern. 1953 [1944]. *Theory of Games and Economic Behavior.* Princeton: Princeton University Press.

Ngunyi, M. 1996. "Resuscitating the Majimbo Project: The Politics of Deconstructing the Unitary State in Kenya," in A. O. Olukoshi and L. Laakso, eds. *Challenges to the Nation-State in Africa.* Uppsala: Nordiska Afrikainstitutet, 183–213.

Nnoli, Okwudiba. 1998. *Ethnic Conflicts in Africa.* Dakar: CODESRIA.

Nohlen, D. et. al, 1999. *Elections in Africa: A Data Handbook.* Oxford: Oxford University Press.

Nyangira, N. 1987. "Ethnicity, Class and Politics in Kenya," in M. G. Shatzberg, ed. *The Political Economy of Kenya.* New York: Praeger, 15–31.

Nyang'oro, J. E. 2000. "Civil Society, Structural Adjustment, and Democratization in Kenya," in R. B. Kleinberg and J. A. Clark, eds. *Economic Liberalization and Civil Society in the Developing World.* New York: St. Martin's Press, 91–108.

——. 1997a. "Critical Notes on Political Liberalization in Africa," in E. I. Udogu, ed. *Democracy and Democratization in Africa.* Leiden: Brill, 112–124.

——. 1997b. "The Depth of Democratic Change in Africa," in J. N. K. Mugambi, ed. *Op. Cit.,* 129–154.

Nyerere, J. K. 1974. *Freedom and Unity: Uhuru na Umoja.* Dar es Salaam: Oxford University Press.

Nyong'o, A. 2002. "Hazards of Transition from Authoritarian Governments," *Sunday Nation,* Nairobi, March 31.

——. 1989. "State and Society in Kenya: The Disintegration of the Nationalist Coalition and the Rise of Presidential Authoritarianism, 1963–78," *African Affairs,* 88, 351, 229–251.

Nzongola-Ntalaja, 1989. "The African Crisis: The Way Out," *African Studies Review,* 32, 1, 115–128.

Ochieng, W. R. 1995. "Structural and Political Changes" in B. A. Ogot and W. R. Ochieng, eds. *Decolonization and Independence in Kenya, 1940–93*. London: James Currey, Nairobi: E.A.E.P., Athens: Ohio University Press, 83–109.

O'Donnell, G. 1994. "Delegative Democracy," *Journal of Democracy,* 5, 55–69.

Ogachi, O. 1999. "Economic Reform, Political Liberalization and Economic Ethnic Conflict in Kenya," *Africa Development,* 24, 1–2, 83–107.

Okoth, P. G. 1992. *United States of America's Foreign Policy Toward Kenya, 1952–1969*. Nairobi: Gideon S. Were Press.

——., and B. A. Ogot, eds. 2000. *Conflict in Contemporary Africa*. Nairobi: Jomo Kenyatta Foundation.

Okoth-Ogendo, H. W. O. 1991. "Constitutions without Constitutionalism: Reflections on an African Political Paradox," in Issa G. Shivji, ed. *State and Constitutionalism: An African Debate on Democracy*. Harare: SAPES Trust.

Oloo, A. 2004. "Changing Roles: The Politics of Constitution Making in Kenya," in 47th/37th Annual Meeting of the African Studies Association/Canadian Association of African Studies, New Orleans, November 11–14.

Olson, M, Jr. 1965. *The Logic of Collective Action*. Cambridge: Harvard University Press.

Olukoshi, A. 1999. "State, Conflict, and Democracy in Africa: The Complex Process of Renewal," in R. Joseph, ed., *Op. Cit.,* 451–465.

——., and Lisa Laakso, eds. 1996. *Challenges to the Nation-State in Africa*. Uppsala: Nordiska Afrikainstitutet.

Omolo, K. 2002. "Political Ethnicity in the Democratisation Process in Kenya," *African Studies,* 61, 2, 209–221.

Orvis, S. 2003. "Kenyan Civil Society: Bridging the Urban-Rural Divide?" *Journal of Modern African Studies,* 41, 2, 247–268.

——. 2001a. "Moral Ethnicity and Political Tribalism in Kenya's 'Virtual Democracy,'" *African Issues,* XXIX, 1&2, 8–13.

——. 2001b. "Civil Society in Africa or African Civil Society?" in S. N. Ndegwa, ed., *Op. Cit.,* 17–38.

Orwenyo, J. N. 1977. "Problems of Ideology in Independent Kenya: Soviet Background and Repercussions in Some Aspects of Nation-Building," in Historical Association of Kenya Annual Conference, August 25–28.

Osei-Hwedei, B. 1998. "The Role of Ethnicity in Multiparty Politics in Malawi and Zambia," *Journal of Contemporary African Studies,* 16, 2, 227–247.

Ottaway, M. 1999. "Ethnic Politics in Africa; Change and Continuity," in R. Joseph, ed., *Op Cit.,* 299–317.

——. 1997. "African Democratization and the Leninist Option," *Journal of Modern African Studies,* 31, 1, 1–15.

Owiti, J. 2000. "Political Aid and the Making and Re-making of Civil Society," Research Report. Institute of Development Studies, UK.

Owiti, O. and K. Kibwana, eds. 1994. *Good Governance and Accountability in Kenya: The Next Step Forward*. Nairobi: Claripress.

Owuoche, S. and F. Jonyo, 2002. *Political Parties & Civil Society in Governance and Development: A Synthesis*. Nairobi: Birds Printers.

Oyugi, W. O. 1998. "Ethnic Politics in Kenya," in O. Nnoli, *Ethnic Conflicts in Africa*. Dakar: CODESRIA, 287–309.

——. 1997. "Ethnicity in the Electoral Process: The 1992 General Elections in Kenya," *African Journal of Political Science*, 2, 1, 41–69.

——. 1992. "Inter-Ethnic Relations in Kenya," in CODESRIA Workshop on 'Ethnic Conflict in Africa' Nairobi: November 16–18.

Perlas, N. 1999. *Shaping Globalisation: Civil Society, Cultural Power, and Threefolding*. Quezon: Centre for Alternative Development Initiatives.

Phiri, I. 1999. "Media in 'Democratic' Zambia: Problems and Prospects," *Africa Today*, 46, 2, 53–65.

Pietrowski, M. 1994. "The One-Party State as a Threat to Civil and Political Liberties in Kenya," in E. McCarthy-Arnolds et al. eds. *Africa, Human Rights and the Global System: The Political Economy of Human Rights in a Changing World*. Westport: Greenwood Press, 131–146.

Posner, D. N. 2003. "The Colonial Origins of Ethnic Cleavages: The Case of Linguistic Divisions in Zambia," *Comparative Politics*, 35, 2, 127–146.

Putnam, R. C. et. al. 1988. "Institutional Performance and Political Culture: Some Puzzles About the Power of the Past," *Governance: An International Journal of Policy and Administration*, 1, 3, 221–244.

Republic of Kenya. 1992. *Report of the Parliamentary Select Committee to Investigate Ethnic Clashes in Western and other Parts of Kenya*. Nairobi: Government Printer.

Republic of Zambia. 1995. *Constitutional Review Commission and Government Reaction to the Report*. Lusaka: Government Printer.

Reynolds, A. and T. C. Sisk, 1998. "Elections and Electoral Systems: Implications for Conflict Management," in T. C. Sisk and A. Reynolds, eds. *Elections and Conflict Management in Africa*. Washington, DC: United States Institute of Peace, 11–36.

Rodney, W. 1982. *How Europe Underdeveloped Africa*. Washington, DC: Howard University Press.

Rotberg, R. I. 2002. *Ending Autocracy Enabling Democracy: The Tribulations of Southern Africa, 1960–2000*. Washington, DC: Brookings Institution.

Rutto, S. K. and G. K. Njoroge, 2001. *The Democratization Process in Africa*. Nairobi: Quest & Insight Publishers/Friends-of-the-Book Foundation.

Sabar, G. 2002. *Church, State and Society in Kenya: From Mediation to Opposition, 1963–1993*. London: Frank Cass.

Sandbrook, R. 1993. *The Politics of Africa's Economic Recovery*. Cambridge: Cambridge University Press.

——. 1987. *The Politics of Africa's Economic Stagnation*. London: Cambridge University Press.

——. 1975. *Proletarians and African Capitalism: The Kenyan Case, 1960–1972*. London: Cambridge University Press.

Scarritt, J. A. 1998. "Communal Conflict and Contention for Power in Africa South of the Sahara," in T. R. Gurr, *Minorities at Risk: A Global View of Ethnopolitical Conflicts*. Washington, D.C: United States Institute of Peace, 252–289.

Schedler, A. 1998. "What is Democratic Consolidation?" *Journal of Democracy*, 9, 2, 91–107.

Sichone, O. B. 1999. "The Sacred and the Obscene: Personal Notes on Political Ritual, Poverty and Democracy in Zambia," in J. Hyslop, ed. *African Democracy in the Era of Globalisation.* Johannesburg: Witwatersrand University Press, 152–166.

——. 1995. "The National Question, Ethnicity and the State in Zambia," *Southern Africa Political and Economic Monthly,* 8, 6, 54–58.

Simon, D. J. 2002. "Can Democracy Consolidate in Africa amidst Poverty? Economic Influences upon Political Participation in Zambia," *Commonwealth and Comparative Politics,* 40, 1, 23–42.

Simone, A. M. and Santi, P. K. 1998. "South African Civil Society State of the Art Review," in UNDP/CODESRIA Eastern and Southern Africa Sub-Regional Workshop on Empowering Civil Society for Poverty Reduction in Sub-Saharan Africa, Silver Springs Hotel, Nairobi, Kenya, October.

Sisk, T. C. and A. Reynolds, eds. 1998. *Elections and Conflict Management in Africa.* Washington, DC: United States Institute of Peace.

Sørensen, G. 1998. *Democracy and Democratization: Processes and Prospects in a Changing World.* Boulder: Westview Press.

Szeftel, M. 1982. "Political Graft and the Spoils System in Zambia—the State as a Resource in Itself," *Review of African Political Economy,* 24, 4–21.

Takougang, J. 1997. "The 1992 Multiparty elections in Cameroon: Prospects for Democracy and Democratization," in E. I. Udogu ed. *Democracy and Democratization in Africa.* Leiden: Brill, 52–65.

Tester, K. 1992. *Civil Society.* London: Routledge.

The Free Africa Foundation. 2002. "African Kleptocracies: Kenya," accessed on July 3, 2002, at: http://www.freeafrica.org/looting3.html

Throup, D. and C. Hornsby. 1998. *Multiparty Politics in Kenya.* Nairobi: East African Educational Publishers.

Times of Zambia, January 24, 1981.

Tsebelis, G. 1990. *Nested Games: Rational Choice in Comparative Politics.* Berkeley: University of California Press.

Tordoff, W. ed. *Politics in Zambia.* Berkeley: University of California Press.

——., and R. Molteno. 1974. "Introduction," in W. Tordoff, ed., *Ibid.,* 1–39.

——., and I. Scott. 1974. "Political Parties: Structures and Policies," in W. Tordoff, ed., *Ibid.,* 107–154.

Turok, B. 1989. *Mixed Economies in Focus: Zambia.* London: Institute for African Alternatives.

Udogu, E. I. ed. 1997. *Democracy and Democratization in Africa.* Leiden: Brill.

Vengroff, R. and M. Kone. 1995. "Mali: Democracy and Political Change," in J. A. Wiseman, ed. *Democracy and Political Change in Sub-Saharan Africa.* London: Routledge, 45–70.

Venter, D. 1995. "Malawi: The Transition to Multiparty Politics," in J. A. Wiseman, ed. *Democracy and Political Change in Sub-Saharan Africa.* London: Routledge, 152–188.

Walle, N. van de. 2003. "Presidentialism and Clientilism in Africa's Emerging Party Systems," *Journal of Modern African Studies,* 41, 2, 297–321.

——. 1999. "Economic Reform in a Democratizing Africa," *Comparative Politics,* 32, 1, 21–41.

Wallerstein, I. 1979. *Capitalist World Economy.* Cambridge, England: Cambridge University Press.

Wamba-dia-Wamba. 1991. "Discourse on the National Question," in I. G. Shivji, ed. *State and Constitutionalism: An African Debate on Democracy.* Harare: SAPES Trust, 57–70.

Wanbali, P. 2001. "Civic Education Debate Dishonest," *Daily Nation,* Nairobi, August 7.

Wanyama, F. O. 2000. "The Role of the Presidency in African Conflicts," in P. G. Okoth and B. A. Ogot, *Op. Cit.,* 30–43.

Wanyande, P. 2002. "The Power of Knowledge: Voter Education and Electoral Behaviour in a Kenyan Constituency," in L. Chweya, *Op Cit.,* 52–75.

Wanyonyi, P. K. 1997. "A Historical Reflection on the Electoral Process in Post-Colonial Africa," in O. Ogunba, ed. *Governance and the Electoral Process.* Lagos: ASAN, 21–36.

Warah, R. 2004. "Ngugi in Exile: Home is Where the Art Is," *The East African,* August 30th—September 5th.

Weekly Review, Nairobi, November 21, 1986.

Wele, P. 1995. *Zambia's Most Famous Dissidents: From Mushala to Luchembe.* Solwezi, Zambia: PMW.

Widner, J. A. ed. 1994. *Economic Change and Political Liberalization in sub-Saharan Africa.* Baltimore: Johns Hopkins University Press.

——. 1994. "Political Reform in Anglophone and Francophone African Countries," in J. A. Widner, ed., *Ibid.,* 49–79.

——. 1992. *The Rise of a Party-State in Kenya: From 'Harambee!' to 'Nyayo!'* Berkeley: University of California Press.

Wiseman, J. A. 1996. *The New Struggle for Democracy in Africa.* Aldershot, UK: Averbury.

——. 1995. "The Movement towards Democracy: Global, Continental, and State Perspectives," in J. A. Wiseman, ed., *Ibid.,* 1–10.

Woldring, K. 1984. "Survey of Recent Inquiries and their Results," in K. Woldring and C. Chibaye, eds. *Beyond Political Independence: Zambia's Development Predicament in the 1980s.* Berlin: Mouton.

World Socialist Organization, 2002. "Zambia's Tribalist Politics," http://www.worldsocialism.org/zambia3.htm accessed on February 27, 2003.

Young, C. 1999. "The Third Wave of Democratization in Africa: Ambiguities and Contradictions," in R. Joseph, *Op Cit.,* 15–38.

——. 1994. "Democratization in Africa: The Contradictions of a Political Imperative," in J. A. Widner, ed., *op. Cit.,* 230–250.

Zagare, F. C. 1984. *Game Theory: Concepts and Applications.* Newbury Park, CA: Sage Publications.

Zakaria, F. 1997. "The Rise of Illiberal Democracy," *Foreign Affairs,* 76, 6, 22–43.

Zolberg, A. R. 1966. *Creating Political Order: The Party-States of West Africa.* Chicago: Rand McNally.

Index

For Product Safety Concerns and Information please contact our EU
representative GPSR@taylorandfrancis.com Taylor & Francis Verlag GmbH,
Kaufingerstraße 24, 80331 München, Germany

Printed and bound by CPI Group (UK) Ltd, Croydon, CR0 4YY
11/04/2025
01843977-0002